MW00582019

The Unsolid South

PRINCETON STUDIES IN AMERICAN POLITICS

HISTORICAL, INTERNATIONAL, AND COMPARATIVE PERSPECTIVES

Ira Katznelson, Eric Schickler, Martin Shefter, and Theda Skocpol,
Series Editors

A list of titles in this series appears at the back of the book

The Unsolid South

Mass Politics & National Representation
in a One-Party Enclave

Devin Caughey

PRINCETON UNIVERSITY PRESS

PRINCETON AND OXFORD

Copyright © 2018 by Princeton University Press
Published by Princeton University Press,
41 William Street, Princeton, New Jersey 08540
In the United Kingdom: Princeton University Press,
6 Oxford Street, Woodstock, Oxfordshire OX20 1TR

press.princeton.edu

All Rights Reserved

LCCN 2018941290

ISBN 978-0-691-18179-0

ISBN (pbk.) 978-0-691-18180-6

British Library Cataloging-in-Publication Data is available

Editorial: Eric Crahan and Pamela Weidman
Production Editorial: Natalie Baan
Production: Erin Suydam
Publicity: Tayler Lord
Copyeditor: Theresa Kornak
Jacket photo: U.S. senatorial candidate Lyndon B. Johnson
addresses a crowd in Johnson City, Texas, June 28, 1941.
Courtesy of the LBJ Presidential Library

This book has been composed in Sabon LT Std
Printed on acid-free paper. ∞

Printed in the United States of America

1 3 5 7 9 10 8 6 4 2

Contents

Illustrations

Figures

Tables

Preface

THIS IS A BOOK ABOUT A PARTICULAR (and unique) place and time—the Southern United States in the 1930s–50s. But, like many who have studied the South, I believe that it not only is important in itself, but also has valuable lessons to teach us about politics generally. I have thus tried to write this book in a way that interests not only scholars in my own niche of American political development, but also political scientists in other fields, political historians and sociologists, and even (dare I hope?) lay readers. I have also tried to marshal diverse forms of evidence, from statistical analyses to archival documents to vivid historical anecdotes, with the goal of engaging and convincing this diverse range of readers. I have aimed for a broad audience because even as the one-party (Democratic) South is passing out of living memory, its legacy and lessons live on—not least in the form of the contemporary resurgence of one-party (Republican) dominance in much of the region.

This book began life as my dissertation, completed at the University of California–Berkeley under the supervision of Eric Schickler. But its origins go back to my undergraduate days at Yale, to a post-class conversation with David Mayhew (Eric's dissertation advisor) in which I asked him to, in essence, "explain the South" to me. David pointed me toward the work of *his* thesis advisor, V. O. Key, which was enough to get me hooked on Southern politics for the next decade (and counting). The next, unlikely stop on my Southern intellectual journey was Cambridge, England, where I wrote a master's thesis, guided by the political historian Anthony Badger, on three midcentury Southern senators. Studying at Cambridge helped me make the transition from history, my undergraduate major, to political science, and gave me an invaluable foundation for my doctoral work at Berkeley. Anyone who reads this book will notice the palpable influence of these four great scholars, and I am grateful to each for their tutelage and support (even if it was, in the case of Key, from beyond the grave).

I am lucky that the sub-subfield of Southern political development is filled with brilliant and—more importantly—generous scholars. Chief among these are Robert Mickey and Ira Katznelson, who more than anyone else directly inspired my own work and provided templates for how to do rigorous, big-stakes work on Southern politics. Rick Valelly has also been extremely positive, helpful, and encouraging. The historian Sam Webb and his wife Ann even put me up at their house during my archival trip to Tuscaloosa. In political science more broadly, I thank James Snyder, Stephen Ansolabehere, John Mark Hansen, and Shigeo Hirano for sharing their data; Josh Clinton for flying from Nashville to Boston in January to attend my book conference; and Michele Epstein, Marty Gilens, Chuck Cameron, Brandice Canes-Wrone, Tali Mendelberg, and other folks at Princeton University's Center for the Study of Democratic Politics, who provided critical intellectual and financial support near the end stages of this project. At various points, I received helpful feedback on this project from discussants and audience members at Harvard, MIT, Yale, Princeton, Cornell, University of California–San Diego, Boston University, University of Toronto, and several political science conferences. And, of course, I am grateful to Eric Crahan and Princeton University Press for agreeing to publish the final product.

At Berkeley, I was fortunate not only in my dissertation chair, Eric Schickler, but also in the other members of my committee—Jas Sekhon, Laura Stoker, Sean Farhang, and Kevin Quinn—all of whom contributed in different ways to this project and my intellectual development. I am particularly grateful to Kevin for teaching me about item response theory models (and Bayesian statistics generally). I also learned a great deal about political parties from David Karol, about Congress from Rob Van Houweling, about historically informed political science from Paul Pierson, about formal modeling from Bob Powell and Sean Gailmard, and about whatever he wanted to spiel about from Nelson Polsby. I am grateful to Henry Brady for the training and financial support of the Integrative Graduate Education and Research Traineeship program, and to Jack Citrin and Terri Bimes for the support and welcoming community of the Institute for Governmental Studies. Berkeley also surrounded me with a wonderful group of fellow graduate students, including John Henderson, Sara Chatfield, and Peter Ryan, with and from whom I learned about American politics; Allan Dafoe, who provided coauthorship and intellectual companionship; Danny Hidalgo, who is nearly as fascinated by Southern politics as I am; Erin Hartman, Adrienne Hosek, Chloe Thurston, and Abby Wood, who helped keep me on track and with whom I shared the dank glory of the carrels; Kristi Govella, who listened patiently over coffee at A Musical Offering; Peter Hanson, who explained to me how Congress actually works; Mark Huberty, who created and maintained the Berkeley political science computing cluster; Ruth Bloch Rubin, who shared insights into the workings of the Southern caucus; Alex Theodoridis, who occasionally let me beat him at basketball; and Sara Newland (more on her later).

I owe huge thanks to Chris Warshaw, my friend, collaborator, and erstwhile colleague at MIT, for working with me to develop the dynamic group-level IRT model, without which this book really would not have been possible. My other MIT colleagues have also been unfailingly supportive, including Andrea Campbell, Charles Stewart, Kathy Thelen, and especially Adam Berinsky, who has been an exemplary senior faculty mentor. I also want to acknowledge my colleague David Singer, for reminding me how important acknowledgments are. At MIT I have been fortunate to collaborate with several stellar graduate students: Yiqing Xu, Tom O'Grady, and especially James Dunham, who helped Chris and me develop the dgo package. I've also benefitted from working with several wonderful research assistants/collaborators, particularly Mallory Wang and Melissa Meek, both of whom made important substantive contributions to this project.

My grandfather Winslow Caughey was an early patron of my love of books, and he later told me that part of him always wanted to be a political scientist, rather than the "real" scientist that he ended up becoming. I wish that he had lived to see this book in print. I am grateful to my parents for their support and patience during my somewhat winding journey toward academia and political science. Thanks also to them and my siblings—Robert, Ben, and Willa—for being the kind of family I look forward to spending time with, though that now happens all too infrequently. Although they're not technically family, I want to express my appreciation to Ann McNamee and Magen Solomon, professors both, who kept the pressure on me to finish my PhD. And finally, Sara Newland: you are the core of my life, and nothing I have accomplished would be possible without you. I am so proud and honored to be associated with you, and so grateful that you have decided to share your life with me. I am also so very grateful for our children Milo and Hazel, and I am looking forward to watching them grow up with you.

The Unsolid South

CHAPTER 1

Introduction

> The South really has no parties. Its factions differ radically
> in their organization and operation from political parties.
> The critical question is whether the substitution of factions
> for parties alters the outcome of the game of politics. The
> stakes of the game are high. Who wins when no parties
> exist to furnish popular leadership?[1]
>
> —V. O. Key (1949)

ON FEBRUARY 22, 1937, Representative James P. Buchanan of Texas's
10th congressional district suffered a fatal heart attack. The special election triggered by the long-serving congressman's death attracted seven
candidates—all Democrats, as was the norm in the one-party state of
Texas. Among these was the ambitious young director of the state branch
of the National Youth Administration, one of the many government agen-
cies created by President Franklin Roosevelt's New Deal. As a 28-year-old
making his first run for elected office, Lyndon Baines Johnson sought to
compensate for his youth and lack of name recognition by distinguishing himself as "Roosevelt's man" in the race. Johnson did everything he
could to tie himself to the immensely popular president. The centerpiece
of Johnson's campaign was his support for FDR's controversial court-
packing plan, which conservatives assailed as a dictatorial power grab
but district residents reportedly favored seven-to-one.[2] On election day,
Johnson's strategy of all-out support for Roosevelt paid off. With about
a quarter of the eligible white population voting, Johnson earned 28% of
ballots cast, enough for a plurality victory.

---

[1] V. O. Key Jr., *Southern Politics in State and Nation* (New York: Knopf, 1949), 299.
[2] Robert A. Caro, *The Path to Power* (New York: Vintage Books, 1981), 395.

At first, Johnson proved himself a loyal and effective New Dealer. Only on bills related to civil rights for African Americans, who at that time were effectively disenfranchised in Texas and across the South, did Representative Johnson, like nearly all his fellow Southerners in the House, toe an unwaveringly conservative line. During his first term he helped secure the passage of bills funding dam construction, rural electrification, farm tenancy reduction, and crop control, all of which brought concrete material benefits to the residents of his relatively poor district. He was even among the few Southern representatives to support the passage of the landmark Fair Labor Standards Act (FLSA), which established national minimum wages and maximum hours. Rebuffing critics who feared that the FLSA would undermine the South's economic advantages as a low-wage region, Johnson declared, "If an industry cannot pay decent wages, I do not want it in my district."[3]

The 1938 elections, however, in addition to reducing the Democrats' House majority by 72 seats, also brought the primary defeat of Johnson's fellow Texan and FLSA supporter, Representative Maury Maverick. Johnson interpreted the defeat of the outspokenly liberal Maverick, who represented the adjoining 20th district, as a sign of his constituents' increasing conservatism. The next year, when pressed by White House counsel Jim Rowe to support an administration priority, Johnson replied, "You know, look where your old friend and my old friend Maury Maverick is, he's not here. The first problem we've got is to get re-elected. I don't want to go that way." Throughout his career Johnson continued to cite Maverick as a cautionary tale, insisting, "I can go [only] so far in Texas. Maury forgot that and he is not here.... There's nothing more useless than a dead liberal."[4]

Although Johnson remained a relative progressive by Texas standards, he continued to tack to the right over the course of the 1940s. His conservative drift culminated in the Republican-controlled 80th Congress, when, along with nearly all Southern congressmen, he voted for the Taft–Hartley Act of 1947.[5] Johnson's support for Taft–Hartley's partial dismantlement of the pro-union New Deal labor regime earned him the enmity of organized labor, but given his constituents' anger over wartime strikes and unions' growing power, it was "good central Texas politics."[6]

---

[3] Joe B. Frantz, "Opening a Curtain: The Metamorphosis of Lyndon B. Johnson," *Journal of Southern History* 45, no. 1 (1979): 10.

[4] Jordan A. Schwartz, *The New Dealers: Power Politics in the Age of Roosevelt* (New York: Vintage Books, 1993), 264; James H. Rowe Jr., "Interview by Joe B. Frantz" (Interview I, transcript, Lyndon Johnson Oral History Collection, Lyndon Johnson Presidential Library, Washington, DC, September 9, 1969), 15, http://millercenter.org/scripps/archive/oralhistories/detail/2952.

[5] Irwin Unger and Debi Unger, *LBJ: A Life* (New York: Wiley, 1999), 126–127.

[6] Frantz, "Opening a Curtain," 13.

It also proved crucial to his razor-thin election to the Senate the following year over the conservative governor Coke Stevenson, who ran on a platform of "less government, lower taxes, states' rights, and 'the complete destruction of the Communist movement in this country.'"[7] Famously, Johnson also benefitted from election fraud in south Texas. But as Stevenson's gubernatorial successor Allan Shivers later observed, it was support for Taft–Hartley that "enabled Johnson to get close enough in votes to where [fraud] could make the difference."[8] Once in the Senate, Johnson maintained the careful centrism he had cultivated in the House, balancing the leftward pull of party loyalty and national ambitions against his constituents' (and financial backers') skepticism toward many aspects of New Deal liberalism.

* * * *

Lyndon Johnson's career in the House is not merely an intriguing prelude to his subsequent career as Senate leader, vice president, and ultimately president. It is also emblematic of the contemporaneous careers of members of Congress (MCs) across the South.[9] Like Johnson, the Southern congressional caucus—which numbered almost two dozen senators and a hundred-odd House members—underwent a dramatic ideological transformation between the mid-1930s and late 1940s, even as almost every single one remained, as Johnson did, a member of the Democratic Party. The consequences of this transformation were momentous at the time and continue to reverberate today.

A rich scholarly literature has documented Southern MCs' critical role in American political development during and after the New Deal. After many years as the dominant faction in a minority party, Southern Democrats' position in national politics was radically altered by the Great Depression. The Depression not only devastated the already-poor and underdeveloped South, but also in 1933 handed the Democratic Party unified control of the national government for the first time in a generation. Amidst the economic emergency, Southern MCs relaxed their traditional opposition to external intervention and gave overwhelming support to President Roosevelt's New Deal, which vastly expanded the federal government's role in the nation's economic and social life.

In the late 1930s, as the economic emergency receded and traditional fears of federal power resurfaced, Southern MCs' support for New Deal liberalism began to ebb. Though the South remained a one-party region,

[7] Robert Dallek, *Lone Star Rising: Lyndon Johnson and His Times, 1908–1960*, Vol. 1 (New York: Oxford University Press, 1991), 315.
[8] Frantz, "Opening a Curtain," 14.
[9] Unless otherwise noted, this book defines "the South" as the 11 states of the former Confederacy.

4 ◀─── Chapter 1

its representatives in Congress began allying with Republicans to block liberal reforms and even roll back elements of the New Deal regime. By the mid-1940s, with the passage of landmark laws such as Taft–Hartley, this conservative coalition had become a durable feature of congressional politics.[10] Southern Democrats did not fully abandon New Deal liberalism, however. Rather, balancing party loyalty and desire for federal aid against fear of external intervention, they came to occupy a centrist position in congressional politics, "holding the balance of power between the two great parties" on questions of economic policy.[11]

From this pivotal position, Southern MCs exercised profound influence over the scope and structure of the American state and political economy.[12] Even in the heyday of the New Deal, Southern MCs made their support for federal welfare and regulatory programs contingent on minimizing the federal government's interference with the region's racialized political economy. Southern MCs sought to limit spending on social welfare benefits, which undermined black laborers' dependence on low-wage agricultural employment. They also pushed for statutory exclusions and local discretion that ensured that programs such as Social Security, means-tested welfare, and veterans benefits were administered in a racially discriminatory fashion. These policy designs had important long-term effects on the development of the U.S. welfare state.[13]

---

[10] James T. Patterson, *Congressional Conservatism and the New Deal: The Growth of the Conservative Coalition in Congress, 1933–1939* (Lexington: University of Kentucky Press, 1967); David W. Brady and Charles S. Bullock III, "Is There a Conservative Coalition in the House?," *Journal of Politics* 42, no. 2 (1980): 549–559.
[11] Cortez A. M. Ewing, *Primary Elections in the South: A Study in Uniparty Politics* (Norman: University of Oklahoma Press, 1953), 106; see also Ira Katznelson, Kim Geiger, and Daniel Kryder, "Limiting Liberalism: The Southern Veto in Congress, 1933–1950," *Political Science Quarterly* 108, no. 2 (1993): 283–306; Ira Katznelson and Quinn Mulroy, "Was the South Pivotal? Situated Partisanship and Policy Coalitions during the New Deal and Fair Deal," *Journal of Politics* 74, no. 2 (2012): 604–620.
[12] For a sweeping synthesis, see Ira Katznelson, *Fear Itself: The New Deal and the Origins of Our Time* (New York: Liveright, 2013).
[13] Jill Quadagno, *The Color of Welfare* (New York: Columbia University Press, 1994); Robert C. Lieberman, *Shifting the Color Line: Race and the American Welfare State* (Cambridge, MA: Harvard University Press, 1998); Lee J. Alston and Joseph P. Ferrie, *Southern Paternalism and the American Welfare State: Economics, Politics, and Institutions in the South, 1865–1965* (New York: Cambridge University Press, 1999); Michael K. Brown, *Race, Money, and the American Welfare State* (Ithaca, NY: Cornell University Press, 1999); Ira Katznelson, *When Affirmative Action Was White: An Untold History of Racial Inequality in Twentieth-Century America* (New York: Norton, 2005). However, for accounts that emphasize the nonracial rationales for the policy designs, see Gareth Davies and Martha Derthick, "Race and Social Welfare Policy: The Social Security Act of 1935," *Political Science Quarterly* 112, no. 2 (1997): 217–235; Julian E. Zelizer, "The Forgotten Legacy of the New Deal: Fiscal Conservatism and the Roosevelt Administration, 1933–1938," *Presidential Studies Quarterly* 30, no. 2 (2000): 331–358;

The South's pivotal position was perhaps most consequential on issues related to labor markets, where the region's dependence on a low-wage, racially segmented labor force made it particularly sensitive to federal intervention.[14] Although Southern MCs expressed little overt opposition to the 1935 Wagner Act, which created a legal environment highly favorable to labor unions, their sensitivity on labor issues was already evident in the 1938 House vote on the FLSA, which most Southerners opposed. As unions grew in power, assertiveness, and racial inclusiveness, Southern MCs viewed them with increasing alarm, prompting cooperation with Republicans to rein in organized labor. These efforts culminated in 1947 with the Taft–Hartley Act, which passed over President Truman's veto thanks to overwhelming support from Southern Democrats. Taft–Hartley's retrenchment of the New Deal labor regime not only inhibited further union growth, but also arguably marked a crucial turning point in U.S. history away from European-style social democracy.[15]

Yet Southern Democrats stopped far short of a full alliance with Republicans, many of whom exhibited a "zealously sincere desire to dismantle the New Deal."[16] Rather, they joined with non-Southern Democrats to block more radical conservative reforms and consolidate liberal achievements. Southern MCs like House Ways and Means chair Wilbur Mills (D-AR), for example, were key to devising a fiscally and politically sustainable foundation for New Deal programs such as Social Security in the 1940s and 1950s.[17] In doing so, they helped institutionalize

---

Larry DeWitt, "The Decision to Exclude Agricultural and Domestic Workers from the 1935 Social Security Act," *Social Security Bulletin* 70, no. 4 (2010): 49–68.

[14] On the South's isolation from the national labor market and the threat the New Deal posed to this isolation, see Gavin Wright, *Old South, New South: Revolutions in the Southern Economy since the Civil War* (New York: Basic Books, 1986).

[15] Nelson Lichtenstein, "From Corporatism to Collective Bargaining: Organized Labor and the Eclipse of Social Democracy in the Postwar Era," in *The Rise and Fall of the New Deal Order, 1930–1980*, ed. Steve Fraser and Gary Gerstle (Princeton: Princeton University Press, 1989), 122–152; Sean Farhang and Ira Katznelson, "The Southern Imposition: Congress and Labor in the New Deal and Fair Deal," *Studies in American Political Development* 19, no. 1 (2005): 1–30; cf. Karen Orren and Stephen Skowronek, "Regimes and Regime Building in American Government: A Review of Literature on the 1940s," *Political Science Quarterly* 113, no. 4 (December 1998): 689–702.

[16] This quote was originally used to describe Ohio senator Robert Taft, arguably the preeminent congressional Republican in the 1940s and early 1950s; James T. Patterson, *Mr. Republican: A Biography of Robert A. Taft* (Boston: Houghton Mifflin, 1972), 314.

[17] Julian E. Zelizer, *Taxing America: Wilbur D. Mills, Congress, and the State, 1945–1975* (New York: Cambridge University Press, 1998); Alan Jacobs, "Policymaking as Political Constraint: Institutional Development in the U.S. Social Security Program," in *Explaining Institutional Change: Ambiguity, Agency, and Power*, ed. James Mahoney and Kathleen Thelen (New York: Cambridge University Press, 2010), 94–131.

a durable New Deal order that, although it fell short of progressive ambitions, was still a transformative achievement.[18]

Southern MCs' turn to the right in the 1930s and 1940s, coupled with their continued support for many elements of the New Deal order that they had helped construct, thus ranks among the most important political developments of the twentieth century. However, while scholars have described in great detail how these developments played out in Congress, much less is known about what drove them in the first place. Did Southern MCs' insulation from partisan competition give them the autonomy to base their decisions on their own personal policy preferences? Or, as is more commonly assumed, were Southern MCs acting as agents of the planters and other economic elites who controlled the one-party system? Or were they, like MCs outside the South, subject to an electoral connection that induced them to cater to ordinary voters?[19] In short, whom did Southern MCs *represent*? It is this question that is my focus in this book.

1.1 EXISTING PERSPECTIVES

Perhaps the most common answer to this question is that MCs from the one-party South represented the region's economic elite, especially plantation owners and other low-wage employers. This perspective, which I label *elite dominance*, often goes hand in hand with a characterization of the one-party South as an authoritarian enclave within a national democratic regime.[20] As one review summarizes, the elite dominance account holds that the South's "shriveled, conservative electorate" stymied mass participation in politics, and its lack of electoral competition gave politicians "few incentives to respond to whatever popular pressures did emerge."[21] Southern elites, through their command of economic and

---

[18] David Plotke, *Building a Democratic Political Order: Reshaping American Liberalism in the 1930s and 1940s* (Cambridge: Cambridge University Press, 1996); see also Alonzo L. Hamby, *Beyond the New Deal: Harry S. Truman and American Liberalism* (New York: Columbia University Press, 1973).

[19] David R. Mayhew, *Congress: The Electoral Connection* (New Haven, CT: Yale University Press, 1974).

[20] Edward Gibson and Robert Mickey have most fully developed the idea of Southern states as authoritarian enclaves; Edward L. Gibson, *Boundary Control: Subnational Authoritarianism in Federal Democracies* (New York: Cambridge University Press, 2012); Robert W. Mickey, *Paths out of Dixie: The Democratization of Authoritarian Enclaves in America's Deep South* (Princeton: Princeton University Press, 2015). Mickey, however, is careful to avoid the suggestion that authoritarianism necessarily implies domination by a cohesive elite; indeed, intra-elite conflict is central to his account.

[21] Jeff Manza, "Political Sociological Models of the U.S. New Deal," *Annual Review of Sociology* 26 (2000): 309.

social resources, were able to control Democratic nominations and thus, given the lack of Republican opposition, install their preferred candidates in office. Southern primaries provided "a semblance of political choice and electoral competition," but in the end they merely served to justify and entrench "complete planter dominance through the Democratic Party."[22]

The elite dominance account underlies most treatments of Southern MCs' role in national politics during this period. The influential analyses of Ira Katznelson and his collaborators, for example, presume that Southern MCs, as agents of "an authoritarian... political system," were "free from the constraints of a conventional reelection imperative" and represented "the interests of economic and political elites," whose policy preferences they largely shared.[23] These analyses thus implicitly attribute Southern Democrats' evolving position in congressional politics to Southern elites' changing calculus regarding the costs and benefits of federal power. Similar assumptions about elite dominance undergird the accounts of such scholars as Richard Bensel, Robert Lieberman, and Margaret Weir in political science; Lee Alston and Joseph Ferrie in economics; and Jill Quadagno and William Domhoff and Michael Webber in sociology.[24]

---

[22] G. William Domhoff and Michael J. Webber, *Class and Power in the New Deal: Corporate Moderates, Southern Democrats, and the Liberal-Labor Coalition* (Stanford, CA: Stanford University Press, 2011), 59.

[23] Farhang and Katznelson, "Southern Imposition," 1, 6; Katznelson, Geiger, and Kryder, "Limiting Liberalism," 284. Farhang and Katznelson "assume... that there was a very close mapping of personal and voting constituency [i.e., elite] preferences in the South in this era"; see Farhang and Katznelson, "Southern Imposition," 9, footnote 38. In his latest work Katznelson has taken a somewhat softer line, acknowledging that Southern politicians such as Mississippi senator Theodore Bilbo depended on the support of lower-income whites; see Katznelson, *Fear Itself.*

[24] Bensel describes the New Deal coalition as an alliance "between the southern plantation elite and northern working class." Alston and Ferrie characterize the Southern Democratic Party as "controlled by landowners and merchants in the counties dominated by plantation agriculture—the black belt elites," who "used Congressmen as their political agents." According to Quadagno, national "social policy was shaped by the ability of the southern planter class to wield a disproportionate share of political power in the broader nation-state. Southern planters gained political power through the establishment of a one-party South, which effectively stifled opposition to the dominant planter class." Likewise, Lieberman argues that Southern MCs opposed universalistic social policies because they threatened to give black laborers independence from "the planter elite and the political institutions that it dominated," and Weir makes similar claims about the threat that federal control posed to "the planter elite that had dominated the region's political and economic life for over half a century." Finally, Domhoff and Webber claim the most important New Deal policies were allowed to pass only after Southern Democrats—"the party of the Southern white rich"—shaped them "to fit the needs of plantation capitalists and large agricultural interests." See Richard Bensel, *Sectionalism and American Political Development: 1880–1980* (Madison: University of Wisconsin

All of these authors attribute the behavior of Southern MCs overwhelmingly if not exclusively to the interests and preferences of regional elites, with most stressing specifically the dominance of plantation owners.

All analyses require simplification, and for some analytic purposes treating Southern MCs as agents of the Southern elite may be satisfactory. But the elite dominance model runs into difficulty when confronted with the vigorous contestation within the South on economic issues. As Lyndon Johnson's congressional career demonstrates, Southern MCs not only changed ideologically over time, but also took divergent positions at any given place and time. Johnson's narrow plurality in 1937 or his 87-vote margin in 1948, both over more conservative opponents, are hardly suggestive of tight elite control of their congressional agents. Nor does the apparent appeal of court packing and minimum wages to many voters in Johnson's district bespeak a monolithic conservatism in the Southern electorate. This ideological diversity and contestation is amply documented in fine-grained accounts of Southern politics, as exemplified by V. O. Key's 1949 magnum opus on the subject.[25]

Notwithstanding Key's attention to the South's internal heterogeneity, the overall message of his *Southern Politics* is the inadequacy of one-party politics. The region's lack of partisan competition, Key argues, inhibited government responsiveness not only to disenfranchised blacks and poor whites, but to the eligible electorate as well. This model of Southern politics, which I will call *ruptured linkages*, acknowledges the contestation within the one-party system and the political participation of many nonelite whites. But it holds that without parties to foster issue-based conflict, facilitate collective responsibility, and provide low-cost information, voters cannot make meaningful electoral choices. The consequence, Key argues, is a politics unresponsive to voters' preferences and biased toward the "haves" over the "have-nots."[26] In short, the ruptured linkages suggests a weaker degree of upper-class control than elite dominance

---

Press, 1984), 370; Alston and Ferrie, *Southern Paternalism*, 34; Jill Quadagno, "From Old-Age Assistance to Supplemental Security Income: The Political Economy of Relief in the South, 1935–1972," in *The Politics of Social Policy in the United States*, ed. Margaret Weir, Ann Shola Orloff, and Theda Skocpol (Princeton: Princeton University Press, 1988), 236; Margaret Weir, "The Federal Government and Unemployment: The Frustration of Policy Innovation from the New Deal to the Great Society," in *The Politics of Social Policy in the United States*, ed. Margaret Weir, Ann Shola Orloff, and Theda Skocpol (Princeton: Princeton University Press, 1988), 27; Lieberman, *Shifting the Color Line*, 158; Domhoff and Webber, *Class and Power*, 5.

[25] Key, *Southern Politics*.

[26] Key, *Southern Politics*, chapter 14; for a succinct but more general statement, see Gerald C. Wright, "Charles Adrian and the Study of Nonpartisan Elections," *Political Research Quarterly* 61, no. 1 (2008): 13–16.

does, but otherwise offers a similar view of Southern MCs as relatively unresponsive to ordinary voters.[27]

A third and distinctly minority perspective is summarized by Robert Dahl's characterization of the one-party South as a dual system: "a more or less competitive polyarchy in which most whites were included and a hegemonic system to which Negroes were subject and to which southern whites were overwhelmingly allegiant."[28] I refer to this model of Southern politics as *white polyarchy*, using polyarchy in Dahl's sense of a "relatively (but incompletely) democratized regime" characterized by a high degree of political contestation and participation.[29] The strongest version of this model characterizes the South as a *Herrenvolk* democracy—"democratic for the master race but tyrannical for the subordinate groups."[30] But the white polyarchy model also encompasses the more qualified view of the South as an "exclusive republic" that, while properly classed as nondemocratic, for the white population nevertheless resembled democracy in important respects.[31] Both versions of white polyarchy make

---

[27] For analyses of congressional politics in the South roughly in line with the ruptured linkages view, see Key, *Southern Politics*, chapters 16–17; George Robert Boynton, "Southern Conservatism: Constituency Opinion and Congressional Voting," *Public Opinion Quarterly* 29, no. 2 (1965): 259; Earl Black and Merle Black, *The Rise of Southern Republicans* (Cambridge, MA: Belknap, 2002); Robert K. Fleck, "Democratic Opposition to the Fair Labor Standards Act of 1938," *Journal of Economic History* 62, no. 1 (2002): 25–54.

[28] Robert A. Dahl, *Polyarchy: Participation and Opposition* (New Haven, CT: Yale University Press, 1971), 93–94.

[29] Ibid., 8.

[30] Pierre L. Van den Berghe, *Race and Racism* (New York: Wiley, 1967), 19. On this view, the exclusion and subjugation of blacks was compatible with, or even facilitated, the empowerment of poor whites; cf. Edmund S. Morgan, "Slavery and Freedom: The American Paradox," *Journal of American History* 59, no. 1 (1972): 5–29. This was indeed an argument made, however insincerely, by many turn-of-the-century Southern disenfranchisers. Scholars such as Robert Mickey, however, criticize this view of Southern politics for ignoring the ways that oppression of blacks led also to the oppression of dissident and nonelite whites; Robert W. Mickey, "The Beginning of the End for Authoritarian Rule in America: *Smith v. Allwright* and the Abolition of the White Primary in the Deep South, 1944–1948," *Studies in American Political Development* 22, no. 2 (2008): 148–149. Linz argues that such restrictions are unavoidable in a racial democracy, which "is not only an authoritarian rule over the nonwhites but inevitably leads to increasingly authoritarian rule over those whites who question the policy of the majority and increasing limitations and infringements of the civil liberties and political expression of the dissidents"; Juan J. Linz, "Totalitarian and Authoritarian Regimes," in *Handbook of Political Science*, ed. Fred I. Greenstein and Nelson W. Polsby, Vol. 3: Macropolitical Theory (Reading, MA: Addison-Wesley, 1975), 328.

[31] On exclusive republics, see Philip G. Roeder, "Varieties of Post-Soviet Authoritarian Regimes," *Post-Soviet Affairs* 10, no. 1 (1994): 61–101; compare with the discussion of "diminished subtypes" of democracy in David Collier and Steven Levitsky, "Democracy

a fundamental distinction between Southern blacks, who were wholly barred from political participation, and Southern whites, who even if nonvoting were considered part of the political community. The white polyarchy model thus implies that, at least to a first approximation, Southern MCs represented their white constituents.

Each of these three models of Southern politics—elite dominance, ruptured linkages, and white polyarchy—is theoretically plausible, and the first two especially have undergirded numerous empirical investigations. No study, however, has subjected these three alternative accounts to systematic empirical comparison and evaluation, especially with respect to congressional representation. There are many fine studies of intra-Congress politics, and many also of politics "on the ground," but precious little evidence regarding the linkages among mass opinion, elections, and congressional behavior in the one-party South. To a large degree this has been a consequence of a lack of electoral and especially public opinion data from the one-party period, which has prevented the kind of systematic statistical analysis of representation that is possible in more contemporary studies. Taking advantage of newly available data and specially developed statistical methods, in conjunction with archival and secondary sources, this book conducts the first such analysis. At stake is not merely an answer to the question of representation in the one-party South, but also a deeper understanding of a critical juncture in American history and of mass politics in democratic and authoritarian regimes.

1.2 MY ARGUMENT

Over the course of this book, I will argue that the white polyarchy model provides the best account of congressional representation in the one-party South. To do so, I rely on an analytical framework that encompasses the elite dominance, ruptured linkages, and white polyarchy models as special cases. This framework characterizes the South as an exclusionary one-party enclave, which departed from normal democratic politics in three major respects: its exclusion of many citizens from the franchise, its lack of partisan competition, and its embeddedness within a national democratic regime. Each of these features had important implications for Southern politics.

The exclusion of many citizens changed the selectorate—the subset of citizens who participate in the selection of government officials, and thus to whom officials are accountable—to something less than the full

with Adjectives: Conceptual Innovation in Comparative Research," *World Politics* 49, no. 3 (1997): 430–451.

public.[32] If this had been the only undemocratic feature of Southern politics, we would expect Southern officials to have represented the selectorate about as well as officials in democratic regimes represent the set of all citizens. But the second feature, the South's lack of partisan competition, complicates this expectation by undermining the linkages between citizens and representatives. It did so not by eliminating electoral competition entirely, since Democratic primaries provided an alternative to general elections, but by depriving voters of the low-cost information that party labels convey about candidates' policy positions and relationship to the governing coalition. The third feature of congressional politics in the South, however—its subnational embeddedness—compensated for this informational deficit, at least to a degree. In a crucial difference from state-level politics, which lacked both parties in government and partisan electoral competition, once in office Southern MCs operated in a national political arena structured by partisan competition. Thus, unlike state and local officials, Southern MCs had to take clear and salient policy positions in a party-defined ideological space.

Different claims about these three features correspond to different models of Southern politics. The elite dominance model, for example, follows from the claim that the selectorate was so exclusive as to include only the economic elite. The ruptured linkages model follows from the claims that one-party politics deprived the selectorate, even if broader than the elite, of effective control over elected officials. And white polyarchy follows from the claim that the South's embeddedness in a national partisan regime gave the selectorate—defined as all whites—the information required to hold Southern MCs accountable.

My central thesis that white polyarchy provides the best description of congressional politics in the South rests on a number of empirical premises. Most obviously, it presumes that despite their monolithic partisanship, both Southern MCs and Southern selectorates exhibited meaningful variation in their political preferences. While this premise may be implausible on issues related to race and civil rights, it is quite reasonable on economics.[33] For this reason, I focus on the issues of regulation,

---

[32] I take this definition of *selectorate* from Bruce Bueno de Mesquita et al., *The Logic of Political Survival* (Cambridge, MA: MIT Press, 2003).

[33] The exclusion of blacks removed from the Southern electorate the only constituency with any strong commitment to racial equality. Notwithstanding certain efforts to reform the Jim Crow system and a few maverick politicians' support for civil rights, the bedrock principle of racial segregation was—in public at least—virtually unquestioned among Southern white citizens and politicians until after the Voting Rights Act. For exceptions, see Patricia Sullivan, *Days of Hope: Race and Democracy in the New Deal Era* (Chapel Hill: University of North Carolina Press, 1996); Timothy Werner, "Congressmen of the Silent South: The Persistence of Southern Racial Liberals, 1949–1964," *Journal of Politics*

redistribution, and social welfare at the core of the New Deal agenda, largely bracketing explicitly racial issues except insofar as they intersected with economic policymaking. To measure the preferences of Southern MCs, I estimate a dynamic ideal-point model of House and Senate votes on economics-related roll calls between 1931 and 1963. The resulting estimates of MCs' economic conservatism reveal Southern Democrats' diverse positions on economic issues in this period, as well as their ideological evolution from New Dealers in the 1930s to pivotal centrists after 1945. I also construct analogous measures of economic conservatism at the mass level, using data from hundreds of little-used public opinion polls fielded between 1936 and 1952.[34] These measures reveal patterns that parallel those in Congress: the Southern white public too shifted markedly to the right in the late 1930s and early 1940s, even as it remained internally diverse on questions of economics.

To connect the two arenas of mass opinion and congressional behavior, I develop an account of what I call the *selectoral connection*.[35] I argue that Democratic primaries, by providing a forum for intraparty contestation that was open to most Southern whites, induced Southern MCs to cater to their white constituents. I show that the selectorate in the South, while nearly all white, extended well beyond the economic elite. In fact, voter turnout in the white community was only modestly below turnout among modern-day Southerners of all races. Moreover, electoral competition in congressional primaries was frequent enough to provide a realistic threat of opposition and ideological enough to present voters with meaningful policy-based choices. As a consequence, voters were able to select representative candidates prospectively and sanction out-of-step incumbents retrospectively. The threat of such punishment in turn induced incumbents to anticipate the judgment of voters and adapt their behavior to voters' changing preferences. The end result was congressional representation that was responsive to a broad swath of the white public.

71, no. 1 (2009): 70–81; Kimberly Johnson, *Reforming Jim Crow: Southern Politics and State in the Age before Brown* (New York: Oxford University Press, 2010).
[34] The somewhat shorter range of my public opinion data is largely driven by the fact that the National Science Foundation–funded project to clean and code early public opinion data has not reached beyond 1952. Poll questions on economic issues were also substantially sparser in the 1950s than earlier. For examples of this decline, see Hazel Gaudet Erskine, "The Polls: Some Gauges of Conservatism," *Public Opinion Quarterly* 28, no. 1 (1964): 154–168. Fortunately, the period of greatest movement in Southern whites' economic attitudes (the mid-1930s to the mid-1940s) features particularly rich polling data.
[35] Compare Melanie Manion, " 'Good Types' in Authoritarian Elections: The Selectoral Connection in Chinese Local Congresses," *Comparative Political Studies* 47 (2014): 1–33.

To provide statistical evidence for Southern MCs' representation of their selectorates, I conduct a multifaceted analysis of the relationship between MCs' economic conservatism and the preferences of their constituents. I present evidence that Southern MCs' positions on economics were collectively in step with their selectorates', and that changes in the Southern mass public appear to have preceded those in Congress. I then show that within the South, MCs' conservatism covaried with the conservatism of their white constituents, both cross-sectionally and over time. Southern MCs even responded to the income level of their selectorates: richer selectorates elected more conservative MCs. All of these findings contradict the elite dominance model of Southern politics.

More remarkably—and contrary to the ruptured linkages model—I do not find that MCs in the two-party non-South were systematically more responsive to their selectorates than Southern MCs were. Nor do I find evidence of conservative bias in Southern congressional representation. Rather, owing probably to the effects of party loyalty, Southern MCs were markedly less economically conservative than non-Southern MCs from ideologically similar constituencies. In short, despite the limitations of the one-party politics and the disfranchisement of many whites, Southern MCs appear to have represented their white constituents about as well as non-Southern MCs did theirs. State politics, however, was a very different story: unlike the non-South, economic policies in Southern states bore no relationship to mass conservatism, and were uniformly more conservative than in the non-South. This suggests that it is only because of the unique features of congressional politics in the one-party South—specifically, the fact that in Congress Southern MCs operated within a partisan political arena—that congressional representation approximated white polyarchy.

1.3 IMPLICATIONS

My argument has three major sets of implications. Most directly, it challenges conventional explanations for Southern MCs' pivotal actions in shaping, limiting, and consolidating the New Deal order. Rather than merely reflecting the evolving preferences of Southern planters, Southern MCs were responding to the changing views of the white public at large. A fully satisfying account of this crucial era in American political development thus requires explaining not only the changing calculus of economic elites, but also the causes and contours of mass opinion and electoral politics in the South. If we want to understand Southern MCs' influence on the welfare state and political economy of the United States, we must first understand the evolving preferences and choices of ordinary white Southerners.

My argument also has implications for our understanding of the character and persistence of the South's exclusionary one-party enclaves. As Robert Mickey rightly argues, the suffrage limitations, barriers to political contestation, and other undemocratic restrictions of the one-party South justify its classification as an authoritarian regime.[36] Yet like many other electoral authoritarian regimes, the one-party South's undemocratic features did not preclude internal contestation or responsiveness to mass preferences.[37] Indeed, this very responsiveness may help explain the durability of the one-party system and the fervency of ordinary whites' resistance to external attempts to democratize the South in the 1950s and 1960s. This conclusion must be qualified by the evidence that Southern state politics was far less responsive than congressional politics. Nevertheless, my findings still suggest that the South's authoritarian regime lasted partly because it satisfied whites' preferences on both race *and* economics.

Most speculatively, my argument suggests a revised interpretation of the role that parties play in democracy. While it may seem strange to argue that the "authoritarian" South, which was undemocratic on multiple dimensions, informs our understanding of democracy, many scholars have made this very inference, most notably Key himself. The crux of Key's argument is that if one-party politics undermines representation even of the eligible electorate—and he argues that it does—then we can infer that it would do so even in an otherwise fully democratic regime. More recently, the party theorist John Aldrich has made this same inference to support his claim that a multiparty system is a necessary condition for democracy.[38] Thus, by showing that in some contexts the one-party South *was* responsive to the eligible electorate, my argument undermines the empirical basis for the almost unquestioned maxim that "democracy is unthinkable save in terms of . . . parties."[39]

---

[36] Mickey, "Beginning of the End"; Mickey, *Paths out of Dixie*.

[37] Steven Levitsky and Lucan A. Way, *Competitive Authoritarianism: Hybrid Regimes after the Cold War* (New York: Cambridge University Press, 2010).

[38] John H. Aldrich, *Why Parties? A Second Look* (Chicago: University of Chicago Press, 2011), 310–312; see also John H. Aldrich and John D. Griffin, "Parties, Elections, and Democratic Politics," in *The Oxford Handbook of American Elections and Political Behavior*, ed. Jan E. Leighley (New York: Oxford University Press, 2010), 595–610; John H. Aldrich and John D. Griffin, *Why Parties Matter: Political Competition and Democracy in the American South* (Chicago: University of Chicago Press, 2017); Wright, "Charles Adrian."

[39] E. E. Schattschneider, *Party Government* (Westport, CT: Greenwood, 1942), 1. "No theorist we know of," assert Wright and Schaffner, "has . . . explicitly challenged Schattschneider's . . . proposition"; see Gerald C. Wright and Brian F. Schaffner, "The Influence of Party: Evidence from the State Legislatures," *American Political Science Review* 96, no. 2 (2002): 367.

1.4 PLAN OF THE BOOK

The remainder of this book is organized as follows. Chapter 2 fleshes out the theoretical background for my argument. After clarifying the logic of representative democracy and parties' role within it, it develops a theoretical framework for analyzing electoral politics in an exclusionary one-party enclave such as the one-party South. Using the terms of this framework, it describes the three rival models of Southern politics—"elite dominance," "ruptured linkages," and "white polyarchy"—that structure the empirical analyses in succeeding chapters.

Chapter 3 examines the political attitudes of the Southern mass public in the wake of the Great Depression and the New Deal. Taking advantage of hundreds of public opinion polls conducted beginning in the mid-1930s, it documents Southern whites' collective turn against many aspects of the New Deal as well as their persistent ideological diversity on economic issues. The chapter illustrates these developments with a focus on four policy areas: old-age pensions, minimum wages, union security agreements, and income taxation. It then summarizes these patterns using a dynamic group-level item response theory (IRT) model, which estimates the economic conservatism of demographic subpopulations in each state and year.

Chapter 4 moves from the mass public to the halls of Congress. Paralleling Chapter 3, it describes the ideological evolution and continuing diversity of Southern senators and representatives, focusing again on their positions on economic issues. Using an IRT model similar to that used to estimate mass conservatism, it shows that between the 1930s and 1940s Southern members of Congress (MCs), like the Southern white public, turned sharply but incompletely against New Deal liberalism. By the mid-1940s, Southern Democrats in Congress had come to occupy a pivotal position on economic issues midway between non-Southern Democrats and Republicans, giving them outsized influence over national policymaking in the wake of the New Deal. The chapter illustrates these developments with three of the four policy areas Chapter 3 examines at the mass level.

Chapter 5 explains how the white primary created a selectoral connection between Southern MCs and the voting public, thus incentivizing them to respond to the preferences of the eligible electorate. It marshals quantitative evidence on competition in Southern primaries as well as qualitative evidence drawn from archives, newspapers, and other historical sources on Southern MCs' representational and accountability relationships with their constituents.

Chapter 6 conducts a systematic statistical analysis of congressional representation in the one-party South. It examines Southern MCs' responsiveness to their white constituents, both cross-sectionally and over time, and compares them to non-Southern MCs. It also shows that Southern MCs responded to the income of the median voter, and examines their ideological bias relative to non-Southern MCs. It then highlights the ways that congressional representation did differ across regions, and concludes by discussing how these findings help resolve the "puzzle" of Southern conservatism.

The final chapter concludes with a discussion of the implications of the revisionist portrait of Southern politics I have proposed. I begin by considering how much the South has changed since the dismantlement of the one-party system. I then explore the my findings' implications for our understanding of American political development, of mass politics in authoritarian regimes, and of the role of parties in democracy.

Replication materials for this book can be accessed at https://press.princeton.edu/titles/13231.html.

CHAPTER 2

The One-Party South

An Analytic Framework

[T]he existence of two parties—which is by no means the
same as a twoparty *system*—remains the standing pattern
throughout the United States, if only in exogenous and
incomplete terms, that is, on account of the
superimposition of the national twoparty system.[1]

—*Giovanni Sartori (1976)*

THIS CHAPTER DEVELOPS A THEORY OF ELECTORAL POLITICS AND REPRE-
SENTATION IN THE ONE-PARTY SOUTH, conceptualized as an exclusionary
one-party enclave. I begin with a stylized description of the logic of electoral democracy and how it induces government to represent its citizens.
Next, I consider the role of political parties, especially partisan competition, in democratic theory and practice. Having developed this framework
with respect to democratic regimes, I then propose a modified version of
it to describe electoral politics in the one-party South. I focus on three
important factors distinguishing the South from democratic regimes: its
political exclusion of many citizens, its lack of partisan competition, and
its status as a subnational enclave embedded in a national democratic
regime. The chapter concludes with a discussion of the empirical implications of this theoretical framework and what we can learn through
examination of the one-party South.

2.1 THE LOGIC OF REPRESENTATIVE DEMOCRACY

In this work, I employ a procedural definition of *democracy*, defining it
as a system for collective decision making that treats all participants as

---

[1] Giovanni Sartori, *Parties and Party Systems: A Framework for Analysis* (New York:
Cambridge University Press, 1976), 83–84.

political equals. More precisely, I follow Dahl in arguing that a democratic process requires equal and effective opportunities for participants to learn about political alternatives, express their views, influence the agenda, and vote on alternatives, as well as the political inclusion of all competent adult citizens.[2] In addition, I conceive democracy as an ideal type that actual regimes may approach to varying degrees on different dimensions of democracy. Chief among these dimensions of democracy are (1) *inclusiveness*, the extent of political participation, and (2) *contestation*, the extent of political competition.[3] Between the poles of democracy and totalitarianism lie intermediate regimes that may be considered hybrids with both democratic and authoritarian characteristics.[4]

Democracy can be justified from a variety of perspectives. John Stuart Mill, for example, argues that democracy serves three purposes: improving the civic character of the governed, facilitating the discovery of solutions to collective problems, and inducing governments to act in the interests of ordinary citizens.[5] This last justification, which Thompson calls "the democratic objective," is common to nearly all theoretical treatments of democracy and is probably the one that has received the most empirical attention as well.[6] The democratic objective encompasses both interests shared by all citizens (usually vis-à-vis their rulers) and situations in which citizens' interests conflict, in which case democracy can be seen as a fair means of aggregating or deciding among these interests.[7] Even if, as Kenneth Arrow shows, there is no uniquely optimal way to aggregate interests, democracy provides citizens with a minimum of control that enables them to reject clearly dispreferred policies and governments.[8]

---

[2] Robert A. Dahl, *Democracy and Its Critics* (New Haven, CT: Yale University Press, 1989), 106–131.

[3] Dahl, *Polyarchy*.

[4] Collier and Levitsky, "Democracy with Adjectives"; Levitsky and Way, *Competitive Authoritarianism*.

[5] John Stuart Mill, *Considerations on Representative Government*, People's edition, (London: Longmans, Green, 1867).

[6] Dennis F. Thompson, *The Democratic Citizen* (Cambridge: Cambridge University Press, 1970), 41. Dahl presents this justification as follows: "to a substantially greater degree than any alternative to it, a democratic government provides an orderly and peaceful process by means of which a majority of citizens can induce the government to do what they most want it to do and to avoid doing what they most want it not to do." See Dahl, *Democracy and Its Critics*, 95.

[7] Adam Przeworski, Susan Carol Stokes, and Bernard Manin, "Introduction," in *Democracy, Accountability, and Representation*, ed. Adam Przeworski, Susan Carol Stokes, and Bernard Manin (New York: Cambridge University Press, 1999), 6.

[8] Kenneth J. Arrow, *Social Choice and Individual Values*, 2nd ed. (1951; New Haven, CT: Yale University Press, 1963); William H. Riker, *Liberalism against Populism*

In its classical form, democracy entails direct citizen participation in policymaking. Notwithstanding the persistence of referenda and other forms of direct democracy, however, democracy in modern large-scale polities takes place instead through the mechanism of representation. In a representative democracy, citizens delegate their policymaking authority to elected officials who formulate policy on their behalf. To the extent that officials *represent* their constituents—that is, act "in the interest of the represented, in a manner responsive to them"—the policies chosen by them will reflect citizens' interests and preferences.[9] Representation thus provides a mechanism for achieving the democratic objective without direct citizen participation in policymaking.

The main tool by which citizens induce officials to represent them is elections. Elections induce representation via two mechanisms, selection and sanctioning, both core concepts of agency theory.[10] Candidates may differ in a variety of ways, such as in their ideology, competence, or corruptibility,[11] and so the goal of selection is to choose "good types" of officials, who share the preferences of their constituents and who competently and honestly pursue desired outcomes. The purpose of sanctioning is to punish poorly performing incumbents by removing them from office. Selection is prospective; sanctioning, retrospective. Under the right circumstances, either mechanism can induce representation.[12] If voters succeed in selecting competent officials who share their preferences, they have no need to sanction them ex post. Likewise, if voters can perceive and punish poor performance, then not only will bad incumbents be removed quickly, but the threat of electoral punishment will give officials an incentive to be representative when they would otherwise shirk.[13] Elections thus create an "electoral connection" between incumbents and the voters they must please to stay in office.[14]

(San Francisco: W. H. Freeman, 1982); Joseph A. Schumpeter, *Capitalism, Socialism and Democracy* (1942; repr., New York: Routledge, 2003).

[9] Hanna Fenichel Pitkin, *The Concept of Representation* (Berkeley: University of California Press, 1967), 209. A *responsive* official is one who chooses policies that citizens signal as preferred; Przeworski, Stokes, and Manin, "Introduction," 9.

[10] This discussion draws heavily on James D. Fearon, "Electoral Accountability and the Control of Politicians: Selecting Good Types versus Sanctioning Poor Performance," in *Democracy, Accountability, and Representation*, ed. Adam Przeworski, Susan Carol Stokes, and Bernard Manin (New York: Cambridge University Press, 1999), 55–97.

[11] Scott Ashworth, "Electoral Accountability: Recent Theoretical and Empirical Work," *Annual Review of Political Science* 15, no. 1 (2012): 186.

[12] Przeworski, Stokes, and Manin, "Introduction," 10.

[13] Compare with the distinction between turnover and anticipation in James A. Stimson, Michael B. MacKuen, and Robert S. Erikson, "Dynamic Representation," *American Political Science Review* 89, no. 3 (1995): 543–565.

[14] Mayhew, *Electoral Connection*.

The effectiveness of both selection and sanctioning in inducing responsiveness depends crucially on the information available to citizens. The mechanism of selection breaks down if citizens cannot predict how candidates are likely to act once in office. This lack of information can come about because citizens have heard nothing about the candidates, or because what they have heard (e.g., in the form of campaign platforms) is not a credible guide to their future behavior.[15] Similarly, sanctioning is ineffective if voters cannot discern representative incumbents from unrepresentative ones. Citizens may lack information about, for example, the policy choices of officials, the relationship between officials' actions and social outcomes, or what policies are in their own best interest.[16] If citizens lack the requisite information, elections alone may be insufficient to induce representation.

2.2 THE ROLE OF PARTIES IN REPRESENTATIVE DEMOCRACY

Parties are thought to play a critical role in making democracy work. The first democratic polities, such as the city-states of ancient Greece, lacked political parties. But today, despite the existence of a few small nations without parties[17] and the United States' and other countries' use of nonpartisan ballots in subnational elections,[18] representative democracy is nearly synonymous with partisan politics. Indeed, many scholars argue that democracy without parties is "unthinkable,"[19] "unworkable,"[20] or simply a contradiction in terms: "modern democracy *is* party democracy."[21]

Why is this so? What exactly do parties do that sustains democracy or makes it possible in the first place? Scholars have offered many

[15] Compare Alberto Alesina, "Credibility and Policy Convergence in a Two-Party System with Rational Voters," *American Economic Review* 78, no. 4 (1988): 796–805; Timothy Besley and Stephen Coate, "An Economic Model of Representative Democracy," *Quarterly Journal of Economics* 112, no. 1 (1997): 85–114.

[16] Fearon, "Electoral Accountability," 83; Ashworth, "Electoral Accountability," 191.

[17] Dag Anckar and Carsten Anckar, "Democracies without Parties," *Comparative Political Studies* 33, no. 2 (2000): 225–247.

[18] Alan Ware, *Citizens, Parties, and the State: A Reappraisal* (Cambridge: Polity, 1987), 59–63.

[19] Schattschneider, *Party Government.*

[20] John H. Aldrich, *Why Parties?* (Chicago: University of Chicago Press, 1995).

[21] Richard S. Katz, *A Theory of Parties and Electoral Systems* (Baltimore: Johns Hopkins University Press, 1980), 1; emphasis added. Susan Stokes, in the course of offering a more skeptical assessment of the role of parties in democracy, notes the possibility "that parties are markers of democracy, inevitable expressions of its advance, without being causally connected to all that is presumed good about democracy"; S. C. Stokes, "Political Parties and Democracy," *Annual Review of Political Science* 2 (1999): 263.

answers to this question,[22] but two common threads run through nearly all of them: alternatives and information. That is, parties provide the alternatives and information that citizens require to exercise meaningful control over their governors. The informational requirements in particular are a weak spot of democracy. Liberal democratic theory "loses its starting point" if citizens lack the information to develop well-ordered preferences and connect them to political outcomes and choices.[23] Given the abundance of evidence that most citizens fall well short of theoretical ideals, well-functioning democracy does indeed require some means of compensating for citizens' informational deficits.

Parties perform these functions in two main venues: within the government and in elections. Parties in government provide mechanisms for coordinating and constraining the behavior of the incumbent officeholders who affiliate with them. Their ability to do so provides stable institutional solutions to social-choice problems endemic to legislatures.[24] Parties also provide means of coordinating the activities of officials across government institutions, a function particularly important in fragmented polities such as the United States. By facilitating coordinated policymaking, parties in government provide a justification for assigning collective responsibility for current policies to the subset of incumbents affiliated with the governing party. Parties also play a key role in legitimizing and institutionalizing opposition to the dominant coalition, both within the state and outside it.[25] Parties, in short, provide a plausible answer to the

---

[22] Diamond and Gunther, for example, identify seven functions of political parties: (1) candidate nomination, (2) electoral mobilization, (3) issue structuring, (4) societal representation, (5) interest aggregation, (6) forming and sustaining governments, and (7) social integration; Larry Diamond and Richard Gunther, "Types and Functions of Parties," in *Political Parties and Democracy*, ed. Larry Diamond and Richard Gunther (Baltimore: Johns Hopkins University Press), 7–8. Snyder and Ting enumerate an analogous list of the purposes parties serve: "providing long-lived organizations through which relatively short-lived politicians can formulate policies, make credible promises to voters, solve collective action problems, and pursue politics as a career; providing low-cost information to voters about the likely policy goals or ideologies of politicians; providing low-cost information about which politicians are responsible for current policy outcomes; providing voters with distinct policy choices; and organizing legislative activity to solve collective choice problems"; James M. Snyder Jr. and Michael M. Ting, "Electoral Selection with Parties and Primaries," *American Journal of Political Science* 55, no. 4 (2011): 782–796.

[23] Christopher H. Achen, "Mass Political Attitudes and the Survey Response," *American Political Science Review* 69, no. 4 (1975): 1220; see also Larry M. Bartels, "Democracy with Attitudes," in *Electoral Democracy*, ed. Michael B. MacKuen and George Rabinowitz (Ann Arbor: University of Michigan Press, 2003), 48–82.

[24] Aldrich, *Why Parties?*

[25] According to Hofstadter, "the full development of the liberal democratic state in the West required that political criticism and opposition be incarnated in one or more

question of who should and should not be held accountable for current policies and conditions.[26]

In addition to clarifying collective responsibility, parties in government also engage in "issue structuring," bundling otherwise unrelated policy positions and interests into particular packages.[27] Control of nominations helps parties ensure that affiliated officials' policy positions are acceptable to all elements of the partisan coalition.[28] Control of the legislative agenda allows parties to limit and structure policy alternatives so as to avoid dividing members of their coalition.[29] As a consequence, partisan politics tends to fall along low-dimensional, often one-dimensional, lines of conflict.[30] This in turn renders political conflict more predictable: politicians who take a "left-wing" (whatever that means in the party system at hand) stance on one issue are likely to do so on other issues as well.

Parties also play an important role at the level of elections. Most fundamentally, a competitive party system ensures that incumbents face electoral opposition, thus providing voters with alternatives from which to choose. But beyond merely ensuring opposition, the information provided by party labels helps make these choices meaningful. As many scholars have noted, party labels provide voters with low-cost information about candidates' policy preferences and their relationship to the governing coalition.[31] This is important because each voter, having

---

opposition parties, free not only to express themselves within parliamentary bodies but also to agitate and organize outside them among the electorate, and to form permanent, free, recognized oppositional structures." Richard Hofstadter, *The Idea of a Party System: The Rise of Legitimate Opposition in the United States, 1780–1840* (Berkeley: University of California Press, 1969), xii.

[26] American Political Science Association, "Toward a More Responsible Two-Party System: A Report of the Committee on Political Parties," *American Political Science Review* 44, no. 3, Part 2, Supplement (1950): 1–96; Morris P. Fiorina, "The Decline of Collective Responsibility in American Politics," *Daedalus* 109, no. 3 (1980): 25–45.

[27] Diamond and Gunther, "Types and Functions of Parties," 8.

[28] Kathleen Bawn et al., "A Theory of Political Parties: Groups, Policy Demands and Nominations in American Politics," *Perspectives on Politics* 10, no. 3 (2012): 571–597.

[29] Gary W. Cox and Mathew D. McCubbins, *Legislative Leviathan* (Berkeley: University of California Press, 1993).

[30] For empirical evidence, see Jeffery A. Jenkins, "Examining the Bonding Effects of Party: A Comparative Analysis of Roll-Call Voting in the U.S. and Confederate Houses," *American Journal of Political Science* 43, no. 4 (1999): 1144–1165; Wright and Schaffner, "The Influence of Party"; Royce Carroll and Jason Eichorst, "The Role of Party: The Legislative Consequences of Partisan Electoral Competition," *Legislative Studies Quarterly* 38, no. 1 (2013): 83–109.

[31] Anthony Downs, *An Economic Theory of Democracy* (New York: Harper, 1957); Cox and McCubbins, *Legislative Leviathan*; Aldrich, *Why Parties?*; Brian F. Schaffner and Matthew J. Streb, "The Partisan Heuristic in Low-Information Elections," *Public Opinion Quarterly* 66, no. 4 (2002): 559–581; James M. Snyder Jr. and Michael M. Ting, "An Informational Rationale for Political Parties," *American Journal of Political Science* 46, no. 1 (2002): 90–110; Scott Ashworth and Ethan Bueno de Mesquita, "Informative Party

almost no probability of affecting the election outcome, has little reason to acquire more costly information about candidates. If they find it worthwhile to vote at all, voters thus tend to base their choices on whatever heuristic cues are available. By distinguishing the "ins" from the "outs," party labels enable voters to hold governments accountable for policy and social outcomes.[32] In addition, by conveying policy information about ideological differences between candidates, party labels also provide a basis for prospective selection of representative officials.[33] In short, "meaningful party labels allow voters to play a substantial role in selecting the direction of policy and holding politicians accountable."[34]

Not all party labels, however, are equally "meaningful." How much information a party label conveys depends on the character of the party system as a whole. Parties in government can affect the clarity of their "brand" by adopting distinctive policy agendas and positions.[35] Similarly, the informativeness of party labels also increases when parties propose divergent party platforms or purge ideologically heterodox candidates from their ranks.[36]

At the other extreme of informativeness lie elections in which party labels are entirely absent. This situation arises in two main cases: intraparty elections held to choose party nominees and nonpartisan general elections in otherwise partisan regimes. In contexts in which one party is so dominant that nomination is tantamount to election, the first case largely converges with the second. And indeed, party theorists have lodged the same complaints against both kinds of partyless elections: elections without party labels decrease turnout, advantage incumbents, disadvantage the poor, and ultimately result in "ruptured representational linkages" between officials and constituents.[37]

There are reasons to believe, however, that the case against nonpartisan elections has been overstated. First, at a theoretical level, it is not at all clear that democracy without parties is necessarily incoherent or

Labels with Institutional and Electoral Variation," *Journal of Theoretical Politics* 20, no. 3 (2008): 251–273.

[32] V. O. Key, *The Responsible Electorate: Rationality in Presidential Voting 1936–1960* (Cambridge, MA: Harvard University Press, 1966).

[33] Snyder and Ting, "Informational Rationale."

[34] Aldrich and Griffin, "Parties, Elections, and Democratic Politics," 595.

[35] Cox and McCubbins, *Legislative Leviathan*.

[36] Snyder and Ting, "Informational Rationale"; Ashworth and Bueno de Mesquita, "Informative Party Labels."

[37] Wright, "Charles Adrian," 15; See also Key, *Southern Politics*, chapter 14; Willis D. Hawley, *Nonpartisan Elections and the Case for Party Politics* (New York: Wiley, 1973); Sartori, *Parties and Party Systems*; Ware, *Citizens, Parties, and the State*; Brian F. Schaffner, Matthew Streb, and Gerald Wright, "Teams without Uniforms: The Nonpartisan Ballot in State and Local Elections," *Political Research Quarterly* 54, no. 1 (2001): 7–30.

impossible, or even undesirable.[38] Depending on how parties are conceptualized and modeled, they may be seen as diminishing the quality of representation rather than enhancing it.[39] There does seem to be robust support for the idea that responsiveness is increasing in the amount of information that voters possess.[40] But removing party labels does not eliminate all information about candidates. First, partisanship can "spill over" into officially nonpartisan contests, especially when nonpartisan local elections are embedded in a larger partisan system.[41] Second, voters can to some degree rely on alternative ideological cues, such as candidates' socioeconomic status.[42] Moreover, the effectiveness of such heuristic decision making can be enhanced by other features of the institutional environment, such as the activities of interest groups or the media.[43] Finally, there is some recent empirical evidence that nonpartisan elections, perhaps because they lessen incentives for ideological rigidity, do not diminish responsiveness to citizen preferences and may even enhance it.[44]

In summary, parties serve key functions in facilitating and sustaining democracy. Chief among these are the provision of alternatives and of information to citizens, which they perform through their actions both in government and in elections. It is not self-evident, however, that *only* parties—or more specifically, partisan electoral competition—can serve these functions. Rather, it is at least possible for these functions to be served by other institutions, in which case nonpartisan elections may be just as effective as partisan ones. We bear this possibility in mind as we

---

[38] See, for example, C. B. Macpherson, *The Real World of Democracy* (Oxford: Clarendon, 1966); Ware, *Citizens, Parties, and the State.*

[39] Stokes, "Political Parties and Democracy." For pro-party theoretical treatments, see, e.g., James M. Snyder Jr. and Michael M. Ting, "Roll Calls, Party Labels, and Elections," *Political Analysis* 11, no. 4 (2003): 419–444; Dan Bernhardt et al., "On the Benefits of Party Competition," *Games and Economic Behavior* 66, no. 2 (2009): 685–707. For contrary positions, see Brandice Canes-Wrone and Kenneth W. Shotts, "When Do Elections Encourage Ideological Rigidity?," *American Political Science Review* 101, no. 2 (2007): 273–288; Bawn et al., "A Theory of Political Parties."

[40] For a review, see Ashworth, "Electoral Accountability," 191–194.

[41] Ware, *Citizens, Parties, and the State*, 61.

[42] Fred Cutler, "The Simplest Shortcut of All: Sociodemographic Characteristics and Electoral Choice," *Journal of Politics* 64, no. 2 (2002): 466–490.

[43] Arthur Lupia and Mathew D. McCubbins, "The Institutional Foundations of Political Competence: How Citizens Learn What They Need to Know," in *Elements of Reason*, ed. Arthur Lupia, Mathew D. McCubbins, and Samuel L. Popkin (New York: Cambridge University Press, 2000), 47–66.

[44] Chris Tausanovitch and Christopher Warshaw, "Representation in Municipal Government," *American Political Science Review* 108, no. 3 (2014): 605–641; Brandice Canes-Wrone, "From Mass Preferences to Policy," *Annual Review of Political Science* 18, no. 1 (2015): 147–165.

now consider how representation might operate in an exclusionary one-party enclave.

2.3 ELECTORAL POLITICS IN AN EXCLUSIONARY ONE-PARTY ENCLAVE

We have seen that in well-functioning democracies, elections incentivize government officials to represent their constituents, and that competition among multiple parties is nearly always a marker of, if not a necessary condition for, large-scale modern democracy. How then should we understand electoral politics in a regime like the one-party South, which both lacked party competition and featured substantial restrictions on the scope of political participation? Does understanding the South require a totally different analytic framework, or can we modify the model of democratic politics sketched earlier to accommodate nondemocratic electoral systems?

For Edward Gibson, Robert Mickey, Ira Katznelson, and others who have labeled the one-party South an "authoritarian" regime, the answer seems to be that the region's restrictions on political competition and participation were so severe as to require an analytic framework wholly different from that appropriate to democratic regimes.[45] Other theorists, while granting that suffrage restrictions may render a regime undemocratic, nevertheless argue that there is nothing fundamentally undemocratic about a one-party system.[46] Still others, such as Schumpeter, dispute democracy has anything at all to do with the definition of the "populus," and thus characterize exclusionary regimes such as the one-party South as democratic as long as they use elections to allocate political power.[47]

My own view is that one can accept that the one-party South failed to meet democratic standards and yet still make use of frameworks developed with reference to democratic regimes. Doing so, however, requires careful specification of the ways in which the South fell short of democracy. This section develops such a framework, focusing on the three most important ways that the pre-1960s South differed from a national democratic regime. This first is the exclusion of nearly all Southern blacks as well as many poorer whites from the electorate. The second is its lack of

---

[45] Gibson, *Boundary Control*; Mickey, *Paths out of Dixie*; Farhang and Katznelson, "Southern Imposition."
[46] Macpherson, *The Real World of Democracy*; Jean Blondel, *An Introduction to Comparative Government* (New York: Praeger, 1969); Ware, *Citizens, Parties, and the State*.
[47] Schumpeter, *Capitalism, Socialism and Democracy*, 244, 269.

partisan electoral competition. And the third is the fact that the one-party South was a subnational regime embedded in a national two-party democratic system. Each of these characteristics has important implications for how we should understand and analyze Southern politics. They are encapsulated in my preferred term for the South's one-party regime: an *exclusionary one-party enclave*.[48] The remainder of this section develops a theory of electoral politics in exclusionary one-party enclaves.

2.3.1 *The Selectorate*

The exclusionary nature of Southern politics constituted a severe restriction on one of Dahl's two dimensions of polyarchy: the scope of political participation. Through a variety of formal and informal suffrage barriers, the Southern electorate was purged of nearly all blacks, especially before 1944, as well as many poor whites. As a consequence of these restrictions, election into political office did not require the support of a majority of adult citizens, as it would in a full democracy, but rather a nonrepresentative subset of them. Following Bueno de Mesquita et al., we may call this subset the *selectorate*.[49]

There are several important things to note about the Southern selectorate. The first is that the social composition of the selectorate differed markedly from that of the general Southern public. Most obviously, the selectorate was nearly entirely white. But because poll taxes, literacy tests, and other disenfranchising devices fell most heavily on the poor and uneducated, even relative to the white public the Southern selectorate was biased toward those of higher socioeconomic status. Because Southerners' interests differed by race and class, the biased demographic composition of the selectorate translated into biases in its political preferences, in turn biasing the incentives and behavior of Southern elected officials. As we will see in Chapter 3, the selectorate's bias was greatest on issues of segregation and civil rights, where Southern blacks and whites held

---

[48] This term is most closely related to Huntington's notion of *exclusionary one-party systems*, which he argues arise in "bifurcated" societies as an institutional means by which a dominant group "mobiliz[es] support from their constituency while at the same time suppressing or restricting political activity by the subordinate social force"; Samuel P. Huntington, "Social and Institutional Dynamics of One-Party Systems," in *Authoritarian Politics in Modern Society: The Dynamics of Established One-Party Systems*, ed. Samuel P. Huntington and Clement H. Moore (New York: Basic Books, 1970), 15. The term *enclave* I borrow from Edward Gibson and Robert Mickey's work on subnational authoritarianism; Edward L. Gibson, "Boundary Control: Subnational Authoritarianism in Democratic Countries," *World Politics* 58, no. 1 (2005): 101–132; Gibson, *Boundary Control*; Mickey, "Beginning of the End"; Mickey, *Paths out of Dixie*.

[49] Bueno de Mesquita et al., *The Logic of Political Survival*.

extremely divergent preferences, but it was also to some degree evident on economic issues.

It is essential to recognize, however, that Southern suffrage restrictions operated very differently for blacks and whites. At a fundamental level, even nonvoting whites were part of the political community in a way that African Americans were not. Southern states blatantly and unapologetically disenfranchised blacks, at least within the limits of the U.S. Constitution. Notwithstanding these constitutional limits, in practice blacks found suffrage barriers nearly insurmountable until the mid-1940s, when the white primary was struck down, and even afterwards black voting remained extremely difficult except in urban areas and where blacks composed a small fraction of the population. For whites, however, suffrage barriers were much more surmountable, given sufficient motivation and mobilization.[50] The white electorate was consequently much more elastic than the black electorate, and turnout variation within the South was largely a function of the number of whites who voted.

In sum, through the 1950s the selectorate in nearly all parts of the South consisted of a class-biased subset of the white community. Just how large a subset varied across time and place, depending on legal constraints, electoral competitiveness, political mobilization, and other factors. But as in fully democratic polities, the set of Southern citizens who actually voted, and even the set that registered to vote, was a conservative estimate of the *potential* electorate—the electorate whose responses politicians must anticipate when making political decisions.[51] Even if politicians responded more to actual than potential voters, it is fair to characterize the Southern selectorate as lying somewhere between the set of registered voters and all white adults, with substantial local and temporal variation. And while the electorate came after 1944 to include some African Americans, black voting remained marginal and inelastic enough that outside a few pockets the selectorate was effectively all-white.

2.3.2 Political Competition

Political participation does not by itself guarantee citizens a voice in the selection of officials and the formulation of policies. In some regimes, for example, the selectorate is large but the "winning coalition" consists of a tiny few who make the real decisions.[52] Without at least the potential for

---

[50] By 1950, all Southern states had literacy rates above 92% (pooling blacks and whites together), so literacy tests disenfranchised relatively few citizens. By then many Southern states had also abolished their poll taxes.
[51] R. Douglas Arnold, *The Logic of Congressional Action* (New Haven, CT: Yale University Press, 1990).
[52] Bueno de Mesquita et al., *The Logic of Political Survival*.

open political competition, "the right to 'participate' is stripped of a very large part of [its] significance."[53] As we have seen, one of the most important functions of parties is to provide such competition, in the form both of opposition within the government and of contestation in the electoral arena. It is commonly assumed that because general elections in the South were uncompetitive, the region lacked political competition entirely.[54] But while parties may be the most effective means of ensuring political competition, they are not a necessary condition for it, for competition can take place between candidates with the same (or no) party affiliation.

The institutional mechanism for such nonpartisan electoral competition in the South was the Democratic primary. By the early 1900s, all Southern Democratic parties had adopted the direct primary as a means of selecting nominees, replacing the previous system of elite-dominated caucuses. The primary was simultaneously a disenfranchising and democratizing reform. Until 1944, blacks could be legally excluded from intraparty elections, making the so-called white primary the "most efficacious method of denying the vote to African Americans."[55] At the same time, however, by opening up Democratic nominations to all white voters, primaries forced politicians to cultivate a popular following and provided a means by which ordinary whites could press their interests.

Primaries, in short, replaced general elections as the real elections in the one-party South. Though open only to whites, they did in fact provide a genuine forum for political competition, largely compensating for the absence of general-election competition.[56] And since the Democratic nomination was tantamount to election, this gave Southern selectorates real power over government officials.

2.3.3 Embeddedness

The final distinguishing characteristic of Southern politics is that the region's exclusionary one-party regimes were embedded in a national democratic polity featuring two-party competition. As Giovanni Sartori emphasizes, the fact that the one-party South was a subnational regime

---

[53] Dahl, *Polyarchy*, 5.
[54] See, e.g., Timothy Besley, Torsten Persson, and Daniel M. Sturm, "Political Competition, Policy and Growth: Theory and Evidence from the US," *Review of Economic Studies* 77, no. 4 (2010): 1329–1352.
[55] Alexander Keyssar, *The Right to Vote: The Contested History of Democracy in the United States* (New York: Basic Books, 2000), 249.
[56] Stephen Ansolabehere et al., "More Democracy: The Direct Primary and Competition in U.S. Elections," *Studies in American Political Development* 24, no. 2 (2010): 190–205.

rendered it qualitatively different from national one-party systems such as Mexico or Tanzania.[57] It did so in three major ways: by *constraining* the South's undemocratic tendencies, by *linking* the South to national politics, and—most relevant to my argument—by influencing the *informational* context of Southern politics.

Most fundamentally, the South was constrained by its embeddedness in a national legal and constitutional order. Notwithstanding national acquiescence to the South's creation of one-party enclaves and imposition of de facto disenfranchisement and de jure segregation, the South could not fully abandon the forms and procedures of democratic politics without inviting external intervention.[58] Blatantly unconstitutional restrictions, such as Oklahoma's grandfather clause and Texas's earlier, more overt version of the white primary, were subject to invalidation by the Supreme Court.[59] Violence and lawlessness could trigger congressional responses such as anti-lynching bills. The Constitution's Guarantee Clause, though largely toothless, precluded the outright abandonment of elections. These national constraints, even if rarely binding in practice, put limits on the authoritarianism of Southern state governments.

One of the main functions of a single-party regime is to monopolize linkages with external actors and present a united front in the enclave's "foreign relations" with the rest of the country.[60] In the case of the one-party South, alliance with the national Democratic Party came with both opportunities and dangers. After the Democrats became the national majority party in the early 1930s, for example, the South's national representatives used their influence in Congress particularly to shape the New Deal to the region's benefit. But Southern Democrats also faced recurring trade-offs between empowering the national government to aid and develop the South while also shielding Jim Crow from external interference.[61] The Democratic Party's monopolization of external linkages influenced Southern politics in other ways as well. It encouraged upwardly mobile politicians to hew to the national party line,[62] for example, and limited Southern whites' capacity to exit the party,

---

[57] Sartori, *Parties and Party Systems*, 83–84.
[58] Huntington notes that even national exclusionary one-party regimes depend on "a sympathetic or indifferent international environment that does not challenge the legitimacy of the system"; Huntington, "Social and Institutional Dynamics of One-Party Systems," 18.
[59] Michael J. Klarman, *From Jim Crow to Civil Rights: The Supreme Court and the Struggle for Racial Equality* (New York: Oxford University Press, 2004), 152.
[60] Gibson, *Boundary Control*; Key, *Southern Politics*, 315.
[61] Katznelson, Geiger, and Kryder, "Limiting Liberalism."
[62] Consider, for example, the careers of such presidential and vice-presidential aspirants as Alben Barkley, John Sparkman, Estes Kefauver, Albert Gore, and Lyndon Johnson.

undermining their voice within it.[63] In short, the Democratic Party was a two-way street, providing Southern enclaves with a mechanism for influencing national politics but also opening avenues of national intervention into the region.

For my purposes, however, the most important implication of the South's being embedded in a national two-party democracy is its effect on the informational context of Southern politics. These informational implications played out very differently for congressional politics, my focus in this work, than for state and local politics. In both settings, electoral politics in the South was conducted without parties. Party organizations, even of the dominant Democrats, played essentially no role in the recruitment of candidates, the running of campaigns, or the mobilization of voters, and voters chose among candidates without party labels to guide them. Congressional as well as state and local politics were thus equally deprived of the role of parties in providing voters with alternatives and information in the electoral arena.

Where congressional politics differed crucially from state and local is with respect to parties-in-government. State and local officials not only were elected without parties, but once in office they organized the government on a nonpartisan basis. The consequences, as Key forcefully articulates, were political instability and incoherence, a lack of clear responsibility for social and policy outcomes, and a bias toward the conservative status quo resulting from the difficulty of coordinating individual officials in pursuit of collective policy ends. It is on the basis of an analysis of state politics that Key rests his influential brief against no-party politics.[64] In short, notwithstanding the ways that national partisan politics could "spill over" at the subnational level, state and local politics in the South closely approximated the ideal type of a politics entirely without parties.

By contrast, Southern MCs, though elected without partisan competition, went on to serve in a national political environment structured by partisan conflict. Once in office, Southern MCs were forced to take positions and make choices in a political space largely defined by Democratic and Republican poles.[65] This not only imbued MCs' positions with an easily understood ideological meaning—which, in the 1930s–50s,

---

[63] In 1948, for example, national Democratic strategists persuaded President Truman to embrace civil rights on the logic that since "the South can be considered safely Democratic . . . it can be safely ignored"; Harvard Sitkoff, "Harry Truman and the Election of 1948: The Coming of Age of Civil Rights in American Politics," *Journal of Southern History* 37, no. 4 (1971): 597.

[64] Key, *Southern Politics*, especially chapter 14.

[65] On the low dimensionality of congressional roll call voting and the primacy of partisanship in defining the main dimension of conflict, see Keith T. Poole and

revolved largely around the role of government in the economy—but also defined their relationship to the majority (and thus to some degree "responsible") party in Congress. That is, MCs could associate themselves more or less closely with the governing coalition by positioning themselves as partisan loyalists or dissidents. Given the weakness of party discipline in the mid-century U.S. Congress, MCs' ability to differentiate themselves in this way was quite substantial, as we shall see in Chapter 4. Just as crucially, Southern MCs were able—indeed, required—to do so publicly and frequently by taking positions on roll call votes. Although roll calls hardly capture all important decisions, they do provide a salient and largely sincere indication of MCs' policy positions.

In short, whereas state and local politics in the South approximated pure unipartism, congressional politics was in a sense a hybrid of one-party and two-party politics: it lacked parties-in-elections but not parties-in-government. Consequently, the informational context of the two settings was quite different. Voters in congressional primaries, while lacking party labels, nevertheless benefitted from the relative coherence and low dimensionality of political alternatives structured by partisan conflict, and by the requirement that incumbents take frequent positions in a party-defined space.

2.3.4 The Selectoral Connection

We have now identified the essential elements distinguishing the one-party South from national democracies. First, the Southern selectorate consisted not of all adult citizens but rather of a class-biased and racially exclusive subset of them. Second, political competition did not take place between parties but rather within the hegemonic Democratic Party, in the form of primary elections in which all white members of the selectorate could participate. Third, the Southern one-party enclaves were embedded within a national two-party system, which had especially important implications for congressional politics: whereas state and local politics were purely one-party (hence no-party) affairs, in congressional politics only parties-in-elections were absent because once elected MCs operated in a two-party political arena. Congressional politics thus benefited from the informational functions of parties-in-government in ways that state and local politics in the South did not.

By incorporating these elements we can build a modified model of democratic politics to analyze exclusionary one-party enclaves such as the South. The first modification is to treat government officials as agents

Howard Rosenthal, *Ideology & Congress* (New Brunswick, NJ: Transaction Publishers, 2007).

not of the general public, but of a selectorate consisting roughly of the set of potential voters. When political preferences are approximately one-dimensional, we can as a shorthand allow the median member of the selectorate to stand in for the selectorate as a whole.[66] Whether the median is in fact decisive depends on the institutions for selecting party nominees. A caucus system, such as that used by the nineteenth-century Democratic Party, is likely to be dominated by party insiders unrepresentative of the selectorate as a whole. But a direct primary in which each selectorate member has an equal vote and opportunities for contestation are relatively open will more closely approximate majority rule.[67] Finally, the "slack" in the agency relationship between officials and voters is inversely proportional to the information about the former available to the latter.[68] In the absence of party labels, voters' capacity to distinguish candidates ex ante and monitor them ex post hinges on the availability of alternative sources of information.

To summarize: we should expect officials in an exclusionary one-party enclave to be responsive to their selectorates, not to the public. In particular, if nomination (hence election) is determined by an open process with equal votes for all members of the selectorate, officials should be accountable to a majority winning coalition that encompasses the electoral center. The strength of these relationships of accountability and responsiveness should be increasing in the quality of information available to the selectorate. In short, to the extent that these conditions are satisfied, we should expect representatives' actions in office to be rooted in their "selectoral connection" to their voting constituents.

2.4 MODELS OF SOUTHERN POLITICS

The analytic framework just described encompasses as special cases several competing models of Southern politics. It should be emphasized that each of these models is a highly stylized representation of a complex and nuanced reality. Like all models, none of them is "true," but they can be more or less useful for different purposes. By specifying these models in

[66] Even if politics is multidimensional, there are theoretical reasons to expect candidates to converge near the political center; Randall L. Calvert, "Robustness of the Multidimensional Voting Model: Candidate Motivations, Uncertainty, and Convergence," *American Journal of Political Science* 29, no. 1 (1985): 69–95.

[67] Equal voting power is, of course, unlikely to result in fully equal responsiveness unless voters are equal in money, attention, information, and other resources as well.

[68] Compare Sean Gailmard and Jeffery A. Jenkins, "Agency Problems, the 17th Amendment, and Representation in the Senate," *American Journal of Political Science* 53, no. 2 (2009): 324–342.

terms of the framework, we can derive testable implications that can be used to guide the empirical analyses in subsequent chapters.

2.4.1 Model 1: Elite Dominance

The elite dominance model presents Southern officials as agents of the economic elite, particularly plantation owners. As noted in Chapter 1, this model undergirds most existing analyses of the role of Southern MCs in national politics. In terms of the analytic framework sketched earlier, this model stipulates that winning coalitions in the earlier one-party South consisted of a small and cohesive fraction of the total population. The dominance of this small elite has been attributed to a variety of mechanisms: the South's "shriveled, conservative" selectorate, its lack of genuine political competition, and elite manipulation of lower-class whites through racial and symbolic appeals.[69] Regardless of the mechanism, the key feature of the elite dominance model is that Southern officials were responsive not to the general public, or even to those formally eligible to participate (i.e., the selectorate), but rather to a narrow elite with homogeneous and relatively conservative political preferences.

2.4.2 Model 2: Ruptured Linkages

Elite dominance paints a stark vision of a politics controlled by a small and homogeneous group. A less extreme view is one that might be called the *ruptured linkages* model. This is the model closest to Key's position in *Southern Politics* and also to that of scholars, such as Gerald Wright, who have extended Key's critiques to local nonpartisan politics.[70] Compared to elite dominance, the ruptured linkages model places less emphasis on the narrowness and homogeneity of winning coalitions in the South, and more on the defects of politics without partisan competition. On this view, lack of party labels largely deprived voters of the ability to make policy-based choices between candidates, and the feebleness of electoral competition endowed incumbents with relative security once in office. Under the ruptured linkages model, one-party politics may not have completely eliminated responsiveness to the selectorate, but it certainly weakened it relative to a two-party setting.

2.4.3 Model 3: White Polyarchy

The final model I consider, *white polyarchy*, is derived from Dahl's categorization of the one-party South as a polyarchy for whites superimposed

---

[69] Manza, "Political Sociological Models of the U.S. New Deal," 309.
[70] See, for example, the review in Wright, "Charles Adrian."

on a hegemony for blacks.[71] This model does not consider the South fully democratic, or even fully democratic for whites, for such claims would be implausible on their face given the region's formal restrictions on democratic processes. But it does consider Southern MCs to have been at least as faithful agents of their selectorates as non-Southern MCs were. Moreover, it defines the Southern selectorate broadly, as consisting of all adult whites (but no blacks). This model is thus predicated on two premises: first, that the selectorate in the South had political preferences similar to those of the white public as a whole (or at least no more different than those of voters and nonvoters in the non-South), and second, that lack of partisan competition did not materially inhibit responsiveness to the selectorate, relative to the non-South. In short, this model holds that the informational and other conditions for a selectoral connection in the South were substantially satisfied.

2.5 CONCLUSION

As I have emphasized, each of these models is a simplistic representation of reality. Models 1 and 3 in particular are extreme cases whose perfect truthfulness is contradicted by easily observable facts. The real question is which of these models provides the most accurate parsimonious depiction of congressional politics in the one-party South. In the following chapters I will take these models to the data in an attempt to adjudicate among them. As I will show, though there is some evidence of ruptured linkages, on the whole the congressional evidence is most consistent with a model of the South as a polyarchy for whites.

---

[71] Dahl, *Polyarchy*, 93–94.

CHAPTER 3

Public Opinion in South and Nation

"Children, who paved the road in front of your house?"
In response, the chorus, "Roosevelt!"
"Who put electricity into your house for you?"
"Roosevelt!"
"Who gave your uncle a job in the WPA?"
"Roosevelt!"
"Who got your granddaddy an old age pension?"
"Roosevelt!"
"All right, children. Now. Who made you?" After a
moment of silence one little boy asserted stoutly, "God."
Whereupon a gallused, barefoot towhead leaped up in the
back row and yelled, "Throw that sorry Republican out of
here."[1]

— *Joke told in the Depression-era South*

[W]hat is progress at one time may be retrogression at
another. There are times, as in the 1930s, when we need
most an improvement in human welfaring and then
progress must take that direction. There are other times,
and these are such, when we most need to protect or
recover the framework of liberty....[2]

— *John Temple Graves (1946)*

IN FEBRUARY 1937, the Gallup Poll asked the American public, "If there
were only two political parties in this country—one for conservatives and

---

[1] Ferrol Sams Jr., "God as Elector: Religion and the Vote," in *The Prevailing South: Life and Politics in a Changing Culture*, ed. Dudley Clendinen (Atlanta: Longstreet, 1988), 50.
[2] John Temple Graves, "This Afternoon," *Birmingham Post*, August 9, 1946, 8.

one for liberals—which would you join?"[3] Fielded only a few months after FDR's smashing reelection victory, the survey recorded a liberal majority of 55%, marking one of the few moments in U.S. history when more Americans identified with liberalism than conservatism.[4] The majority was even larger among Southern whites, 63% of whom said they would join the liberal party. The South, in fact, was the most liberal region in the country, beating out the West (58%), Northeast (55%), and Midwest (52%).[5] Nine years later, in June 1948, Gallup posed the same question.[6] Although a bare majority of Americans with an opinion still chose the liberal option, the ideological distribution across regions was starkly different from what it had been in 1937.[7] Just 34% of white Southerners said they would join the liberal party, compared to 49% of Midwesterners, 52% of Westerners, and 59% of Northeasterners. In only a decade, the South had transformed from the region most attached to liberalism into a bastion of conservatism.[8]

In this chapter, I explore the sources, scope, and timing of this dramatic and, as I argue later in the book, highly consequential shift in Southern

---

[3] *Gallup Poll* no. 69 (February 17–22, 1937).

[4] Unless otherwise noted, the figures cited in this chapter refer to poll samples weighted to be representative of the voting-eligible public (i.e., excluding Southern blacks). In this case, 53% of the unweighted sample selected "liberal." These percentages do not include the 29% of the weighted respondents who expressed no opinion or whose responses are otherwise missing. Since the mid-1970s, the percentage of Americans identifying as liberal (excluding moderates) has ranged between 32% and 40%; see Christopher Ellis and James A. Stimson, "Symbolic Ideology in the American Electorate," *Electoral Studies* 28, no. 3 (2009): 388–402.

[5] Unless otherwise noted, I use the following regional classification for states:

- Midwest: OH, MI, IN, IL, WI, MN, IA, MO, ND, SD, NE, KS, KY, OK
- Northeast: ME, NH, VT, MA, RI, CT, NY, NJ, PA, MD, DE, WV
- South: NC, SC, VA, GA, AL, AR, FL, LA, MS, TN, TX
- West: MT, AZ, CO, ID, WY, UT, NV, NM, CA, OR, WA

[6] *Gallup Poll* no. 421 (July 16–21, 1948).

[7] The number of missing/no-opinion responses was 46%, substantially higher than in 1937.

[8] Many observers have noted the South's shift from most liberal to most conservative region. See, e.g., Everett Carll Ladd and Charles D. Hadley, *Transformations of the American Party System: Political Coalitions from the New Deal to the 1970s* (New York: Norton, 1975); David A. Breaux and Stephen D. Shaffer, "Southern Political Attitudes," in *The Oxford Handbook of Southern Politics*, ed. Charles S. Bullock III and Mark J. Rozell (New York: Oxford University Press, 2012), 235–254, as well as the more qualified discussion in V. O. Key Jr., *Public Opinion and American Democracy* (New York: Knopf, 1961), 103–104. What is not often recognized is that much of this shift took place in just a few short years between the mid-1930s and mid-1940s.

white opinion. In doing so I rely heavily on a rich but underused data source: hundreds of public opinion surveys fielded by commercial polling firms between 1936 and 1952. In addition to analyzing responses to individual questions, I also take advantage of recently developed statistical methods to estimate different geographic and demographic groups' general economic conservatism. Based on this and other evidence, I argue that the South's turn to the right was driven partly by the increasingly urban and union-oriented character of New Deal liberalism, which alienated rural areas throughout the nation, and partly by white Southerners' growing sense of threat to their region's system of racial hierarchy. Southern conservatism was most evident on issues related to the region's racialized labor markets, such as minimum wages, work relief, and organized labor. At the same time, on other issues, including redistributive taxation, public power, and old-age insurance, Southern whites remained at least as liberal as other Americans. Moreover, like Americans elsewhere, white Southerners were divided along class and urban–rural lines in their attitudes toward New Deal liberalism. Unlike the rest of the country, however, these ideological divisions were not reflected in white Southerners' party identification (PID), which remained overwhelmingly Democratic, though this is less true of presidential vote. In short, even as white Southerners turned against the New Deal they remained committed to the one-party system, but this partisan unanimity masked persistent ideological diversity on economic issues.

3.1 THE NEW DEAL AND THE SOUTH

When the stock market crashed in 1929, the South was a poor and underdeveloped region already mired in a general agricultural downturn. Following the crash, farm income in the region fell by a further 50%, and in many areas manufacturing declined at least as precipitously.[9] With miserly state and local governments and a per capita income half as high as that of the rest of the country, Southerners had little to cushion them from the devastation of the ensuing Great Depression. The severity of the economic emergency prompted many Southern whites to abandon, if only temporarily, their traditional hostility to outside intervention in their region. "[S]o desperately did the region require relief," writes one historian, "that the southern people and the very leaders who had long championed the 'state's rights' tradition, demanded federal action in

---

[9] Sullivan, *Days of Hope*, 20.

the thirties."[10] Indeed, some of the more radical responses to the Depression, from Louisianan Huey Long's "Share Our Wealth" movement to Alabamian Hugo Black's proposal for a mandatory 30-hour work-week, originated in the South.[11]

Franklin Delano Roosevelt, the upstate New Yorker inaugurated as president when the Depression was already in its fourth year, had long enjoyed a special relationship with the South.[12] In 1924 he began making regular visits to Warm Springs, Georgia, whose therapeutic baths eased his polio symptoms. FDR's second home in Warm Springs also served a valuable political purpose, as "a kind of embassy . . . to the Southern wing of his party."[13] Roosevelt's cultivation of Dixie politicians paid off handsomely in 1932, when the support of Southern delegations proved critical to his fourth-round convention victory over his rivals for the Democratic presidential nomination, Texas's John Nance Garner and New York's Al Smith.

From the outset, FDR enjoyed enormous popularity in the South. "I don't imagine you could have found a white man in Georgia," one Southern politician later recalled, "that would have admitted publicly in '32 that he was against Roosevelt."[14] Southern support for Roosevelt continued unabated after the election. One year into his administration, one Texas editor observed that "the popularity of President Roosevelt not only is general but . . . is unprecedented in intensity."[15] The new president drew support from Southern whites of all classes. Roosevelt's patrician gentility appealed to the Southern gentry, who saw the New York country squire as something of a kindred spirit.[16] But FDR's popularity was even greater among ordinary Southern farmers and laborers, many of whom expressed a profound devotion to the president. "You are our Moses,"

[10] Bruce J. Schulman, *From Cotton Belt to Sunbelt: Federal Policy, Economic Development, and the Transformation of the South, 1938–1980* (Durham, NC: Duke University Press, 1994), 14.

[11] George Brown Tindall, *The Emergence of the New South, 1913–1945* (Baton Rouge: Louisiana State University Press, 1967), 390.

[12] For a general discussion, see William Edward Leuchtenburg, *The White House Looks South: Franklin D. Roosevelt, Harry S. Truman, Lyndon B. Johnson* (Baton Rouge: Louisiana State University Press, 2005).

[13] David M. Kennedy, *Freedom from Fear: The American People in Depression and War, 1929–1945* (New York: Oxford University Press, 1999), 97.

[14] This quote is from Georgia politician Herman Talmadge, whose father Eugene had been among the earliest and most vituperative Southern critics of the New Deal; quoted in Leuchtenburg, *White House Looks South*, 39.

[15] Quoted in Tindall, *Emergence of the New South*, 390.

[16] Robert A. Garson, *The Democratic Party and the Politics of Sectionalism, 1941–1948* (Baton Rouge: Louisiana State University Press, 1974), 1–2; Leuchtenburg, *White House Looks South*, 37.

wrote one South Carolina textile worker. "Leading us out of the Egypt of depression to the promised land of prosperity."[17] If anything, ordinary Southerners' enthusiasm waxed over the course of FDR's first term. In 1936 Senator Josiah Bailey (D-NC), himself no great fan of the president, reported that "the masses of the people are very strong [for Roosevelt], and while he has lost support with a limited number of business men, he has gained very greatly with the smaller business man, the farmers, clerks, and general run of the voters."[18]

Although Southerners enjoyed less influence in the executive branch than under the last Democratic president, Woodrow Wilson, the raft of policies that composed FDR's New Deal were nevertheless crafted with Southern sensibilities in mind.[19] Given the desperate condition of the Southern economy, the relief spending, farm subsidies, and expanded access to credit brought by the early New Deal were a godsend to the region. So too were the infrastructure investment and economic development delivered by such programs as the Rural Electrification Administration (REA), Tennessee Valley Authority (TVA), and Public Works Administration (PWA).[20] As Gavin Wright has argued, New Deal spending in the South not only stabilized its devastated economy but also greatly accelerated the region's economic modernization over the longer term.[21]

Moreover, federal aid in the 1930s came with few overt strings attached, especially when it came to the South's system of racial hierarchy. In addition to lacking explicit antidiscrimination provisions,[22] New Deal policies were designed in ways that limited their interference with the South's racialized political economy. In particular, most federal programs were either administered locally or included racially biased statutory exclusions. The Social Security Act (SSA) of 1935 is a well-studied example of this phenomenon. The means-tested welfare programs created by the SSA (Old-Age Assistance and Aid to Dependent Children) permitted substantial local discretion in administration, which in practice led to the withholding of benefits during the cotton harvest and other

---

[17] Leuchtenburg, *White House Looks South*, 51.
[18] Quoted in Tindall, *Emergence of the New South*, 390.
[19] Tindall, *Emergence of the New South*, 390; Michael Perman, *Pursuit of Unity: A Political History of the American South* (Chapel Hill: University of North Carolina Press, 2009), 231; more generally, see Roger Biles, *The South and the New Deal* (Lexington: University Press of Kentucky, 1994).
[20] Schwartz, *The New Dealers*; Jason Scott Smith, *Building New Deal Liberalism: The Political Economy of Public Works, 1933–1956* (New York: Cambridge University Press, 2006).
[21] Gavin Wright, "The New Deal and the Modernization of the South," *Federal History* 2010, no. 2 (2010): 58–73.
[22] Katznelson, *When Affirmative Action Was White*, 22–23.

forms of discrimination against African Americans. The SSA's system of old-age insurance (OAI), on the other hand, could not effectively be decentralized in this way, but instead OAI excluded the two most common occupations among Southern blacks, farm laborers and domestic servants.[23]

As a number of scholars have noted, some of these policy designs had compelling nonracial rationales, and the degree to which they can be attributed to Southern racism is subject to debate.[24] Furthermore, these policy designs did not prevent African Americans from receiving substantial benefits from New Deal programs. About a fifth of all recipients of federal relief, for example, were black, mostly from the rural South— double their proportion of the population, though probably less than their share of the needy.[25] More generally, the New Deal also "stirred the stagnant economic and political relationships" of the South and "implicitly threatened the culture of dependency that had secured an abundant, cheap labor supply."[26] On the whole, however, while the New Deal contributed mightily to the development of the Southern economy, it did little in the short term to disturb either Jim Crow or the one-party system.[27] For these reasons, the New Deal, like the president himself, was widely popular among white Southerners through the end of Roosevelt's first term. "An overwhelming majority of the people are for it," one Mississippi newspaper editor commented in 1936, "stronger than horseradish."[28]

Support for the New Deal was not universal, however. "It must not be assumed," wrote another editor, "that because South Carolina [is] overwhelmingly for the nomination and reëlection of Roosevelt, the Administration is without criticism. Criticism is remarkably free and unrestrained."[29] Indeed, some white Southerners opposed the New Deal wholesale from the outset. Prominent among these early critics were manufacturing groups such as the Southern States Industrial Council, which bitterly criticized Roosevelt's policies for driving up wages and encouraging labor unrest (most spectacularly, the huge and violently suppressed

---

[23] Quadagno, *Color of Welfare*; Lieberman, *Shifting the Color Line*; Katznelson, *When Affirmative Action Was White*.
[24] Davies and Derthick, "Race and Social Welfare Policy"; Zelizer, "Forgotten Legacy"; DeWitt, "The Decision to Exclude."
[25] Kennedy, *Freedom from Fear*, 164.
[26] Sullivan, *Days of Hope*, 3.
[27] Anthony J. Badger, "How Did the New Deal Change the South?," in *New Deal/New South* (Fayetteville: University of Arkansas Press, 2007), 31–44; Wright, "The New Deal and the Modernization of the South."
[28] Frederick Sullens, "The South Is Still Solid: Mississippi," *Review of Reviews* 93 (January 1936): 39.
[29] William E. Gonzales, "The South Is Still Solid: South Carolina," *Review of Reviews* 93 (January 1936): 39.

textile strike of 1934, which involved nearly 200,000 employees of Southern mills). Many Southern planters shared these concerns, though they also benefitted greatly from New Deal farm programs as well as from agricultural exceptions included in many New Deal laws. Other early critics, mostly old Wilsonians, opposed the New Deal out of a principled commitment to laissez faire. Only a few isolated voices, most prominently Governor Eugene Talmadge of Georgia, did so on explicitly racial grounds.[30]

More common than blanket opposition to the New Deal was opposition to, or at least lack of enthusiasm for, particular policies. This unevenness of Southern support for liberal policies is evident in a pair of large-scale surveys of newspaper editors conducted in late 1934 and early 1936 by the National Industrial Conference Board (NICB). These surveys asked editors to report "whether public opinion in their communities favored or disapproved" of a number of actual and proposed policies.[31] These assessments of community opinion reveal the South to have been more liberal than the nation on most issues, but not all of them. The region's liberalism relative to the nation was clearest on redistributive taxation, government control of the money supply, and agricultural price supports and production controls.[32] On some policies, however, especially those related to national regulation of labor markets (compulsory unions, minimum wages, and unemployment insurance), Southern communities

[30] Garson, *Democratic Party*, 3–4; Patterson, *Congressional Conservatism*; Tindall, *Emergence of the New South*, 615–617. Many Southern business owners, however, supported the New Deal for increasing access to credit and generally subsidizing the development of the region. See, e.g., the portrait of Jesse H. Jones, chairman of the Reconstruction Finance Corporation and later Secretary of Commerce, in Schwartz, *The New Dealers*.

[31] These surveys, based on a questionnaire sent to every editor in the country and returned by several thousand, were fielded by the National Industrial Conference Board, a moderately progressive association of business leaders; see National Industrial Conference Board, *A Statistical Survey of Public Opinion: Regarding Current Economic and Social Problems as Reported by Newspaper Editors in August and September, 1934*, Study no. 205 (New York: National Industrial Conference Board, 1934); National Industrial Conference Board, *A Statistical Survey of Public Opinion: Regarding Current Economic and Social Problems as Reported by Newspaper Editors in the First Quarter of 1936*, Study no. 222 (New York: National Industrial Conference Board, 1936).

[32] According to two pioneering national (though not fully representative) surveys of "housewives" conducted in late 1933 by a consortium of psychologists in 40 cities and towns, the South was also clearly the region most positive toward the National Recovery Administration. Fifty-five percent of Southern housewives agreed that the NRA was "working well" in their community, 11 points above the national average and 8 points above the next most supportive region, the Far West. See Henry C. Link, "A New Method for Testing Advertising and a Psychological Sales Barometer," *Journal of Applied Psychology* 18, no. 1 (1934): 24.

were actually more conservative than average. Within the South, the East South Central states (TN, AL, MS, and KY) were generally the most conservative—often more so than the national average—and the West South Central states (AR, TX, LA, and OK) were the most consistently liberal.[33]

Given the limitations of such indirect measures of public opinion, considerable uncertainty surrounds our understanding of mass policy attitudes in Roosevelt's first term. Nevertheless, it seems clear that, notwithstanding concerns about particular policies, the New Deal as a whole was broadly popular in the South—probably more so than in any other region of the country. Roosevelt's triumphant reelection in 1936, in which he racked up majorities in Southern states that were extraordinary even by the standards of the "solid South," offers further evidence of Southern voters' satisfaction with Roosevelt's first term.[34] Fortunately, we do not need to rely on indirect measures to chart Southern whites' political evolution after 1936, for that year marks the emergence of a powerful new window into the attitudes of ordinary Americans: the public opinion poll.[35]

3.2 POLITICAL ATTITUDES IN THE SOUTHERN WHITE PUBLIC, 1935–52

In the mid-1930s, George Gallup and other pioneering pollsters began fielding the first national opinion surveys of the American public. By 1952, when the first national academic surveys were conducted, Gallup's American Institute of Public Opinion (AIPO), Hadley Cantril's Office of Public Opinion Research (OPOR), Elmo Roper's eponymous firm, and other commercial organizations had conducted in-person interviews with nearly a million Americans across hundreds of surveys. These early polls included hundreds of distinct questions on respondents' partisan, ideological, and policy attitudes.[36] The remainder of this chapter uses these invaluable data to examine the diversity and evolution of Southern whites' political attitudes in the wake of the New Deal. I begin with an

---

[33] The NICB's reports broke down opinion by nine-category census divisions, of which three included Southern states (in bold): South Atlantic (**VA, NC, SC, GA, FL**, DE, MD, WV), East South Central (**TN, AL, MS, KY**), and West South Central (**AR, TX, LA**, OK).

[34] Historically, Southern whites' identification with the Democratic Party had not guaranteed loyalty in presidential elections. Indeed, just eight years earlier the South had given nearly half its presidential votes to the Republican Hoover over another anti-prohibition (but Catholic) Democrat from New York, Al Smith.

[35] The first national public opinion polls were conducted in 1935, but the earliest polls whose individual-level data are available date from 1936.

[36] For an account of the development of mass opinion surveys, see Jean M. Converse, *Survey Research in the United States: Roots and Emergence* (Berkeley: University of California Press, 1987).

analysis of individual survey questions, followed by an analysis of broad ideological trends.

Public opinion polling arrived at a turning point in Roosevelt's political standing in the South and in the nation at large. After legislative triumphs of the 74th Congress—chief among them the Social Security Act and National Labor Relations (or Wagner) Act—and the Democrats' historic majorities in the 1936 congressional and presidential elections, the president's fortunes had nowhere to go but down. And indeed, the remainder of Roosevelt's presidency witnessed the stalling of domestic reform, the successive whittling of Democratic majorities, and the flowering of a "conservative coalition" between Republicans and Southern Democrats in Congress.

Changes at the mass level were equally striking. Against the backdrop of a national turn to the right, the geographic bases of New Deal liberalism shifted dramatically, with the South transforming from the most economically liberal region in the country to the most conservative. Both nationally and in the South, these changes were most conspicuous on issues related to organized labor, whose growth in membership, power, and assertiveness following the Wagner Act prompted a powerful reaction in the mass public.[37] Yet, crucially, white Southerners did not turn against all aspects of the New Deal state, and on many issues they remained at least as supportive of liberal policies as non-Southerners. To illustrate these transformations I focus primarily on four issues, two concerning labor policy and two unrelated: old-age pensions, the minimum wage, right to work, and tax cuts. The first two issues were most salient in the mid-to-late 1930s, whereas the second pair rose to prominence in the early-to-mid-1940s. Together, these four issues highlight the scope and timing of white Southerners' ideological transformation, which largely took place in the decade following Roosevelt's reelection.

Before turning to the South's ideological transformation, it is worth emphasizing what did not change between these years: white Southerners' attachment to the Democratic Party. As the solid line in Figure 3.1 shows, Democrats composed at least 85% of major-party identifiers in the white South throughout the 1937–52 period.[38] Even the 1952 presidential election, when Republican Dwight Eisenhower won four Southern states,

---

[37] Eric Schickler and Devin Caughey, "Public Opinion, Organized Labor, and the Limits of New Deal Liberalism, 1936–1945," *Studies in American Political Development* 25, no. 2 (2011): 1–28.

[38] These estimates are based on analyses that use a consistent set of demographic variables—including occupation, phone ownership, urban/rural status, and gender—to weight polls. The use of a consistent set of variables means that education, which is first included in polls in 1943, is not used to weight the polls. The estimated percentage of Democrats increases by a couple of points if education weights are used for the subset of polls for which they are available.

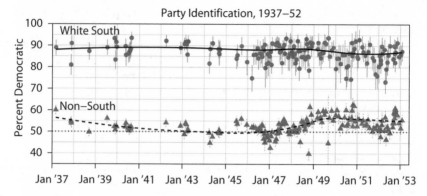

Figure 3.1. Democratic percentage of major-party identifiers in polls fielded between 1937 and 1952. *Source for poll data*: Roper Center for Public Opinion Research.

did not materially increase the percentage of Republican identifiers in the white South, though Independents did tick up to around 20% of identifiers. Among non-Southerners, by contrast, the Democratic advantage undulated between 50% and 60% of major-party identifiers. In short, white Southerners' ideological transformation took place against the backdrop of persistent Democratic hegemony in the mass public.

The earliest opinion polls confirm that the South was also the region most strongly supportive of President Roosevelt. In January 1936, for example, nearly half of Southerners agreed that "Roosevelt's reelection is essential for the good of the country," a figure twice as high as in the rest of the country. Another third of Southerners conceded some mistakes on FDR's part but still agreed that "there is no one else who can do so much good."[39] For a time, Roosevelt's popularity in the South carried over into support for his policy initiatives, even ones that provoked great controversy. FDR's February 1937 proposal to enlarge the Supreme Court (no doubt with supporters of the New Deal), dubbed the "court packing" plan by its opponents, is a case in point. The president's gambit "generated an intensity of response unmatched by any legislative controversy of this century," and editorial opinion ran heavily against it.[40] Within three months of the plan's announcement, public opinion in the non-South had

---

[39] Hadley Cantril, ed., *Public Opinion, 1935–1946*, prepared by Mildred Strunk (Princeton: Princeton University Press, 1951), 755. These percentages are unweighted and include undecideds in the denominator.
[40] William E. Leuchtenburg, "Franklin D. Roosevelt's Supreme Court 'Packing' Plan," in *Essays on the New Deal*, ed. Harold M. Hillingsworth and William F. Holmes, The Walter Prescott Webb Memorial Lectures (Austin: University of Texas Press, 1969), 76;

turned against court packing. In the South, however, despite a good deal of elite opposition to the plan, a majority of whites continued to back it until Roosevelt himself gave up the fight at the end of the summer.[41] Southern whites' support for court packing was surely in part due to the fact that Roosevelt's name was attached to it, but it also reflected their general support for New Deal policies imperiled by a conservative Supreme Court. In November 1936, for example, well before Roosevelt announced his court packing proposal, 75% of white Southerners wanted the Court to "be more liberal in reviewing New Deal measures," whereas support among non-Southerners was almost 20 points lower.[42]

Among the "New Deal measures" referenced by the foregoing poll, perhaps none was more important than the SSA of 1935. The SSA, whose components included OAI as well as unemployment insurance and welfare benefits for the indigent elderly, was the capstone of Roosevelt's drive to bring greater security and stability to Americans' lives.[43] It was also partly a preemptive response to social movements on the left demanding aid for the elderly. A chief fomenter and mobilizer of such pressures was Louisiana's Huey Long, whose massively redistributive "Share Our Wealth" platform included pensions for the elderly as a key demand.[44] And indeed, though stoutly opposed by nearly all business leaders and organizations,[45] government pensions were broadly popular in the public at large—especially in the South.

According to the NICB surveys discussed earlier, 70% of American communities favored compulsory old-age pensions in 1934, and by 1936 (after the passage of the SSA) the figure had grown to 85%.[46] Consistent regional patterns are hard to discern from these surveys, but clear

Gregory A. Caldeira, "Public Opinion and the U.S. Supreme Court: FDR's Court-Packing Plan," *American Political Science Review* 81, no. 4 (1987): 1145.

[41] White Southerners remained consistently about 10 points more favorable toward court packing than non-Southerners. See *Gallup Poll* no. 68 (February 10–15, 1937), *Gallup Poll* no. 78 (April 14–19, 1937), *Gallup Poll* no. 79 (April 21–26, 1937), *Gallup Poll* no. 80 (April 28–May 3, 1937), *Gallup Poll* no. 81 (May 5–10, 1937), *Gallup Poll* no. 82 (May 12–17, 1937), *Gallup Poll* no. 83 (May 19–24, 1937), *Gallup Poll* no. 84 (May 26–31, 1937), *Gallup Poll* no. 85 (June 3–8, 1937), *Gallup Poll* no. 86 (June 9–14, 1937), *Gallup Poll* no. 91 (July 14–19, 1937), *Gallup Poll* no. 92 (July 21–26, 1937), *Gallup Poll* no. 96 (August 18–23, 1937), *Gallup Poll* no. 97 (August 25–30, 1937), *Gallup Poll* no. 127 (July 4–9, 1938), and *Gallup Poll* no. 128 (July 15–20, 1938).

[42] *Gallup Poll* no. 57 (November 15–20, 1936).

[43] Kennedy, *Freedom from Fear*, 245–247.

[44] Ibid., 138.

[45] Theda Skocpol and Edwin Amenta, "Did Capitalists Shape Social Security?," *American Sociological Review* 50, no. 4 (1985): 572–575; but see Jill S. Quadagno, "Welfare Capitalism and the Social Security Act of 1935," *American Sociological Review* 49, no. 5 (1984): 632–647.

[46] NICB, *Statistical Survey 1934*; NICB, *Statistical Survey 1936*.

divisions emerge in the earliest opinion polls. When the OAI went into effect in January 1937, 85% of white Southerners supported the policy, as compared to a still impressive 72% of non-Southerners.[47] The regional gap narrowed over time as overall support for OAI continued to climb toward unanimity, but through the mid-1940s Southerners remained slightly more favorable than non-Southerners.[48] Similarly, white Southerners were no less overwhelmingly supportive of increasing the generosity of old-age pensions than the rest of the country.[49] Only on the issue of expanding OAI's occupational coverage did white Southerners diverge from the nation. White Southerners differed little from the rest of the country on proposals to expand Social Security to include professionals, the self-employed, government employees, and farmers, all of which received around 70% support nationally. But when asked about domestic servants—who in the South were, not coincidentally, predominantly African Americans—Southerners were 14 points less supportive than non-Southerners.[50]

White Southerners' relative lack of enthusiasm for allowing domestic servants access to Social Security is indicative of their sensitivity toward economic policies that, while nonracial on their face, threatened to disturb the region's racially segmented labor system. On issues related to labor, white Southerners' relative liberalism on other economic issues dissipated, or even reversed. This pattern can be discerned as far back as the 1934 NICB survey, in which compulsory unemployment insurance—unlike the SSA's other major component, old-age pensions—received markedly lower support from Southern communities than from the rest of the country. But Southern distinctiveness on labor issues appears to have intensified in the late 1930s, a trend exemplified by the battle over the last major achievement of the New Deal, the Fair Labor Standards Act (FLSA).

---

[47] *Gallup Poll* no. 56 (November 6–11, 1936) and *Gallup Poll* no. 65 (January 20–25, 1937).

[48] *Gallup Poll* no. 127 (July 4–9, 1938), *Gallup Poll* no. 130 (August 12–17, 1938), *Gallup Poll* no. 144 (January 12–17, 1939), *Gallup Poll* no. 176 (November 10–15, 1939), *Gallup Poll* no. 241 (July 11–16, 1941), and *NORC Poll* no. 226 (August 1–7, 1944).

[49] *RFOR Poll* no. 4 (January 1–7, 1939), *Gallup Poll* no. 143 (January 9–14, 1939), *Gallup Poll* no. 145 (January 22–27, 1939), *OPOR Poll* no. 4 (March 20–25, 1943), and *OPOR Poll* no. 24 (April 7–12, 1944).

[50] In the non-South, support for including domestic servants was higher than for any occupation (82%), whereas in the white South it was lower than any other occupation (67%). When asked whether Social Security should be expanded to all previously excluded occupations, non-Southerners were 5–12% more supportive than white Southerners. See *Gallup Poll* no. 107 (December 30, 1937–January 4, 1938), *Gallup Poll* no. 145 (January 22–27, 1939), *Gallup Poll* no. 299 (July 30–August 5, 1943), *NORC Poll* no. 226 (August 1–7, 1944), *Gallup Poll* no. 337 (December 14–20, 1944), and *Gallup Poll* no. 434 (December 11–16, 1948).

The FLSA was a direct descendent of the National Recovery Administration (NRA), a centerpiece of which was minimum wages for industrial workers.[51] After the Supreme Court invalidated the NRA in 1935, Roosevelt and Southern allies such as Senator Hugo Black (D-AL) resolved to reinstate a national minimum wage through standalone wages-and-hours legislation. For Southern liberals, whose views were embodied in the Roosevelt-sponsored "Report on Economic Conditions of the South" (1938), raising Southern wages was essential for upgrading purchasing power in the South and modernizing its "colonial" economy.[52] Southern manufacturers, on the other hand, vigorously opposed this strategy, arguing—not unreasonably—that bringing Southern wages up to national standards deprived the region of its foremost competitive advantage vis-à-vis the rest of the country.[53] (Political commentator Walter Lippmann described the FLSA as "a sectional bill thinly disguised as a humanitarian reform."[54]) Southern planters, though more muted in their opposition due to the exclusion of agricultural workers from proposed legislation, were also resistant to minimum wages. But beyond the class interests of Southern employers, the racial privileges of Southern whites were also threatened by minimum wage legislation, which would have equalized wage rates between low-wage blacks and whites. As one Florida congressman warned, "You cannot put the Negro and the white man on the same basis and get away with it."[55] In sum, the issue of a national minimum wage implicated not only the class interests of employers, but also the sectional interests of the relatively low-wage South and the racial interests of Southern whites.

In the mass public, support for minimum wages was highly stratified by class, both nationally and among white Southerners. In the six months following the May 1937 introduction of a wages-and-hours bill in Congress, support for the bill nationally ranged from below 50% among upper-class respondents to 80% among relief recipients. Initially, white Southerners were almost as favorable toward minimum wages as non-Southerners, but by April 1938, shortly before the FLSA finally passed, an 8-point gap in regional opinion had opened up. This regional gap reappeared after World War II, when polls began asking about increasing the minimum wage: Southern whites were again about 9 points more conservative on this issue than non-Southerners.

[51] Paul H. Douglas and Joseph Hackman, "The Fair Labor Standards Act of 1938 I," *Political Science Quarterly* 53, no. 4 (1938): 491–2; Kennedy, *Freedom from Fear*, 344–345.
[52] Schulman, *Cotton Belt to Sunbelt*, 49–51.
[53] Garson, *Democratic Party*, 4; Schulman, *Cotton Belt to Sunbelt*, 21–23, 26.
[54] Schulman, *Cotton Belt to Sunbelt*, 54.
[55] Farhang and Katznelson, "Southern Imposition," 14.

Similar patterns appeared in more potent form on issues related to labor unions, which over the course of the late 1930s and 1940s became an increasingly salient point of conflict. Although organized labor's political position had always been more tenuous in the South than outside it,[56] white Southerners had never been completely anti-union. This was partly attributable to the fact that until the 1930s, Southern labor unions were exclusively white, and the relatively conservative craft unions that composed the American Federation of Labor (AFL) expressed little to no interest in challenging Jim Crow.[57] Moreover, though the proportion of Southern whites who declared themselves generally "in favor of labor unions" fell from an average of 70% in the 1930s to 64% in the 1940s, a solid majority continued to do so in nearly every poll between 1937 and 1952.[58]

The 1935 formation of the Congress of Industrial Organizations (CIO), however, profoundly disturbed Southern views toward unions. Motivated both by the interracial imperatives of industrial unionism and by principled ideological commitments, the CIO quickly became the leading white-led organization in pushing for civil rights for blacks. The dramatic rise of the CIO as a political force thus created an indelible (and frightening) link between labor unions and civil rights in the minds of white Southerners.[59] Thus, while the AFL remained largely "respectable" in the South,[60] the CIO—along with its forceful and controversial founder, John L. Lewis—became something close to anathema in the region. Between 1938 and 1944, for example, the proportion of white Southerners who said they would vote *against* a candidate endorsed by the CIO rose from 58% to 82%, as compared to an increase from 51% to 61% in the non-South (most of the remaining responses indicated that

---

[56] Gerald Friedman, "The Political Economy of Early Southern Unionism: Race, Politics, and Labor in the South, 1880–1953," *Journal of Economic History* 60, no. 2 (2000): 384–413.

[57] Biles, *The South and the New Deal*, 9.

[58] See *Gallup Poll* no. 88 (June 23–28, 1937), *Gallup Poll* no. 135 (October 10–15, 1938), *Gallup Poll* no. 158 (May 20–25, 1939), *Gallup Poll* no. 166 (August 10–15, 1939), *Gallup Poll* no. 177 (November 17–22, 1939), *Gallup Poll* no. 193 (May 5–10, 1940), *Gallup Poll* no. 195 (May 18–23, 1940), *Gallup Poll* no. 238 (May 31–June 4, 1941), *Gallup Poll* no. 249 (October 3–8, 1941), *Gallup Poll* no. 295 (May 14–20, 1943), *Gallup Poll* no. 365 (February 15–20, 1946), *Gallup Poll* no. 400 (July 4–9, 1947), *Gallup Poll* no. 434 (December 11–16, 1948), and *Gallup Poll* no. 483 (December 9–14, 1951).

[59] Robert Korstad and Nelson Lichtenstein, "Opportunities Found and Lost: Labor, Radicals, and the Early Civil Rights Movement," *Journal of American History* 75, no. 3 (1988): 786–811; Eric Schickler, *Racial Realignment: The Transformation of American Liberalism, 1932–1965* (Princeton: Princeton University Press, 2016), chapter 3.

[60] Biles, *The South and the New Deal*, 101.

the endorsement would make no difference). The CIO was so unpopular in the South that some devious politicians would seek financial support from its political action committee but suggest that the organization publicly endorse their opponent.[61]

It is important to recognize, however, that rising anti-union sentiment was not confined to the South, nor was the antipathy of Southern whites attributable solely to racism. The antilabor reaction may have been especially virulent in the South, but it was widespread in the non-South as well, even among Democrats.[62] The sit-down strikes of 1936–37, work stoppages during the war, and a general sense that labor unions were becoming too militant and powerful all contributed to the national backlash. Unions' deepening unpopularity was particularly acute in rural and agricultural areas, where it reflected a general dissatisfaction with liberalism's growing focus on the problems of cities and industrial workers.[63] The foremost agricultural interest group of the era, the primarily Midwest-based American Farm Bureau Federation, harbored profound suspicions toward organized labor, an antipathy that was "representative of the views of the average American farmer" and that intensified in the late 1930s and early 1940s. Foremost among the Farm Bureau's specific grievances were wages-and-hours legislation, which drove up the cost of labor and the price of goods, and pro-union practices such as the closed shop, which the Bureau attacked with "extreme bitterness."[64]

The closed shop and other union security agreements requiring union membership as a condition of employment were a focal point of the antilabor reaction of the late 1930s and 1940s. Despite their uncertain constitutional status under the Wagner Act, state "right-to-work" laws proscribing some or all union security agreements were passed in five states between 1944 and 1946 (Arizona, Arkansas, Florida, Nebraska, and South Dakota), followed by nine more in 1947.[65] Notably, the

---

[61] Daniel A. Powell, "PAC to COPE: Thirty-Two Years of Southern Labor in Politics," in *Essays in Southern Labor History: Selected Papers, Southern Labor History Conference, 1976*, ed. Gary M. Fink and Merle E. Reed (Westport, CT: Greenwood Press), 247.
[62] Schickler and Caughey, "Public Opinion."
[63] See, e.g., Western progressives' disaffection with the New Deal after 1936; Anthony J. Badger, *The New Deal: The Depression Years, 1933–1940* (Chicago: Ivan R. Dee, 2002), 275.
[64] Theodore Saloutos, "The American Farm Bureau Federation and Farm Policy: 1933–1945," *Southwestern Social Science Quarterly* 28, no. 4 (1947/1948): 325–7. In this era the Farm Bureau did grow rapidly in the South, which constituted 11% of its membership in 1935, 25% in 1940, and 32% in 1945; ibid., 313.
[65] The drafters of the Wagner Act apparently intended to leave union security to the states, but the question of whether state or federal law controlled was not a settled legal issue until the passage of the Taft–Hartley Act in 1947; Harry A. Millis and Harold A. Katz, "A

Arkansas and Florida laws were passed in 1944 by popular referenda, both by a 55% to 45% margin.[66] These referendum outcomes closely matched the results of a 1943 poll, in which 13 of 18 white respondents who hailed from Arkansas or Florida supported amending their state constitution to ban the closed shop. Opinion on this issue was more lopsided among all white Southerners, nearly three-quarters of whom supported such an amendment (as compared to about half of non-Southerners).[67] In fact, in no poll between 1938 and 1947, when the Taft–Hartley Act explicitly sanctioned right-to-work laws, did Southern whites offer more than 35% support for any form of union security. Moreover, the white South averaged about 10% less supportive than the non-South, making it the region by far the most receptive to right-to-work legislation.[68]

The examples of minimum wages and right-to-work might give the impression that in the late 1930s, white Southerners utterly abandoned their previous support for New Deal liberalism. For some vocal dissenters, particularly those who saw the growth of federal power as a threat to Jim Crow, this was undoubtedly true. A "little group of left-wing advisers," accused one Georgia editor, was seeking to "wipe out the traditional Democracy of this section," reviving "that reconstruction fear of 'black heels on white necks.'" A Mississippi newspaper went further: "The New Deal," it declared, "has stolen the Republican thunder and absolved

Decade of State Labor Legislation 1937–1947," *University of Chicago Law Review* 15, no. 2 (1948): 290–1; Gilbert J. Gall, *The Politics of Right to Work: The Labor Federations as Special Interests, 1943–1979* (New York: Greenwood Press, 1988), 19, 41–43.

[66] Southern industrial interests and the Farm Bureau spearheaded the drive for the amendments. In Florida at least, their campaigns did not overtly emphasize racial concerns; John G. Shott, *How 'Right-to-Work' Laws Are Passed: Florida Sets the Pattern* (Washington, DC: Public Affairs Institute, 1956); Gilbert J. Gall, "Southern Industrial Workers and Anti-Union Sentiment: Arkansas and Florida in 1944," in *Organized Labor in the Twentieth-Century South*, ed. Robert H. Zieger (Knoxville: University of Tennessee Press, 1991), 228–238.

[67] *Gallup Poll* no. 294 (April 29–May 5, 1943). One caveat is that this question was asked only of the 62% of respondents who answered (correctly or not) a preceding question asking "what is meant by 'closed shop.'" Only half of Southern white respondents offered an answer, and their probability of doing so was strongly related to their class status. However, among Southern whites asked the amendment question, support for a right-to-work amendment was essentially uncorrelated with class. Urban respondents, however, were 16% less supportive of the amendment than respondents in rural areas.

[68] *Gallup Poll* no. 89 (June 30–July 4, 1937), *Gallup Poll* no. 158 (May 20–25, 1939), *Gallup Poll* no. 249 (October 3–8, 1941), *Gallup Poll* no. 252 (November 7–12, 1941), *Gallup Poll* no. 254 (November 27–December 2, 1941), *Gallup Poll* no. 275 (August 27–September 1, 1942), *Gallup Poll* no. 294 (April 29–May 5, 1943), *Gallup Poll* no. 319 (May 25–31, 1944), *Gallup Poll* no. 351 (July 14–19, 1945), *Gallup Poll* no. 375 (July 26–31, 1946), *Gallup Poll* no. 385 (November 29–December 4, 1946), *Gallup Poll* no. 436 (January 22–29, 1949), and *Gallup Poll* no. 437 (February 11–16, 1949).

southerners from any further obligation of loyalty to a party that has betrayed its most loyal adherents."[69] These alarmist views, however, were not shared by all or even most white Southerners. In fact, a majority of whites in the South remained not only loyal Democrats, but also relative liberals on many economic issues, particularly those unrelated to labor markets and unions.

On taxation, for example, white Southerners remained more liberal than the rest of the country, favoring a more progressive tax system and expressing greater skepticism toward tax cuts. In 1938–39, when congressional conservatives pushed for tax reductions for businesses and high-income individuals, white Southerners were about 8% less supportive on average than non-Southerners. When proposals to cut corporate taxes resurfaced in 1945, white Southerners were again about 6% less supportive.[70] Southern support for corporate and high-income taxation was surely due in part to the fact that very few Southerners paid such taxes. But even across-the-board income tax cuts were relatively unpopular in the South. In 1946, by which point almost all working Americans submitted tax returns and a majority paid some income tax, Republicans made a pledge of a 20% across-the-board income tax cut a central plank of their campaign to retake control of Congress.[71] Tax cuts then became, along with revising the Wagner Act, Republicans' top priority in the 80th Congress.[72] On the whole, the non-Southern public was more receptive to these proposals than white Southerners were. For example, on a series of poll questions pitting income tax cuts against debt reduction in 1946–47, white Southerners were consistently around 9% less supportive of tax cuts than non-Southerners.[73]

---

[69] Editorials from the *Macon Telegraph* (August 26, 1938) and the *Fayette-Chronicle* (September 26, 1937); quoted by Rayford W. Logan, ed., *The Attitude of the Southern White Press toward Negro Suffrage 1932–1940* (Washington, DC: Foundation Publishers, 1940), 37, 46.

[70] *Gallup Poll* no. 114 (March 10–15, 1938), *Gallup Poll* no. 155 (April 21–26, 1939), *Gallup Poll* no. 156 (May 4–9, 1939), and *Gallup Poll* no. 347 (May 17–23, 1945).

[71] W. Elliot Brownlee, *Federal Taxation in America: A Short History*, 2nd ed. (Washington, DC and New York: Woodrow Wilson Center Press/Cambridge University Press, 2004), 115; A. E. Holmans, *United States Fiscal Policy, 1945–1959: Its Contribution to Economic Stability* (London: Oxford University Press, 1961), 58.

[72] Robert Mason, *The Republican Party and American Politics from Hoover to Reagan* (New York: Cambridge University Press, 2012), 116.

[73] *Gallup Poll* no. 380 (October 12–17, 1946), *Gallup Poll* no. 384 (November 15–20, 1946), *Gallup Poll* no. 390 (February 14–19, 1947), *Gallup Poll* no. 395 (April 25–30, 1947), and *Gallup Poll* no. 397 (May 23–28, 1947). In an unweighted Roper poll from 1939, support for cutting taxes "to increase prosperity" was 4% lower among white Southerners than among non-Southerners; *RCOM Poll* no. 9 (April 1–7, 1939). Only on a December 1947 question pitting tax cuts against foreign aid—about which white Southerners were generally unenthusiastic—did regional differences disappear; *Gallup Poll*

Thus, even within the broad area of economic policy, white Southerners' ideological evolution differed across issue areas. On old-age insurance and income taxation, white Southerners were at least as liberal as non-Southerners, though they became relatively more conservative over time. By contrast, minimum wages and union security agreements, policies that threatened the South's agricultural, low-wage, and racially stratified labor system, received a chilly reception in that region, and its relative conservatism on these issues intensified in the late 1930s and early 1940s. Examining individual issues, however, provides only a partial perspective on ideological trends in the South. For a more holistic perspective, we must summarize dynamics across many issues. To do so we turn to a recent methodological innovation: dynamic group-level item-response models.

3.3 IDEOLOGICAL EVOLUTION AND DIVERSITY

Item response theory (IRT) is a statistical framework for estimating some unobserved trait—in this case, economic conservatism—from subjects' responses to binary questions. The basic idea is to model subjects' response to a given question as a function of their latent conservatism and two question-specific characteristics: its "difficulty" (the baseline probability of a conservative response) and its "discrimination" (how much liberals and conservatives differ in their probability of a conservative response). Because IRT models account for these differences between questions, they make it possible to compare subjects' conservatism even if they do not answer the same questions. One requirement of conventional IRT models, however, is that every subject answer multiple questions, preferably at least 15. This requirement is unfortunately not met by the vast majority of early opinion polls, each of which typically included only two or three economic policy questions.

However, since I am interested in aggregate rather than individual-level patterns, I can still use the IRT framework if I estimate conservatism at the level of demographic *groups* rather than individual respondents. The specific method I use to do so, which is detailed in Appendix 3.A of this chapter, is the dynamic group-level IRT (DGIRT) model implemented in the statistical program R using the dgo package.[74] Rather than focusing

---

no. 409 (December 12–17, 1947). For Southerners' foreign policy views, see Alfred O. Hero, *The Southerner and World Affairs* (Baton Rouge: Louisiana State University Press, 1965).

[74] James Dunham, Devin Caughey, and Christopher Warshaw, *dgo: Dynamic Estimation of Group-Level Opinion. R package version 0.2.3.*, 2016, https://

on a few continuous question series, the DGIRT model enables me to take advantage of data from more than 450 distinct issue questions across hundreds of public opinion polls. I use these rich data to estimate the economic conservatism of demographic groups and geographic units in each year beween 1936 and 1952.

For an initial perspective on these estimates, consider Figure 3.2, which illustrates economic conservatism's evolving association with socioeconomic status (SES), urban–rural residence, region, and race. Each panel displays an attribute's association with economic conservatism in each year, holding other predictors constant.[75] The top row plots two indicators of SES, phone ownership and professional occupation, both of which are strong predictors of economic conservatism. The middle row compares farmers and urbanites with residents of small towns (the excluded category), revealing that all else equal, farmers were more conservative and urbanites were more liberal. Aside from a temporary decrease in ideological differences across demographic categories around 1940, the coefficients related to socioeconomic and urban–rural divisions are quite stable across the 1936–52 period.

Finally, the bottom pair of panels illustrate the racial and regional bases of economic conservatism. The left panel plots the conservatism of non-Southern blacks relative to the excluded category of non-Southern whites, and the right panel plots the analogous quantity for Southern whites. Throughout the period, African Americans were substantially more supportive of New Deal liberalism than the baseline category of non-Southern whites—even controlling for the fact that non-Southern blacks were poorer and more urban than their white counterparts.[76] Initially, the same was true of white Southerners. Consistent with their greater preference for the liberal party in the February 1937 Gallup poll, Southern whites' economic policy preferences were significantly less

---

jamesdunham.github.io/dgo/; cf. Devin Caughey and Christopher Warshaw, "Dynamic Estimation of Latent Opinion Using a Hierarchical Group-Level IRT Model," *Political Analysis* 23, no. 2 (2015): 197–211.

[75] The coefficient estimates in Figure 3.2 are derived from a modified DGIRT model in which group conservatism is modeled as a function of demographic predictors only, and not as a function of its lagged value. For a precise description of this model, see Caughey and Warshaw, "Dynamic Estimation." The coefficients in Figure 3.2 are scaled such that each unit difference on the vertical axis corresponds to the standard deviation of economic conservatism across indviduals in the typical year. This scale must be interpreted cautiously, however, because ideological variation was much larger in some years than others. Opinion was most polarized in 1936, when the standard deviation was twice that of the typical year, and least polarized in 1940, when it was less than one-third as dispersed as the typical year.

[76] The coefficient for Southern blacks is not shown but their conservatism is similar to that of non-Southern blacks.

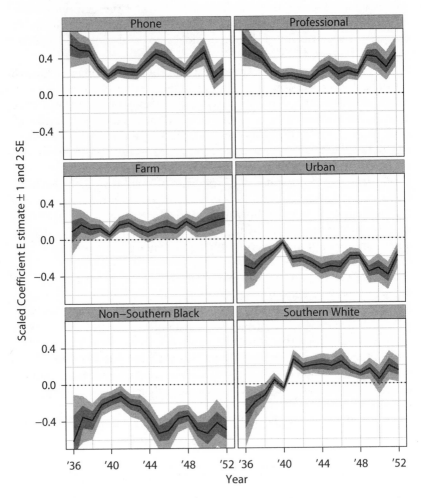

Figure 3.2. Predictors of economic conservatism, 1936–52. In the top row, the baseline categories are, respectively, people without a phone and nonprofessionals. In the middle row, the baseline for both coefficients is rural nonfarmers. In the bottom row, the baseline is non-Southern white (coefficient for Southern black not shown). Coefficients are scaled by the standard deviation of economic conservatism across indviduals in the typical year. *Source for poll data*: Roper Center for Public Opinion Research.

conservative than those of demographically similar non-Southern whites until 1939. In contrast to all other attributes, however, the conditional association between conservatism and being a white Southerner switched sign over this time period. White Southerners' relative conservatism increased rapidly between 1936 and 1941, and by the early 1940s being a white Southerner was actually associated with greater conservatism.

The years around 1940 were a time of transition for the American public outside the South as well. At the same time as white Southerners moved to the right, the American public as a whole temporarily became less ideologically polarized. This depolarization is evidenced by the fact that class, urbanness, and race all became less predictive of economic conservatism leading up to 1940.[77] Whether because of the brewing wartime atmosphere, the ideological flux of the white South, or other factors, survey questions that divided demographic groups in the late 1930s and after the early 1940s were much less divisive in 1940. Unlike white Southerners, however, working-class, urban, and black Americans quickly resumed their disproportionate support for New Deal liberalism.

The temporary decline in class, urban–rural, and racial cleavages around 1940 was accompanied by corresponding depolarization across state and regional lines. This geographic depolarization can be seen in Figure 3.3, which plots trends in mass conservatism by region. The solid line represents the economic conservatism of the average Southern state (blacks again excluded). Consistent with the patterns in Figure 3.2, whites in the typical Southern state were less conservative than other Americans through 1938. In 1939–40 state and regional differences in economic conservatism all but disappeared, but in 1941 the South reemerged as the most conservative region. Aside from a brief blip in 1951, it remained so through the end of the Truman administration.

It is important to emphasize, however, that even as white Southerners as a whole moved to the right, they remained internally diverse. Indeed, demographic cleavages within the white South were about as powerful as they were outside the South. Among both Southern and non-Southern whites, professionals and phone owners were each about a third of a standard deviation (SD) more conservative than nonprofessionals and those without phones, averaged over the 1936–52 period.[78] The difference between farmers and rural nonfarmers was also about the same

---

[77] Public approval of President Roosevelt exhibited the same pattern of depolarization along class lines beginning in 1941; Matthew A. Baum and Samuel Kernell, "Economic Class and Popular Support for Franklin Roosevelt in War and Peace," *Public Opinion Quarterly* 65, no. 2 (2001): 198–229.

[78] These figures are based on region-specific multivariate ordinary least squares models controlling for professional status, phone ownership, urban status, farm status, and year.

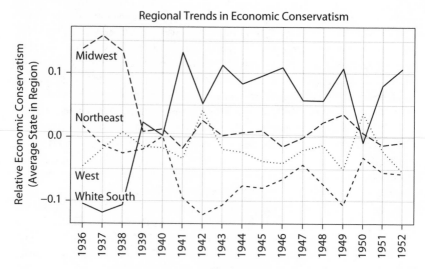

Figure 3.3. Economic conservatism in the average state in each region, relative to the national average, 1936–52. *Source for poll data*: Roper Center for Public Opinion.

in both regions, the former being about 0.15 SD more conservative. Only for urban–rural differences were ideological cleavages slightly less pronounced in the South than in the non-South (0.34 vs. 0.44). In short, the New Deal divided Southern whites along class and urban–rural lines, just as it did non-Southerners.

A crucial difference between the regions, however, is that in the non-South, class and ideological cleavages fell along partisan lines, whereas the situation in the South was more complicated. Before 1960, neither the class status nor economic conservatism was strongly related to the party identification or congressional vote choice of Southern whites.[79] This is partly due to the fact that Democratic dominance persisted in both categories into the early 1960s.

Ideological cleavages were much clearer in presidential voting, probably because the parties' presidential candidates took more divergent positions on economic issues than did Democrats and Republicans within the South. As Figure 3.4 shows, Southern whites who voted Republican at the presidential level were much more conservative than Southern Democrats, even as far back as 1936, when the reference point was the Hoover-FDR election of 1932. In fact, throughout this period white

---

[79] Byron E. Shafer and Richard Johnston, *The End of Southern Exceptionalism: Class, Race, and Partisan Change in the Postwar South* (Cambridge, MA: Harvard University Press, 2006), 28.

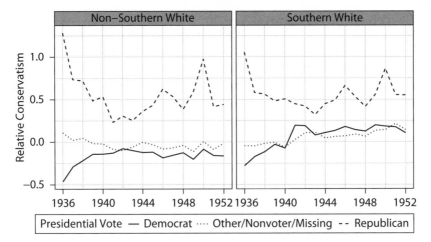

Figure 3.4. Conservatism by region and presidential vote, among whites only. Each line represents the average conservatism of the group, relative to all groups in that year (including blacks by region and partisanship—not shown). *Source for poll data*: Roper Center for Public Opinion Research.

Southern Republicans were just as conservative as white Republicans in the non-South. White Southern Democrats, on the other hand, were originally nearly as liberal as their non-Southern counterparts, but by the early 1940s had reached a position about midway between the non-Southern wings of the two parties.

Interestingly, Figure 3.4 indicates little ideological difference between white presidential Democrats in the South and whites who did not report voting for either of the two major parties. The latter category consists predominantly of nonvoting whites, though it also includes third-party supporters as well as those whose vote choice is missing. Since Republicans were rare in the South before 1948, the Democratic presidential electorate roughly approximated the Democratic primary electorate for most of this period. The similarity between these two categories of Southern whites provides suggestive evidence that there was not a large conservative bias in the active electorate in the South, relative to the white public as a whole.[80] Thus, contrary to the hopes of V. O. Key and other midcentury reformers, there is little evidence of a large pool of liberal nonvoting whites waiting to be mobilized. This was not, however, true of African Americans in the South, who remained substantially less conservative

---

[80] The similarity between the policy preferences of voters and nonvoters in the white South is consistent with the typical finding that American voters and nonvoters have similar attitudes; Raymond E. Wolfinger and Steven J. Rosenstone, *Who Votes?* (New Haven, CT: Yale University Press, 1980).

than nonvoting whites. In fact, by the 1940s even the small number of Southern blacks who reported voting *against* Roosevelt (not to mention black Democrats and nonvoters) were more supportive of the New Deal than all categories of Southern whites.

Although whites across the South became more conservative after the mid-1930s, the intensity of their reactions against the New Deal differed by state. The conservative shift was most striking in the Deep South states of South Carolina, Georgia, Alabama, Mississippi, and Louisiana. In these states the black population was largest and hence white commitment to Jim Crow and the Democratic Party was the most intense.[81] As long as liberal economic policies did not threaten the South's racial system, whites in these very poor states were free to support the New Deal "stronger than horseradish." Not coincidentally, in the early to mid-1930s the Deep South nurtured such economic populists as Huey Long (Louisiana), Hugo Black (Alabama), and Theodore Bilbo (Mississippi). But Deep South whites were also most sensitive to the racial implications of labor market regulation, pro-union policies, and a generally more assertive national government. As New Deal liberalism turned in this direction, Deep South whites turned against the New Deal. While whites in the Peripheral South were not immune to these concerns, the racial implications of liberal economic policies were less salient in those states.

The implications of these dynamics can be seen in Figure 3.5, which plots the changing relationship between mass conservatism and three state characteristics: percent white (top), percent union (middle), and percent Republican in presidential elections (bottom). Each relationship is shown separately for 1936–38 and 1939–52 because all three relationships changed dramatically after 1938. To enhance comparability across years and to indicate Southern states' position relative to the nation, states' conservatism is expressed in terms of their rank relative to the nation. Relatively conservative states rank higher on the vertical axis.

Before 1939, whites in states with large black populations were clearly less conservative than other state publics (Figure 3.5, top left). This was consistent with, and probably partly a product of, the Deep South's overwhelming attachment to the Democratic Party at the national level in the 1932 and 1936 elections (bottom left). In the 1939–52 period, however, the relationship between conservatism and racial composition completely reversed. With extraordinary rapidity, the Deep South transformed from the most liberal to the most conservative states in the country. Southern states with larger white populations, such as Virginia and Florida, shifted much less relative to the nation. The patterns for unionization are

---

[81] Key, *Southern Politics*.

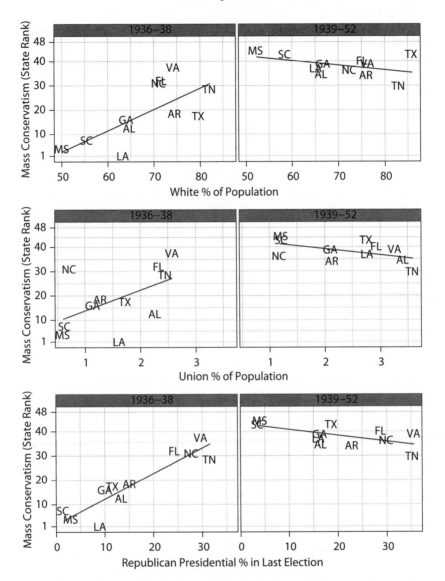

Figure 3.5. Relationship between Southern states' economic conservatism and percent white, percent unionized, and percent Republican, before and after 1939. Estimates of mass conservatism exclude African Americans and are expressed in terms of states' rank relative to other states, with more conservative states ranked higher. *Source for poll data*: Roper Center for Public Opinion Research.

quite similar (middle row). Before 1939, more unionized Southern states were, if anything, more conservative, but after that year the relationship is negative. Over this period union density increased in the South, as it did nationally, but the region remained far less unionized than the rest of the nation.

Significantly, the Deep South's conservative shift was not matched by a shift toward the Republican party in presidential elections before 1952. Rather, the relationship between mass conservatism and presidential Republicanism also switched directions. After 1939, the Deep South remained resolutely hostile to the Republican Party, whereas less conservative states were less so; consequently, Republican states tended to be less conservative, though the relationship is fairly weak within the South. The reversal of the state-level relationship between conservatism and partisanship is paradoxical in light of Figure 3.4, which shows that Southern white Republicans were more conservative than other Southern whites throughout the 1936–52 period. The divergence between the state- and individual-level is due to the fact that the slope of the Republican-conservatism relationship was positive within states, but the intercept was lower in more conservative states.

While paradoxical, the negative relationship after 1939 is also reassuring because it indicates that ideological variation within the South was not purely the result of citizens' adopting the views of the national leaders of their party.[82] To be sure, top-down opinion leadership played a role in the transformation of mass opinion in the South, but it was the cues of state and local, not national, opinion leaders that probably most influenced public opinion. But the partial independence of partisanship and ideology also strengthens the case for taking citizens' survey responses seriously as measures of their policy preferences, rather than simply rote reactions to elite cues.

3.4 VARIATION ACROSS ISSUE DOMAINS

Thus far, my analysis of mass conservatism has not distinguished between different domains of economic policy, nor has it examined attitudes in other areas, such as civil rights. As we saw earlier in this chapter with the analysis of individual issues, white Southerners expressed substantially greater conservatism toward policies related labor markets and, by extension, the racial system of the South. Here, I perform a similar analysis at

---

[82] Cf. John R. Zaller, *The Nature and Origins of Mass Opinion* (New York: Cambridge University Press, 1992); Gabriel Lenz, *Follow the Leader? How Voters Respond to Politicians' Performance and Policies* (Chicago: University of Chicago Press, 2012).

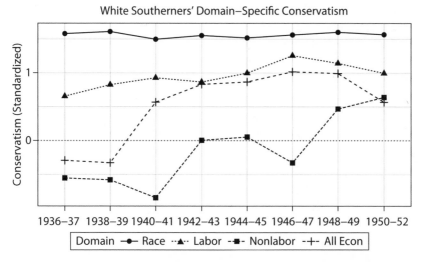

Figure 3.6. Trends in white Southerners' domain-specific conservatism, 1936–52. "Race" is based on civil rights questions; "Labor," economic questions related to labor issues; "All Econ," all economic issue questions; and "Nonlabor," nonlabor economic questions. The vertical axis indicates whites' conservatism in the average Southern state, standardized across all states within each biennium (or triennium, in the case of 1950–52). *Source for poll data*: Roper Center for Public Opinion Research.

a more general level by estimating the DGIRT model separately in three domains: nonlabor economic issues, labor-related economic issues, and racial issues. This yields estimates of domain-specific conservatism, which we can compare with measures of general economic conservatism.

Figure 3.6 plots white Southerners' ideological evolution relative to the nation according to these four measures. Within each biennium beginning in 1936–37, each measure has been standardized to have a mean of 0 and an SD of 1 across all states. Disaggregating in this way reveals important contrasts in opinion dynamics across domains. On racial issues, Southern whites were far more conservative than the national public throughout this period. In March 1939, for example, 60% of white Southerners—compared to 28% of non-Southerners—disapproved of Eleanor Roosevelt's resignation from the Daughters of the American Revolution to protest its refusal to permit African American singer Marian Anderson to perform in its concert hall.[83] Similarly, in polls fielded both before and after the war, white Southerners

---

[83] *Gallup Poll* no. 150 (March 4–9, 1939).

were typically more than 20 percentage points less supportive of federal anti-lynching legislation than non-Southerners.[84] White Southerners' consistent conservatism across all racial issues is reflected in Figure 3.6, which shows that throughout this period the white public in the typical Southern state remained about 1.5 SDs more racially conservative than the average state nationally.

From 1937, when the first labor-related poll questions appeared, white Southerners evinced a similar, though less extreme, conservatism on labor issues. As I noted earlier, this conservatism was most intense on questions related to labor unions, especially the CIO, but it also quickly emerged on nonunion issues such as minimum wages. Though it never matched their extreme racial conservatism, Southern whites' right-wing position on labor issues also intensified over time. As Figure 3.6 shows, in the late 1930s whites in Southern states were already more than half a standard deviation more conservative than the typical state. By 1946–47, after a decade of public controversy over the increased power and assertiveness of labor unions, Southern whites' relative labor conservatism had doubled, to 1.3 SDs above the national average.

On economic questions unrelated to labor issues, Southern whites' shift to the right occurred later and began from a much more liberal starting point. Through 1941, Southern white publics were at least half a standard deviation *less* conservative than the nation on nonlabor issues such as the pension and taxation policies discussed earlier in this chapter. The early war years brought a clear shift to the right, to around the national average, followed by further conservative movement after 1947. By 1952, Southern whites were just as conservative on nonlabor issues as on labor ones, about 1 SD more so than the nation. Labor issues were thus a leading indicator of white Southerners' general shift to the right on economics.

General economic conservatism, indicated by the crosses in Figure 3.6, is, roughly speaking, a weighted average of labor and nonlabor conservatism. The relative weights of the two domains are determined by the number of questions in each domain and how well the questions discriminate between liberals and conservatives. In the 1930s, general economic conservatism corresponded closely with nonlabor conservatism, but by 1942–43 it had converged with labor conservatism. This reflects the growing political salience of labor issues, which increased not only the

---

[84] *Gallup Poll* no. 63 (January 7–12, 1937), *Gallup Poll* no. 96 (August 18–23, 1937), *Gallup Poll* no. 102 (October 30, 1937), *Gallup Poll* no. 104 (November 21–26, 1937), *Gallup Poll* no. 106 (December 15–20, 1937), *Gallup Poll* no. 181 (January 13–18, 1940), *Gallup Poll* no. 182 (January 21–27, 1940), *Gallup Poll* no. 398 (June 6–11, 1947), *Gallup Poll* no. 413 (February 20–25, 1948), *Gallup Poll* no. 414 (March 5–10, 1948), *Gallup Poll* no. 433 (November 26–December 1, 1948), *Gallup Poll* no. 439 (March 19–24, 1949), and *Gallup Poll* no. 451 (January 8–13, 1950).

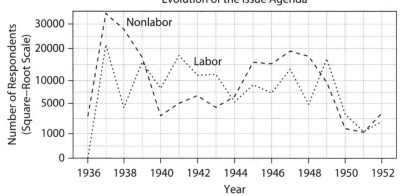

Figure 3.7. Sample size for labor and nonlabor questions, by year. *Source for poll data*: Roper Center for Public Opinion Research.

proportion of labor-related questions pollsters included in their surveys (see Figure 3.7), but also the discrimination of these questions relative to nonlabor questions. The consequence of the higher discrimination of labor questions can be seen in the second half of the 1940s, when Southerners' general economic conservatism remained close to their labor conservatism despite the fact that polls asked more nonlabor than labor questions in those years. In short, the convergence of economic and labor conservatism in the early 1940s reflects the degree to which New Deal liberalism—and conflict between liberals and conservatives—increasingly centered on labor issues.

By contrast, many other elements of the New Deal agenda had either ceased to be controversial (e.g., old-age pensions) or become political non-starters (e.g., government ownership of industry). Rather than a methodological artifact, the relative weights of labor versus nonlabor issues in the estimates of general economic conservatism should thus be considered telling indications of real changes in the content of the political agenda and the structure of political conflict. For this reason, my analysis going forward continues to focus on general economic conservatism, while bearing in mind the different dynamics of labor and nonlabor issues.

3.5 CONCLUSION

Between Roosevelt's triumphant reelection in 1936 and Eisenhower's restoration of unified Republican government in 1952, the Southern white public underwent a dramatic and profoundly consequential ideological transformation. In the 1930s, the South was the region most supportive of

New Deal liberalism. By the early 1940s, it had become the most economically conservative part of the country. This transformation was spearheaded by issues related to labor markets and unions, where the racial
implications of federal interference were most stark and the material
benefits of federal aid to the South's low-wage agricultural economy
were least clear. But skepticism of government activism soon spread to
economic issues unrelated to labor. Notwithstanding their receptivity to a
robust taxation regime and certain other high-level macroeconomic policies, by the 1950s Southern whites had become almost as conservative on
nonlabor economic issues as they were on labor issues.

In its magnitude and rapidity, this transformation was highly unusual,
even unique, in the history of mass opinion in the United States.
Ideological shifts of this magnitude are likely to occur only when citizens
fundamentally change the lens through which they view policymaking in
a given domain. As Katznelson and his collaborators have argued with
respect to Southern members of Congress, just such a change in the "axis
of preferences" occurred in the Southern white citizens' evaluation of liberal economic policies.[85] Whereas they originally viewed the New Deal
through the lens of economic interest and party loyalty, Southern whites
came to see government activism in the economic sphere as threatening
the region's system of racial hierarchy. As the distinction between labor
and nonlabor issues indicates, Southern whites did not view all liberal
policies as equally threatening, and they continued to balance the benefits
of federal aid against the risk to Jim Crow, in many cases concluding that
the former outweighed the latter. Furthermore, Southern whites differed
among themselves about the balance of costs and benefits. For poorer
Southern whites, especially nonfarmers living in urban areas, the material
advantages of the New Deal loomed quite large, leading them (like their
non-Southern counterparts) to be less conservative than their richer and
more rural brethren.

Notably, however, the South's ideological shifts and internal cleavages left almost no trace on partisan identities. As Figure 3.1 illustrated,
the Democratic Party's hold on the loyalties of the Southern white public barely slipped over the 1936–52 period. It is true that just as in
1928, many Southern Democrats bolted to the Republicans in the 1952
presidential election. But this left hardly an echo in Southern whites'
partisan identities or, as we shall see in the next chapter, their votes
for Congress, where for the most part Democratic dominance remained
utterly secure. In short, the mass-level ideological dynamics documented
in this chapter occurred almost wholly within the one-party system. In the

---

[85] Farhang and Katznelson, "Southern Imposition," 2.

following chapter I examine the same themes from a different perspective, moving from the realm of public opinion to the halls of Congress.

3.A APPENDIX: DETAILS OF THE GROUP-LEVEL IRT MODELS

The conservatism estimates used in this chapter were derived from various versions of a group-level IRT model. Like a conventional individual-level IRT model, a group-level one models responses to a given survey question as a function of respondents' score on some latent trait (in our case, conservatism) and the idiosyncratic characteristics of the question. Unlike an individual-level model, a group-level one does not estimate the conservatism of individual respondents, but rather the average conservatism in specified subpopulations. Formally, if n_{gqt} members of group g answered question q in year t, then the number of conservative responses s_{gqt} is distributed

$$s_{gqt} \sim \text{Binomial}\left(n_{gqt}, \ \Phi\left[\frac{\bar{\theta}_{gt} - \kappa_q}{\sqrt{\sigma_q^2 + \sigma_{\theta t}^2}}\right]\right), \tag{3.1}$$

where $\bar{\theta}_{gt}$ is group g's average conservatism in year t, $\sigma_{\theta t}^2$ is the variance of θ within groups, κ_q is the threshold for a conservative answer to question q, and the inverse of σ_q^2 indicates how "ideological" question q is.

All of the conservatism estimates in this chapter were derived from models with equation (3.1) as a component. The models differed, however, in three main respects: the survey data used to estimate them, the definition of subpopulations, and the specification of prior distributions for $\bar{\theta}_{gt}$. The "economic conservatism" scores were estimated based on all available survey questions related to the New Deal. In the analyses reported in Figure 3.6, these questions were classified into "labor" and "nonlabor" domains and groups' conservatism was estimated in each, as well as in questions in the "race" (i.e., civil rights) domain.

As for subpopulations, the analysis reported in Figure 3.2 cross-classified respondents by phone ownership, professional status, farm residence, urban residence, region (South/non-South), and race (black/nonblack) and estimated conservatism in each cell. The analysis reported in Figure 3.4 was based on a model with cells defined by the cross-classification of region, race, and presidential vote. The racial conservatism scores reported in Figure 3.6 were estimated in subpopulations defined by the cross-classification of state, female, phone ownership, and race–region (Southern white/non-Southern white/black), and then poststratified to obtain state-level estimates. The remaining scores in

Figure 3.6 (economic conservatism, labor conservatism, and nonlabor conservatism) were estimated in groups defined by state and race and then also poststratified.

Finally, the models differed in their specification of the prior distribution for $\bar{\theta}_{gt}$. The estimates reported in Figures 3.2 and 3.4, as well as the racial estimates in Figure 3.6, were based on the hierarchical group-level IRT model described by Caughey and Warshaw.[86] In this model, $\bar{\theta}_{gt}$ is given a hierarchical prior whose mean is linear regression of the variables that define the subpopulations (e.g., black, region, etc.). All the other estimates were based on the dynamic group-level IRT model implemented by the R package dgo,[87] which models $\bar{\theta}_{gt}$ as a function of both its demographic attributes and its value in the preceding time period.

[86] Caughey and Warshaw, "Dynamic Estimation."
[87] Dunham, Caughey, and Warshaw, *dgo*.

CHAPTER 4

Southern Democrats in Congress

You'll find that practically every New Deal measure that was enacted into law under President Roosevelt was sponsored by a Southerner, and never could have been passed without the support of Southerners.[1]

—Senator John Sparkman of Alabama (1968)

Four years ago an emergency confronted us.... I voted for every recovery measure...I actively supported every relief appropriation. If today the same conditions existed, I would vote for the same appropriations. But the same conditions do not exist. The recovery program of this administration has accomplished its purpose.... The emergency has passed, and it is now time for us to put our house in order.[2]

—Senator James Byrnes of South Carolina (1937)

The South gets its reputation for conservatism [because] the rest of the world, with party labels in mind, insists on comparing the South with the records of Northern Democrats.... Republicans are expected to be conservative, but Democrats are expected to be liberal and when Southern Democrats are not liberal this fact is made cause for comment.[3]

—William Carleton (1951)

---

[1] John Sparkman, "Interview by Paige E. Mulhollan" (Transcript, Lyndon Johnson Oral History Collection, Lyndon Johnson Presidential Library, Washington, DC, October 5, 1968), 33, http://web1.millercenter.org/poh/transcripts/sparkman_john_1968_1005.pdf.
[2] "Radio Address Delivered by Hon. James P. Byrnes, of South Carolina, on May 3, 1937," 81 Cong. Rec. 1075 (1937).
[3] William G. Carleton, "The Southern Politician—1900 and 1950," *Journal of Politics* 13, no. 2 (1951): 221.

In THIS CHAPTER, I shift my focus from the mass public to political elites, specifically Southern MCs. My goals are threefold. The first is to document the scope and timing of Southern MCs' dramatic but incomplete turn against the New Deal beginning in the late 1930s, which mirrored developments at the mass level. The second is to show that Southern MCs, like the Southern white public, remained ideologically diverse despite maintaining their monolithically Democratic partisanship. My third goal is to highlight the policy consequences of the ideological evolution and diversity of Southern MCs, who, as Ira Katznelson has emphasized, occupied a pivotal position in congressional politics in the wake of the New Deal.[4] I develop these points through the lens of three policy areas discussed in Chapter 2—minimum wages, union security, and income taxes—showing that legislative outcomes in these areas often (but not always) hinged on the distribution of Southern preferences.

Between 1900 and 1950, the Democratic Party won every Senate race held in the former Confederacy and 97% of U.S. House races. Nearly all of the Republican Party's 80 House victories were confined to a handful of anomalous congressional districts in Texas and the Appalachian highlands. While Republicans made a few inroads in the 1950s, Democrats continued to compose well over 90% of Southern House members until after the 1962 elections. Only in 1961 was the first post-Redemption Republican from the former Confederacy, John Tower of Texas, elected to the U.S. Senate.[5] Even as Democrats lost their secure hold on the South in presidential politics after 1948,[6] the vast majority of Democratic

---

[4] Katznelson, Geiger, and Kryder, "Limiting Liberalism"; Katznelson and Mulroy, "Was the South Pivotal?"

[5] Black and Black, *The Rise of Southern Republicans*. Between 1932 and 1965, Republicans won 16% of state presidential elections in the former Confederacy, 7.2% of U.S. House races, 1.5% of U.S. Senate races, and 0% of governorships; Harold W. Stanley and Richard G. Niemi, "Table 1-4 Party Competition, by Region, 1860–2008 (percent)," in *Vital Statistics on American Politics 2009–2010*, ed. Harold W. Stanley and Richard G. Niemi (Washington, DC: CQ Press, 2009), http://library.cqpress.com/vsap/vsap09%5C_tab1-4.

[6] In 1948, protesting President Harry Truman's endorsement of civil rights, four Deep South Democratic parties designated the "Dixiecrat" Governor Strom Thurmond of South Carolina as the official Democratic nominee. Thurmond carried these same four states in the general election. In fact, Harry Truman—the incumbent president!—wasn't even on the ballot in Alabama in 1948; William Warren Rogers et al., *Alabama: The History of a Deep South State* (Tuscaloosa: University of Alabama Press, 1994), 534–535. The Republican Dwight Eisenhower completed the break-up of the Solid South at the presidential level by winning four Southern states in 1952 and five in 1956. One should not overestimate the solidity of the South in presidential elections, however, even at the height of the one-party period. In 1920, Warren Harding carried Oklahoma and Tennessee. In 1928, Herbert Hoover captured Florida, Texas, Oklahoma, Tennessee, North Carolina, and Virginia and came close in several others (e.g., 48.5% in Alabama). The

congressional candidates continued to face at most token opposition in general elections.[7]

Notwithstanding this partisan stability, the 1930s–50s were a period of major change in Southern congressional politics. The Great Depression devastated the South, which was already much poorer than the rest of the nation, and weakened many white Southerners' resistance to outside intervention, at least temporarily. Out of a combination of material interest and party loyalty, Southern Democrats in Congress provided overwhelming support for the recovery policies of the early Roosevelt administration. In the mid-1930s, as the focus of the New Deal turned from short-term relief to more fundamental economic reform, Southern MCs still remained largely loyal to the president, providing overwhelming support for such landmark measures as the 1935 Social Security Act. With few exceptions, Southern conservatives who personally disliked the New Deal swallowed their objections through the end of Roosevelt's first term.[8]

As noted in Chapter 3, Southern support for New Deal programs was facilitated by the fact that they were structured in ways that limited interference with Jim Crow. Even with these protections, however, an expanded and empowered national state still posed dangers, if only in potential form, to Southern autonomy. As a result, in evaluating New Deal–style programs, Southern MCs were confronted with recurring trade-offs between the material benefits of federal aid and the threat of federal interference.[9] Through the mid-1930s, the benefits of federal aid, in conjunction with the pull of party loyalty, were sufficient to convince nearly all Southern MCs to support the New Deal. But cracks in Southern support for Roosevelt began to emerge during the 75th Congress (1937–38), when the first signs appeared of the "conservative coalition" between Southern Democrats and Republicans that would become a fixture of congressional politics for decades to come.[10]

Republican presidential gains of the 1920s were rolled back amid the national resurgence of the Democratic Party in the 1930s, only to reemerge after World War II.

[7] Through the 1950s Democratic primaries, not general elections, remained the main site of electoral contestation in the South; Ansolabehere et al., "More Democracy."

[8] Tindall, *Emergence of the New South*, 390; Patterson, *Congressional Conservatism*, 5–24.

[9] Katznelson, Geiger, and Kryder emphasize Southern MCs' awareness of this tradeoff, whereas Schulman argues that in their zeal for federal aid, Southern conservatives failed to fully "appreciate the potential connections between funds and control"; Katznelson, Geiger, and Kryder, "Limiting Liberalism"; Schulman, *Cotton Belt to Sunbelt*, 110.

[10] On the formation of the conservative coalition, see James T. Patterson, "A Conservative Coalition Forms in Congress, 1933–1939," *Journal of American History* 52, no. 4 (1966): 757–772; Patterson, *Congressional Conservatism*. According to Finley, the 75th Congress also marked the first time the Southern caucus in the Senate formally organized to combat the growing threat of anti-lynching bills and other civil rights legislation; Keith M. Finley,

Southern defections in the 75th Congress were part of a more general congressional reaction against the New Deal. A number of erstwhile progressives from across the nation, particularly from rural constituencies, soured on the increasingly statist, urban, and labor-oriented direction of the New Deal.[11] Indeed, on some issues, such as the 1937 fight over court packing, Democratic opposition to the administration position cut across sectional lines and was not particularly concentrated among Southerners.[12] By the end of the 1930s, however, Southern Democrats had emerged as FDR's chief intraparty antagonists, joining with Republicans to oppose liberal proposals such as the 1937 Housing Act and to advance conservative ones such as a failed resolution to investigate an unpopular wave of sit-down strikes. Even then, Southern conservatives continued to couch their opposition in largely "nonsectional"—that is, nonracial—terms, emphasizing the same charges as non-Southerners: that "the president was usurping his power and that his policies were slowly destroying free competition."[13] The outbreak of World War II, however, brought growing assertiveness on the part of African Americans and racially progressive CIO unions, and the explicitly racial anxieties of Southern whites came increasingly to the fore. These dangers became more concrete with

---

Southern Opposition to Civil Rights in the United States Senate: A Tactical and Ideological Analysis, 1938–1965, PhD dissertation, Louisiana State University, Baton Rouge, 2003, 8. Most scholars have found that the prominence of the CC increased rapidly in the early 1940s and then plateaued. Key reports a marked uptick in CC activity beginning in 1940, the year after Patterson's study ends; Key, *Southern Politics*, 367. Brady and Bullock find that conservative coalition activity increased yearly between 1937 and 1944 and stabilized thereafter; Brady and Bullock, "Is There a Conservative Coalition?," 551. Using data from Democratic conventions as well as from Congress, Reiter dates the regional split to between 1939 and 1944; Howard L. Reiter, "The Building of a Bifactional Structure: The Democrats in the 1940s," *Political Science Quarterly* 116, no. 1 (2001): 107–129. Sinclair identifies 1939 as the break point between the voting alignment of the Depression-era New Deal and that which prevailed through the end of the Truman administration; Barbara Sinclair, *Congressional Realignment: 1925–1978* (Austin: University of Texas Press, 1982), 20–53. By contrast, Poole and Rosenthal report that congressional Southerners' ideological transformation took place more gradually. They find that Southern Democrats first became more conservative than Northern Democrats on the "first dimension" of congressional voting in the early 1940s and "continue[d] to move steadily to the Right until the mid-to-late 1960s"; Poole and Rosenthal, *Ideology & Congress*, 83.

[11] Badger, *The New Deal*, 275; on the rural orientation of New Deal opponents, see Patterson, "Conservative Coalition Forms."
[12] Many non-Southern Democrats, particularly Western progressives such as Senator Burton Wheeler (D-MT), refused to go along with court packing, but a majority of Southern Democrats stood by the president. See, e.g., Albert L. Warner, "Court Bill Battle Opens with Robinson Defying Opposition to Filibuster," *New York Herald Tribune*, July 7, 1937, 1; Leuchtenburg, "Franklin D. Roosevelt's Supreme Court 'Packing' Plan."
[13] Garson, *Democratic Party*, 10.

the 1941 creation of the Fair Employment Practices Committee (FEPC), which, however weakly enforced in practice, enraged Southern conservatives with its endorsement of the principle of nondiscrimination.[14] Over the course of the war, the threats posed by liberal policies, particularly federal regulation of labor markets and encouragement of labor organizing, loomed ever larger in the minds of Southern MCs, whose cooperation with Republicans intensified.[15]

The term "conservative coalition," however, is misleading insofar as it suggests that Southern Democrats became uniformly conservative. This description is apt for issues related to race and civil rights, but not for social welfare, government regulation, and other economic questions at the core of the New Deal issue complex. Even after the emergence of the conservative coalition in the late 1930s, Southern MCs did not turn wholly against New Deal liberalism, but rather continued to weigh the benefits of federal aid (and the pull of party loyalty) against the dangers of federal control.[16] Balancing these trade-offs led Southerners to occupy a centrist position on economic issues, with non-Southern Democrats on their left and Republicans on their right. Moreover, because they collectively "h[eld] the balance of power between the two great parties," the votes of Southern Democrats often determined legislative outcomes on economic issues.[17] The most salient exception to Southerners' economic centrism was labor policy, where by the mid-1940s Southern Democrats had moved into near-complete alliance with Republicans. But the very radicalness of Southern MCs' rightward turn on labor issues offers a particularly stark illustration of their pivotal position in Congress, for labor policy was arguably the area where conservative efforts to dismantle the New Deal, culminating in the 1947 Taft–Hartley Act, were most successful and most consequential over the long term.[18]

Katznelson and his collaborators have offered the most extensive and persuasive analysis of Southern MCs' pivotal status in the 1930s–40s.[19] They show that Southern pivotality—that is, whether the votes of Southern MCs, cast as a bloc, were necessary and sufficient for majority passage of a bill—varied over time and across issue areas.[20] According to

---

[14] Of all civil rights proposals, the Dixiecrats of 1948 were most most critical of the FEPC; Kari Frederickson, *The Dixiecrat Revolt and the End of the Solid South* (London: University of North Carolina Press, 2001), 7.

[15] Farhang and Katznelson, "Southern Imposition."

[16] Katznelson, Geiger, and Kryder, "Limiting Liberalism."

[17] Ewing, *Primary Elections*, 106.

[18] Farhang and Katznelson, "Southern Imposition."

[19] See, most recently, Katznelson and Mulroy, "Was the South Pivotal?"

[20] Katznelson and Mulroy classify Southern Democrats as pivotal on a given roll call if and only if (a) the number of Northern Democratic and Republican "yea" votes were not

their analysis, Southern pivotality appeared first on labor issues but later spread to regulatory and welfare policies as the latter also came to be seen as threatening regional autonomy.

Katznelson and his colleagues' analyses provide a welcome corrective to the literature on the conservative coalition, which they criticize as overly broad and substantively underspecified. Yet their approach, in its reification of the Southern "bloc" as a single "unit of action" in a three-actor model of congressional politics, inherits some of the problems of the conservative coalition measure.[21] In particular, treating Southerners as a

---

sufficient to pass the proposal, and (b) the number of additional votes needed for passage was smaller than the number of Southern Democrats; ibid., 608. On such roll calls, unanimous Southern support would have passed the bill, and unanimous Southern opposition would have blocked it. Katznelson and Mulroy's measure coincides with Shapley and Shubik's classic definition of a pivotal voter (the member of a sequential coalition whose vote is the last needed for the measure to pass) only if Southern Democrats were located ideologically in between non-Southern Democrats and Republicans and if coalitions formed in ideological order, with the most "enthusiastic" voting first; L. S. Shapley and Martin Shubik, "A Method for Evaluating the Distribution of Power in a Committee System," *American Political Science Review* 48, no. 3 (1954): 788, 791–792. Katznelson and Mulroy's measure thus implicitly assumes that Northern Democrats and Republicans are ideologically extreme (thus most "enthusiastic") and Southerners are moderate. If the groups' ideological positions were different on some issue—say, if Southern Democrats are enthusiastic supporters of agricultural subsidies, Republicans are mostly opposed, and Northern Democrats are relatively indifferent—then the pivotality formula might label Southern Democrats as pivotal when substantively they were not. Thus, Katznelson and Mulroy's pivotality measure presumes the same sort of ideological ordering of legislators that spatial models do.

[21] The classic indicator of the conservative coalition, institutionalized by *Congressional Quarterly* in 1958, is a majority of Republicans voting with a majority of Southern Democrats against a majority of Northern Democrats; see, e.g., Key, *Southern Politics*, 355; Brady and Bullock, "Is There a Conservative Coalition?"; John D. Wilkerson and Barry Pump, "The Ties That Bind: Coalitions in Congress," in *The Oxford Handbook of the American Congress*, ed. Eric Schickler and Frances Lee (New York: Oxford University Press, 2011), 618–640. This measure has several problems. First, because it dichotomizes on the basis of an arbitrary threshold, it lacks sensitivity, failing to distinguish between obvious conservative coalition or non–conservative coalition votes and those on the border; for examples, see Eric Schickler and Kathryn Pearson, "Agenda Control, Majority Party Power, and the House Committee on Rules, 1937–52," *Legislative Studies Quarterly* 34, no. 4 (2009): 455–491. Unless each group of legislators is entirely homogeneous (which some analyses do seem to assume, especially with regard to Southern Democrats), the traditional CC measure therefore throws away much information. A second problem is that the CC measure's average value in a given congress depends on the distribution of midpoint locations (viz. the point of indifference between two alternative policy proposals) in that congress. For example, if midpoints tend to be liberal (say, because status quos are moderate and most policy proposals are liberal) and the median Southern Democrat is midway between the medians of the other two groups, then the CC measure will suggest that Southerners are closer ideologically to Republicans. Other measures, such as the cohesion and likeness scores used by Katznelson, Geiger, and Kryder, also depend on the

bloc implies that they either had identical preferences or possessed organizational mechanisms for enforcing collective action.[22] In fact, neither was true. Only in the area of civil rights did Southern MCs engage in formal organization and collective decision making.[23] Even on civil rights, where its preferences were also especially homogeneous, the Southern caucus could not always prevent defection from collective decisions.[24] Southern MCs' capacity for unified collective action was all the lower on economic issues, where they exhibited neither homogeneous preferences nor collective organization. Indeed, on nonracial issues Southern MCs were extraordinarily diverse, ranging from arch-conservatives such as Virginia's Harry Byrd to fervent liberals such as Florida's Claude Pepper.[25]

Taking proper account of the ideological diversity of Southern MCs requires treating them as a collection of individuals, not a reified bloc. I therefore analyze Southern Democrats (along with other MCs) as individuals with possibly distinct preferences, which I estimate using a spatial model similar to that underlying Poole and Rosenthal's NOMINATE scores.[26] One benefit of this approach is that it allows Southern MCs' collective distinctiveness as well as their internal diversity to emerge from the individual-level analysis rather than being imposed a priori. In addition, it focuses on MCs' preferences rather than observed voting alignments, the latter of which are a function of the distribution of legislative proposals as well as of the distribution of preferences. Finally, a spatial model allows MCs to be arrayed as points on a single left–right dimension. This comports with the spatial intuition behind labels such as "liberal" and

---

distribution of midpoints; see Keith Krehbiel, "Party Discipline and Measures of Partisanship," *American Journal of Political Science* 44, no. 2 (2000): 218–20. Percentage support for liberal or administration proposals is another measure with these same drawbacks; for an example of this measure, see Brown, *Race, Money*, 107.

[22] Formal models of the endogenous formation of legislative factions depend critically on the assumption of binding collective decision-making; see Jon X. Eguia, "Endogenous Parties in an Assembly," *American Journal of Political Science* 55, no. 1 (2010): 16–26.

[23] Keith M. Finley, *Delaying the Dream: Southern Senators and the Fight against Civil Rights, 1938–1965* (Baton Rouge: Louisiana State University Press, 2008); Ruth Bloch Rubin, *Building the Bloc: Intraparty Organization in the U.S. Congress* (New York: Cambridge University Press, 2017), chapters 4–5. Bloch Rubin emphasizes that even in the relatively unanimous domain of civil rights, "shared preferences were, on their own, insufficient" to enable Southern MCs to act as a unified bloc, which is why they created formal mechanisms for collective action in this domain; Bloch Rubin, *Building the Bloc*, 117.

[24] In 1957, for example, Southern senators unanimously decided not to filibuster the watered-down Civil Rights Act of that year. They could do little more than fume, however, when Sen. Strom Thurmond (D-SC) broke the agreement and filibustered anyway; Finley, *Southern Opposition*, 215–217.

[25] Key, *Southern Politics*, chapters 16–17; Carleton, "The Southern Politician."

[26] Poole and Rosenthal, *Ideology & Congress*.

"conservative" as well as with the notion of pivotality, which presumes an ordering to legislators.

4.1 THE IDEOLOGICAL EVOLUTION OF SOUTHERN MCS

Since nearly all the empirical analyses in this book involve congressional ideal points, I begin by describing the model that generated them (see Appendix 4.A for technical details). In an ideal-point model, a legislator's probability of voting for a given bill depends on how much they favor the policy proposed by the bill relative to the status quo policy. The legislator's preference is in turn a function of their most-preferred policy—their "ideal point"—and the characteristics of the bill, such as the ideological distance between the two alternatives. Voting "errors" (i.e., mispredicted votes) are assumed to have no systematic pattern once ideal points and bill characteristics are accounted for. The primary goal of ideal-point models is to infer the relative locations of legislators' ideal points from their votes on many bills.

My main focus is evolving distribution of Southern senators' and representatives' positions on economic policies. That is, I require a measure that summarizes MCs' economic liberalism–conservatism at each point in time. The most commonly used publicly available ideal-point estimates, DW-NOMINATE scores, are not ideally suited for this purpose because they are estimated using all roll calls, not just those related to economics. Moreover, DW-NOMINATE requires that any change in a legislator's ideal point be equally apportioned across his or her career, thus ruling out rapid or nonlinear ideological change.[27]

Thus, rather than rely on off-the-shelf scores, I estimate an ideal-point model tailored to the purposes of this study. Specifically, I employ a one-dimensional dynamic item-response model, which allows ideal points to evolve flexibly between congressional terms.[28] Instead of using all roll calls, I use only those related to the issues of social welfare and economic regulation at the heart of the New Deal issue complex.[29] I estimate the

---

[27] Devin Caughey and Eric Schickler, "Substance and Change in Congressional Ideology: NOMINATE and Its Alternatives," *Studies in American Political Development* 30, no. 2 (2016): 128–146.

[28] Andrew D. Martin and Kevin M. Quinn, "Dynamic Ideal Point Estimation via Markov Chain Monte Carlo for the U.S. Supreme Court, 1953–1999," *Political Analysis* 10, no. 2 (2002): 134–153; Andrew D. Martin, Kevin M. Quinn, and Jong Hee Park, "MCMCpack: Markov Chain Monte Carlo in R," *Journal of Statistical Software* 42, no. 9 (2011): 1–21. Quinn and his collaborators have applied this model to the Supreme Court, but to my knowledge, this is the first application of a dynamic IRT model to the U.S. Congress.

[29] Specifically, I used only roll calls classified in the "Government Management" and "Social Welfare" issue categories developed by Aage Clausen and included in roll-call data

model using Bayesian Monte Carlo simulation, which makes it easy to characterize the uncertainty around any parameter (e.g., the identity of the median legislator) by examining the parameter's distribution across simulations.

Figure 4.1 uses these estimates to illustrate the ideological evolution of Republicans, Southern Democrats, and non-Southern Democrats between the 72nd (1931–32) and the 87th (1961–62) congresses. In addition to plotting the median and middle 80% of legislators in each group, the figures also indicate the location of the chamber median and veto pivot in each congress (the veto pivot is the member whose support is necessary and sufficient to override a presidential veto).[30] As this figure shows, Southern Democrats in both chambers began the period at least as liberal on economic issues as their Northern counterparts but became substantially more conservative over time. Contrary to what the moniker "conservative coalition" would suggest, however, Southern Democrats did not fully converge with Republicans. Rather, by the mid-1940s Southern Democrats had arrived at an ideologically moderate position between Republicans and Northern Democrats. This shift occurred later and more rapidly in the Senate than in the House, but ideological trends were broadly similar between the two chambers. As will be explored further later in this chapter, the figure also highlights the diversity of Southern Democrats, who overlapped ideologically with their non-Southern counterparts throughout the period and, at least by the end of the period, did so with Republicans as well.

In the two-party North, as in contemporary American politics, member turnover was the main mechanism of ideological change.[31] Southern Democrats' shift to the right, however, appears to have been driven

downloadable from voteview.com; Aage R. Clausen, *How Congressmen Decide: A Policy Focus* (New York: St. Martin's, 1973); Keith T. Poole and Howard Rosenthal, *HCODES.TXT*, Text file downloaded from http://voteview.com/page2c.htm. 1998; Keith T. Poole and Howard Rosenthal, *Houses 1–106 Outcome Coordinates and Issue Codes*, ftp://voteview.com/h01106xx.dat. Last updated July 3, 2001. Roll calls relating to agriculture, civil liberties, and foreign and defense policy, as well as unclassifiable or unidentifiable votes, were excluded from the dataset.

[30] More precisely, if there is perfect spatial voting along a left–right dimension, the veto pivot is the member with one-third of the chamber to their left if the president is liberal, or to their right if the president is conservative; Keith Krehbiel, *Pivotal Politics: A Theory of U.S. Lawmaking* (Chicago: University of Chicago Press, 1998).

[31] Poole and Rosenthal, *Ideology & Congress*, 72; see also Stephen Ansolabehere, James M. Snyder Jr., and Charles Stewart III, "Candidate Positioning in U.S. House Elections," *American Journal of Political Science* 45, no. 1 (2001): 136–159; David S. Lee, Enrico Moretti, and Matthew J. Butler, "Do Voters Affect or Elect Policies? Evidence from the U.S. House," *Quarterly Journal of Economics* 119, no. 3 (2004): 807–859.

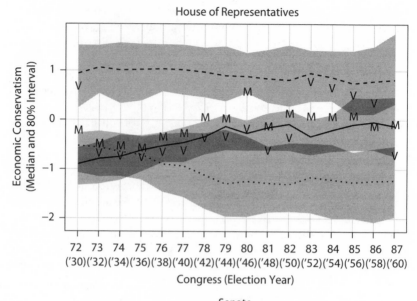

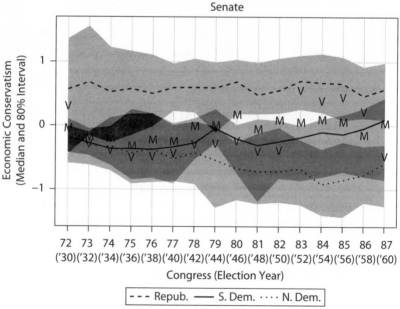

Figure 4.1. Ideological evolution in the U.S. House (top) and Senate (bottom). Lines indicate the median Republican, Southern Democrat, and non-Southern Democrat, respectively. Shaded regions indicate the interval containing the middle 80% of legislators in a group. "M" indicates the location of the chamber median, and "V" the location of the veto pivot.

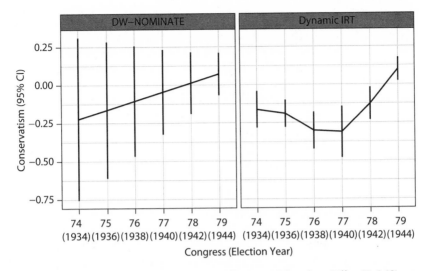

Figure 4.2. The ideological evolution of Senator Theodore Bilbo (D-MS), according to DW-NOMINATE scores (left) and a dynamic IRT model (right). For comparability, both measures have been scaled to range from −1 to +1.

as much by the adaptation of continuing members as by turnover.[32] Figure 4.2 illustrates this point with the case of Senator Theodore Bilbo (D-MS).[33] The left panel of this figure plots Bilbo's DW-NOMINATE score in each congress between 1935 and 1946, and the right panel does the same for estimates from a dynamic item response theory (IRT) model. Both ideal-point measures indicate that Bilbo became substantially more conservative (relative to other continuing members) between the 74th and 79th congresses. Only the dynamic IRT model, however, is able to capture the nonlinearity of Bilbo's shift to the right, which was concentrated entirely between 1941 and 1946.[34]

Bilbo's conservative turn occurred a couple years after most Southern senators', but otherwise his ideological trajectory is emblematic of the evolution of Southern caucus as a whole. Southern MCs did not need

---

[32] Previous evidence on this point is mixed, with Sinclair stressing the importance of adaptation and Reiter and Poole and Rosenthal emphasizing replacement; Sinclair, *Congressional Realignment*, 59; Reiter, "Bifactional Structure"; Poole and Rosenthal, *Ideology & Congress*.

[33] This plot is a modified version of a figure that appears in Caughey and Schickler, "Substance and Change."

[34] The dynamic IRT estimates of Bilbo's ideological evolution are consistent with the account of his career given in Chester M. Morgan, *Redneck Liberal: Theodore G. Bilbo and the New Deal* (London: Louisiana State University Press, 1985).

to be replaced in order to adapt to the ideological times. On average, between-congress differences among continuing members (i.e., adaptation) were only a little smaller than the differences between exiting and entering members (turnover). Because 80–90% of Southern Democrats continued between congresses, however, adaptation among continuing members dominated turnover in terms of its aggregate contribution to ideological change.

4.2 LABOR POLICY: A LEADING INDICATOR

Southern MCs' shift to the right did not play out identically across issue areas. Their ideological transformation came earliest, and was arguably most consequential, on issues related to labor markets and unions. Through the mid-1930s, Southern Democrats viewed organized labor as primarily an issue for the industrialized non-South and were largely willing to defer to non-Southern Democrats on the issue. Although Southern Democrats did not take the lead in sponsoring labor legislation as they had during the Wilson administration, they nevertheless offered overwhelming, if often unenthusiastic, support for labor laws. This remained true through the passage of the 1935 Wagner Act, which helped create "the most hospitable climate ever fashioned in American history for trade unions."[35] Georgia representative Eugene Cox's remarks on the Wagner Act, though perhaps more extreme than most Southerners' views at the time, are indicative of their ambivalent feelings toward the New Deal labor regime:

> I recognize, of course, that the [Wagner] bill raises an issue that must at some time be fought out, and I think it may as well be now as any other time. I have not, therefore, opposed the reporting of the rule by the Rules

---

[35] Farhang and Katznelson, "Southern Imposition," 2. Only three Southern senators opposed the Wagner Act: Harry Byrd (D-VA), Carter Glass (D-VA), and Josiah Bailey (D-NC). The House vote was not recorded. Nevertheless, Southern support was fairly tepid, and several Southern MCs tried to reduce the Wagner Act's pro-labor tilt before ultimately supporting the bill; Biles, *The South and the New Deal*, 87. Many Southerners apparently believed the NLRA would be struck down as unconstitutional and were surprised when it was upheld by the Supreme Court. Southerners' backseat role on labor legislation during the New Deal contrasts with their behavior in the Woodrow Wilson administration, when Southerners had been among the leading sponsors of labor laws like the Clayton and Adamson Acts. The main thrust of the Clayton Act in particular was to remove unions from federal regulation, a purpose that dovetailed with traditional Southern anti-statism better than the much more bureaucratic proposals by New Deal liberals; Melvyn Dubofsky, *The State and Labor in Modern America* (Chapel Hill: University of North Carolina Press, 1994), 110–128.

Committee, and do not and will not oppose the adoption of the rule by
the House.... [B]ut it must be apparent to everyone who has read it that it
carries upon its face the most terrible threat—and I speak deliberately and
advisedly—to our dual form of government that has thus far arisen.... It is
not what appears upon the face of the bill that disturbs me, it is the intent
and purpose carried by the measure which the language used is intended to
conceal.... It is intended by this measure through the use of the commerce
clause of the Constitution to sap and undermine that great document to
the extent of ultimately striking down and destroying completely all State
sovereignty....[36]

The fact that the conservative Cox opposed the Wagner bill on
principle but nonetheless declined to block it in committee reflects his
and other Southerners' initial willingness to defer to pro-union non-
Southerners. Soon, however, Southern ambivalence toward New Deal
labor legislation would soon transform into outright hostility, and labor
legislation became one of the earliest and most consistent areas of collaboration between Southerners and Republicans in Congress.[37] Figure 4.3
illustrates the evolution of this collaboration. Between 1935 and 1947,
Southern Democrats shifted from being nearly as pro-union as their non-
Southern counterparts to being nearly as anti-union as Republicans. This
shift began with a series of high-profile congressional investigations in
the late 1930s targeting a highly unpopular wave of sit-down strikes
and subsequently the National Labor Relations Board. In the 1940s, it
burgeoned into increasingly ambitious efforts by Republicans and Southern Democrats to pass legislation limiting wartime strikes and reining in
union power more generally. Although presidential vetoes largely frustrated the passage of anti-union legislation through 1946, conservatives
finally mustered supermajority support in the Republican-controlled 80th
Congress, which passed the Taft–Hartley Act of 1947.

Why was the antilabor turn of Southern members apparently so
much more rapid and extreme than their shift to the right on economic issues generally (see Figure 4.1)? Farhang and Katznelson attribute
Southern MCs' anti-labor turn to a shift in the "axis of preferences"
they used to evaluate labor issues. "In the 1930s," they argue, "union
and labor market issues were arrayed primarily on the ideology-party
dimension, while, in the 1940s, southern Democrats came to understand labor questions mainly as issues that concerned the durability of

---

[36] National Labor Relations Board, *Legislative History of the National Labor Relations
Act, 1935*, reprint of the 1959 edition, Vol. II (Washington, DC: U.S. Government Printing
Office, 1985), 3103.
[37] Brady and Bullock, "Is There a Conservative Coalition?"; Sinclair, *Congressional
Realignment*; Schickler and Pearson, "Agenda Control."

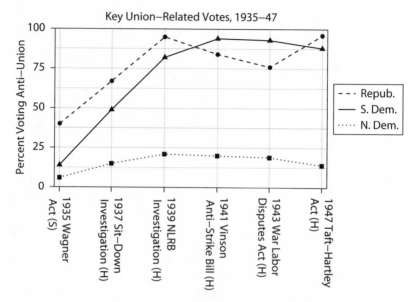

Figure 4.3. Percentage of different groups in Congress voting antilabor on key union-related roll calls. "S" indicates a Senate vote, "H" a House vote. Note that the 1937 and 1939 investigations are not classified as Government Management or Social Welfare roll calls and thus were not used to estimate members' ideal points.

Jim Crow."[38] This characterization contains a large degree of truth, but it should be qualified in two respects. First, the anti-union backlash was a national rather than purely Southern phenomenon. This is apparent from Figure 4.3, which shows that support for pro-union positions also fell among Republican MCs at the same as the Republican share of non-Southern seats increased dramatically after 1938. Resentment of unions and pro-union policies was particularly intense in rural and agricultural constituencies throughout the nation, not just the South.[39] For these reasons it would be an overstatement to attribute Southern MCs' opposition to unions solely to racial concerns.

Second, rather than being fundamentally distinct from other economic issues, labor policy is better viewed as a leading indicator of the broader ideological changes described in Section 4.1. Sinclair, for example, argues

---

[38] Farhang and Katznelson, "Southern Imposition," 2.
[39] Saloutos, "American Farm Bureau"; Edwin Amenta and Theda Skocpol, "Redefining the New Deal: World War II and the Development of Social Provision in the United States," in *The Politics of Social Policy in the United States*, ed. Margaret Weir, Ann Shola Orloff, and Theda Skocpol (Princeton: Princeton University Press, 1988), 118.

that voting alignments on labor issues in the 1930s came in the 1940s "to characterize voting on all social welfare issues."[40] Similarly, Poole and Rosenthal find that labor roll calls began to load on a second, regional dimension in addition to the first (partisan) dimension beginning in the 75th Congress (1937–38). But the importance of this second dimension peaked in 1941–42 and then declined until 1947–48 (the 80th Congress), after which labor votes again became almost entirely first-dimensional.[41]

The dynamic IRT model paints a similar picture. Between the 76th and 78th congresses (1939–44), roll calls on labor-related bills tended to distinguish less well between liberals and conservatives than other economic roll calls.[42] Further, much of the off-dimensional voting that occurred in these years was the result of antilabor defections by Southern Democrats. By the end of the war, however, labor votes had become just as strongly related to members' general economic conservatism as nonlabor ones. Thus, when Southern Democrats voted in 1947 to retrench the pro-union regime they had helped construct a dozen years before, their votes were almost completely in line with their more conservative position on economic issues generally.

Does this contradict the claim that Southern MCs turned against the New Deal labor regime partly because they came to view it as a potential threat to their racial system? No, because similar concerns animated their increasing conservatism on economic issues generally. Just as labor unions threatened the South's political and economic autonomy, so too did federally funded schools and housing projects, price controls, national health insurance, and other liberal programs. Growing Southern conservatism may have been apparent earlier on labor issues, but they were primarily a leading indicator for Southerners' more general shift to the right.

4.3 A "THEY," NOT AN "IT": SOUTHERN DIVERSITY

In his classic portrait of the 1950s Senate, the journalist William White wrote:

> Though [the Southern caucus] is on some issues thoroughly divided, having its right and left wings on tax policy, housing and the like, there is in it at the last analysis a oneness found nowhere else in politics.... A Byrd of Virginia

---

[40] Sinclair, *Congressional Realignment*, 55.

[41] Poole and Rosenthal, *Ideology & Congress*, 137–139.

[42] In more technical terms, the discrimination parameters β_j of labor roll calls tended to be smaller in absolute value than those of nonlabor roll calls. For an extended analysis of the dimensionality of labor roll calls, see Devin Caughey, "Congress, Public Opinion, and Representation in the One-Party South, 1930s–1960s" (PhD dissertation, University of California, Berkeley, 2012), 70–78.

may look with troubled eyes upon the economic heresies of a Sparkman of Alabama, and a Sparkman may somberly return the gaze at what he thinks is the aura of parsimony rising about the seat of the senior Senator from Virginia. Nevertheless, when all is said and done, all are in the same clan, in a way that goes deeper than political ideas and even political conviction.

This quotation illustrates an important tension, that between South- erners' "oneness" on fundamental issues and their internal diversity on many others. On one hand, a few mavericks aside, Southern MCs exhib- ited near-perfect unity on the necessity of preserving racial segrega- tion and the one-party system.[43] Before the 1960s, Southern Democrats were almost monolithic in their opposition to even the mildest civil rights proposals.[44] In addition, beginning in the 75th Congress, Southern preference unanimity on racial issues was reinforced by formal organi- zation to coordinate the caucus's tactical response to civil rights bills.[45] As a result, Southern Democrats did indeed form a "coherent cluster" in ideological space—conservative on civil rights but moderate-to-liberal on other issues.[46]

The limitations of treating Southern Democrats as a single "bloc" of voters loom larger outside of civil rights. On most issues Southerners were, to borrow a phrase, a "they," not an "it."[47] On bills unrelated to civil rights, the Southern caucus did not routinely engage in organized collec- tive action; at best, Southern leaders might act as cue givers on votes where their colleagues were otherwise indifferent.[48] And as White's description

---

[43] As Finley emphasizes, however, in practice Southern MCs did not always agree over how much a policy proposal threatened the "Southern way of life"; Finley, *Delaying the Dream*. In 1944, for example, Representative (later Senator) John Sparkman of Alabama, even as he declaimed his support for states' rights, broke with the dominant Southern position to vote for a bill making it easier for soldiers serving overseas to register and vote; Henry James Walker, "Beyond the Call of Duty: Representative John Sparkman of Alabama and World War II, 1939–1945," *Southern Historian* 11 (1990): 33.

[44] Two partial exceptions to the overwhelming racial conservatism of Southern Democrats were senators Claude Pepper (FL) and Frank Graham (NC), both of whom were defeated for renomination in 1950. For other exceptions, see Anthony J. Badger, "Southerners Who Refused to Sign the Southern Manifesto," *The Historical Journal* 42, no. 2 (1999): 533–534; Werner, "Congressmen of the Silent South."

[45] Robert A. Caro, *Master of the Senate* (New York: Vintage Books, 2002); Finley, *Delaying the Dream*; Bloch Rubin, *Building the Bloc.*

[46] Katznelson and Mulroy, "Was the South Pivotal?," 606; see also Poole and Rosenthal, *Ideology & Congress.*

[47] Kenneth A. Shepsle, "Congress Is a 'They,' Not an 'It': Legislative Intent as Oxymoron," *International Review of Law and Economics* 12, no. 2 (1992): 239–256.

[48] This is not to say that individual Southerners, such as House Rules Chairman Howard Smith (D-VA) or Senator Richard Russell (D-GA), did not influence their fellow Souther- ners and occupy positions of institutional power. Rather, their influence on economic issues was generally episodic and limited. Clapp, for example, claims that on issues where

suggests, Southern MCs were much more diverse on questions of economics, mirroring a regional Democratic Party that "encompasse[d] all shades of political attitude" on issues other than civil rights.[49]

On the caucus's right stood figures such as Senator Josiah Bailey of North Carolina and Representative Howard Smith of Virginia, who on most economic issues were indistinguishable from conservative Republicans.[50] In 1937 Bailey, an early opponent of the New Deal, circulated what was dubbed a "conservative manifesto" calling for tax cuts, a balanced budget, states' rights, and reliance "upon the American system of private enterprise and initiative."[51] Smith too was an ardent fiscal conservative, and from his perch as Rules chair he helped coordinate Southern cooperation with conservative Republicans on a bill-by-bill basis.[52] Between the late 1930s and early 1960s, Smith led efforts to crack down on labor unions; cut public works; restrict welfare eligibility; and oppose federal spending on housing, health care, and education.

Conservatives faced opposition from more liberal Southern Democrats, such as Alabama's Lister Hill. As a representative, Hill was an architect of the Tennessee Valley Authority and a strong New Dealer. He broke with most of the Southern caucus to support federal regulation of wages and hours, and news of his 1937 victory in a Senate special election helped dislodge what became the Fair Labor Standards Act from the recalcitrant House Rules Committee.[53] Along with other "committed spenders" from the South, Hill fought to expand federal welfare programs, sponsoring legislation to provide federal aid to hospitals, housing, libraries, and schools.[54] In 1947, Hill was among a handful of Southern MCs to oppose the Taft–Hartley Act. During the Eisenhower administration the senator

---

Southern preferences were weak, Smith could sway about a third of Southern members to his side; Charles L. Clapp, *The Congressman: His Work As He Sees It* (Garden City, NY: Anchor Books, 1963), 363. According to Jackson, however, Smith and other leading Southern MCs were primarily "spokesmen rather than cue-givers." Overall, he finds little evidence that such spokesmen influenced the votes of Southern senators in the 1961–63 period; John E. Jackson, *Constituencies and Leaders in Congress: Their Effects on Senate Voting Behavior* (Cambridge, MA: Harvard University Press, 1974), 77–78, 83–84. Compare with Brady and Bullock's argument that "the basis for the CC [was] issue agreement among conservatives," not organizational capacity or institutional power; Brady and Bullock, "Is There a Conservative Coalition?," 559.

[49] Key, *Southern Politics*, 360.

[50] Carleton, "The Southern Politician."

[51] Tindall, *Emergence of the New South*, 624–625.

[52] Nelson W. Polsby, *How Congress Evolves: Social Bases of Institutional Change* (New York: Oxford University Press, 2004), 10–11.

[53] Mayhew, *Electoral Connection*, 71–72.

[54] Brown, *Race, Money*, 107; Virginia Van der Veer Hamilton, *Lister Hill: Statesman from the South* (Chapel Hill: University of North Carolina Press, 1987).

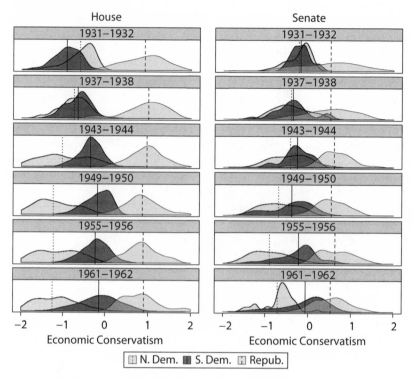

Figure 4.4. Ideological diversity in the U.S. House (left) and Senate (right), 1931–62. Vertical lines indicate the average conservatism in each group of legislators in a given congress, and filled density contours indicate the distribution of ideal points within groups.

spearheaded the creation of an organized "liberal caucus" in the Senate, and in 1965 he supported the creation of Medicare and Medicaid.[55]

Figure 4.4 graphically illustrates the ideological diversity of Southern Democrats. For most of the 1930s, the distribution of ideal points of Southern and non-Southern Democrats overlapped almost completely with each other, and much less so with Republicans (who, particularly

---

[55] "Stewart E. McClure: Chief Clerk, Senate Committee on Labor, Education, and Public Welfare (1949–1973)" (Oral History Interviews, Senate Historical Office, Washington, 1982–1983), 33–34; Gregory Michael Markley, "Senators Hill and Sparkman and Nine Alabama Congressmen Debate National Health Insurance, 1935–1965" (master's thesis, Auburn University, Department of History, 2008).

in the Senate, were extremely heterogeneous). The next decade witnessed Southern Democrats' shift to the right as well as the disappearance of most liberal Republicans. By the end of the 1940s, the Southern caucuses in both chambers—but especially the Senate—included members who voted like mainstream Northern Democrats, as well as members who would have felt at home in the Republican caucus.[56] In short, even as Southern Democrats transformed into a swing group in congressional politics, they became if anything more ideologically diverse.

4.4 THE PIVOTAL SOUTH

As we saw in Figure 4.1, by the 1940s the typical Southern MC had come to occupy an ideological position midway between the typical Republican and non-Southern Democrat. At the same time, as Figure 4.4 shows, Southern MCs remained ideologically diverse on economic issues. An implication of this combination of collective centrism and internal diversity is that the precise *distribution* of Southern preferences was often critically important. In conjunction with two other factors—the partisan breakdown among non-Southern MCs and the size of the majority required for bill passage—the distribution of Southern preferences frequently determined the set of feasible economic policy outcomes.

Scholars have long noted that for much of the 1930s–50s, Southern votes were collectively both necessary and sufficient for the passage of legislation that divided the two parties. "When southerners and nonsouthern Democrats both approved measures they became law," observes DiSalvo. "When southerners dissented, they failed or were rewritten with Republicans."[57] Previous analyses have generally focused on whether Southern

---

[56] Republicans and Northern Democrats were internally diverse as well—in the House, substantially more so than Southern Democrats. After 1940, the standard deviation of ideal points among Southern House Democrats was about half that of Northern Democrats and of Republicans. This fact would appear to conflict with Katznelson, Geiger, and Kryder's finding that House Republicans and especially non-Southern Democrats were more cohesive than Southerners; Katznelson, Geiger, and Kryder, "Limiting Liberalism," 289–292. However, the source of this discrepancy lies in their use of Rice voting cohesion scores rather than ideal point estimates. As noted earlier, cohesion scores are sensitive to the empirical distribution of the roll-call "cutpoints" that separate supporters from opponents. When cutpoints are concentrated in the ideological middle, as they likely were in this period, they will disproportionately divide moderates such as Southern Democrats.
[57] Daniel DiSalvo, "Party Factions in Congress," *Congress & the Presidency* 36, no. July (2010): 42; see also Ewing, *Primary Elections*; Brown, *Race, Money*; Katznelson and Mulroy, "Was the South Pivotal?" The parties divided most frequently over economic issues, the main axis of partisan conflict throughout most of American history; see Poole and Rosenthal, *Ideology & Congress*. Southerners were not pivotal on other issues, most

votes, cast as a bloc, would make difference between a majority for and a majority against a given bill.[58] While useful, this approach has two limitations. First, as previously noted, Southern Democrats possessed neither the ideological homogeneity nor the collective-action mechanisms required to vote as a bloc. Second, the location of the pivotal voter in a chamber depended on the ideological direction of proposed policy change and on the relevant vote threshold. Specifically, liberal (conservative) proposals under Democratic (Republican) presidents required only a simple majority, whereas conservative (liberal) proposals required two-thirds support to surmount a presidential veto.

I therefore instead adopt an individual-level perspective on pivotality, focusing on two kinds of pivotal voters in each chamber: the median (50th-percentile member) and the veto pivot (67th-percentile member on the president's side of the median).[59] This analysis provides a more contingent view of Southern pivotality, which depended not only on Southern MCs' ideal points but also on the partisan composition of Congress and the presidency as well as the ideological content of legislative proposals. As these conditions varied, so too did the probability of various pivotal voters being Southern Democrats. More to the point, the *kind* of Southern Democrat who was pivotal—a relative liberal or a relative conservative—varied as well, which in turn determined the ideological content of feasible policy changes.

Consider a hypothetical bill that would move the policy to the left relative to the status quo. If the president is a liberal Democrat, as was the case for 10 successive congresses between 1933 and 1952, then a veto

---

notably civil rights, on which Western Democrats or Midwestern Republicans usually held the balance of power; see, e.g., Caro, *Master of the Senate*; Sean Farhang, "The Political Development of Job Discrimination Litigation, 1963–1976," *Studies in American Political Development* 23, no. 1 (2009): 23.

[58] See especially Katznelson and Mulroy, "Was the South Pivotal?"

[59] This approach is borrowed from Krehbiel, whose framework also incorporates a second super-majority requirement, the three-fifths threshold for invoking cloture in the Senate (the filibuster pivot); Krehbiel, *Pivotal Politics*. I ignore the filibuster pivot for two reasons. First, the threshold for invoking cloture at the time was the same as to override a presidential veto (two-thirds), so in the case of conservative (liberal) proposals under Democratic (Republican) presidents, the filibuster and veto pivots were identical. Second, lawmaking in the Senate was substantially more majoritarian in this period than it is in the contemporary Congress, in which filibustering is nearly costless and 60 votes are nearly always required for passage; David R. Mayhew, "Supermajority Rule in the U.S. Senate," *PS: Political Science & Politics* 36, no. 1 (2003): 31–36; Gregory J. Wawro and Eric Schickler, *Filibuster: Obstruction and Lawmaking in the U.S. Senate* (Princeton: Princeton University Press, 2006). Thus, except on issues where preferences were intense, such as civil rights, in practice the Senate median was usually pivotal during the years under examination here.

is unlikely and the bill will become law if it receives majority support in the House and the Senate. Thus, the median is the pivotal voter in both chambers. This was the usual state of affairs in Roosevelt's first term: most successful bills moved policy to the left relative to the status quo and were supported (or at least not vetoed) by the president. The situation changed in the late 1930s, with the rise of serious efforts to roll back parts of the New Deal. In general, then, these bills sought to move policy to the right, and in most (but not all) cases would be met with a veto from Roosevelt or his Democratic successor Truman. As such, the pivotal voter in each chamber was no longer the median, but rather, since veto overrides require a two-thirds supermajority, the member in the 67th percentile of liberalism. Of course, the structural setting was reversed when the Republican Dwight Eisenhower succeeded Harry Truman, just as it had been under Roosevelt's Republican predecessor, Herbert Hoover. In sum, when thinking about Southern pivotality, we need to take account of the identity of the president and the ideological direction of the proposed policy change.

With this in mind, we can begin by asking, at each point in time, what were the respective probabilities that the median and veto pivot in each chamber were Southern Democrats?[60] Figure 4.5 summarizes the answer. In the early New Deal congresses, when the leftward direction of policy changes meant that simple majorities sufficed, there was only about a one-third chance in both chambers that the median was a Southern Democrat. As Southern MCs moved rightward, this probability climbed, exceeding 75% in the 79th Congress (1945–46) and remaining above 50% for almost the entire rest of the period. The main exception was the GOP-controlled 80th Congress (1947–48), in which the median House (but not Senate) member was definitely a Republican. The 80th also stands out for its certainty about the partisan identity of the median. In other congresses, there is substantially more uncertainty. After the early 1940s, the median in most congresses was probably a Southern Democrat and almost certainly not a Northern Democrat, but owing to the partisan overlap in Congress there was a nontrivial probability that a moderate Republican was the median voter.

For the most part, the more relevant pivotal voter after the 1930s was not the median, but rather the left veto pivot, for this was the legislator whose support was required for liberals to stave off conservative attacks

---

[60] The probability can be estimated by identifying the pivotal legislator in each MCMC sample and calculating the proportion of samples in which the pivot was a non-Southern Democrat; see Joshua Clinton, Simon Jackman, and Douglas Rivers, "The Statistical Analysis of Roll Call Data," *American Political Science Review* 98, no. 2 (May 2004): 359–361.

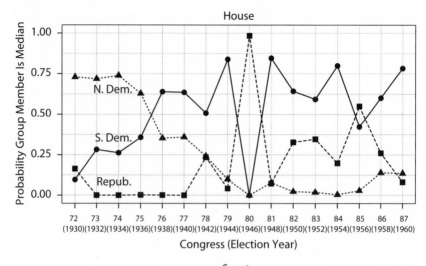

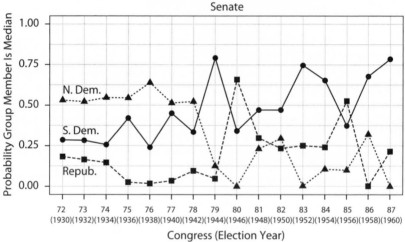

Figure 4.5. Probabilities that the median legislator on economic issues is a member of different groups, in the House (top) and the Senate (bottom), 1931–62

on the New Deal. The likelihood that this pivot was a Southern Democrat was more stable over time, generally ranging between 40% and 60%, with a peak around 80% in the 80th House.[61] According to both of these measures, then, Southerners' pivotality waxed and waned as their relative

---

[61] During the Eisenhower administration, the right veto pivot needed to pass liberal legislation over a presidential veto was almost certainly a Republican in every congress

ideological positioning and the partisan composition of Congress changed over time, but at no point was the pivotal member of both chambers definitely a Southern Democrat.

Given the ideological overlap between groups illustrated in Figure 4.4, however, the regional and partisan identity of a single pivotal voter is arguably not the most meaningful quantity to focus on. More revealing is how the location of Southern Democrats relative to the median altered the proportion and type of Southern Democrats whose support was required for a bill to pass. Insight into this question is provided by Figure 4.6, which plots the percentage of Southern representatives and senators who were more conservative than the median and veto pivots in each congress. In other words, in the case of the solid line (median), this is the fraction of Southern Democrats whose support was necessary and sufficient for majority passage of a conservative bill, assuming perfect spatial voting. Conversely, liberal bills required 100% minus this percentage. Analogously, the dashed line (left veto pivot) indicates the fraction of Southern support needed to overcome a veto by a Democratic president.

The first thing to notice about Figure 4.6 is that the solid (median) and dashed (left veto) lines are almost never at 0 or 100, which implies that during Democratic presidencies, the support of at least *some* Southern Democrats was required to pass either liberal or conservative legislation. In the early to mid-1930s, when Democratic majorities were enormous and the party's regional wings differed little from each other, liberal bills that provoked left–right cleavages were unlikely to pass unless they received the support of nearly all Southern MCs. By contrast, in the 75th (1937–38) and 81st (1949–50) congresses, when Democratic majorities were still large but Southern Democrats more conservative, liberal bills needed the support of somewhere between half and two-thirds of the Southern caucus. Veto-proof conservative bills, on the other hand, generally required the support of at least half of Southern MCs throughout the entire period. In the House, this percentage hit a low point in the 80th Congress (1947–48), when surmounting a Truman veto required only two-fifths of Southern representatives (though three-fifths of Southern senators). Amid these changes, however, it remained true that when a Democrat was president, the pivotal voter was almost always located somewhere within the ideological distribution of Southern Democrats.

What these shifts did affect was the *kind* of Southerner whose support was required for a given bill. Consider, for example, the differences between the 79th (1945–46) and 80th (1947–48) congresses. In the

---

except the 86th (1959–60), when the probability that it was a Southern Democrat rose to around half.

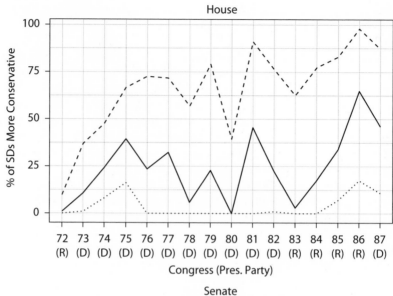

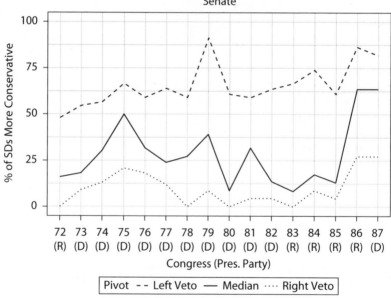

Pivot — — Left Veto —— Median ···· Right Veto

Figure 4.6. Percent of Southern Democrats more conservative than the median and veto pivots in the House (top) and Senate (bottom), 1931–62. The left (right) veto pivot is the member in the 33rd percentile of conservatism (liberalism) in the chamber—that is, the legislator whose support was required to override the veto of a Republican (Democratic) president.

79th House, the median was very likely a fairly conservative Southern Democrat like north Georgia congressman Malcolm Tarver, who ranked in the 78th percentile of conservatism in the caucus. The veto pivot, on the other hand, was considerably more liberal, more likely than not a Southerner like Alabamian Albert Rains, a committed "TVA liberal" who was in the bottom fifth of conservatism among his regional peers.[62] After Republicans captured the House in 1946, both the median and the veto pivot shifted sharply to the right. In fact, the median in the 80th Congress was almost certainly a Republican, meaning that moving policy leftward required the support of even the most conservative Southern Democrat—who in this congress was probably Ezekiel "Took" Gathings, a loyal agent of the Arkansas Delta elite and "among the most vocal anti-Truman Democrats"—as well as at least some Republicans.[63] The veto pivot, who from the perspective of liberals seeking to preserve the New Deal was the more important legislator, was also substantially less liberal than in the previous congress. In all likelihood, he was a Southern Democrat like Rep. Watkins Abbitt, a solid conservative and key lieutenant of Virginia's Byrd Organization.[64]

As this example illustrates, the character of Southern pivotality was not constant; it could change markedly even in successive congresses. As the partisan composition of Congress shifted, so too did the location of the pivotal voters. This in turn determined the proportion and ideological type of Southern Democrats whose support was needed for legislative victory.

4.5 PIVOTALITY IN ACTION: WAGES, UNIONS, AND TAXES

To say that Southern MCs were pivotal is to claim that a different distribution of Southern preferences would have led to different policy outcomes. To understand whether different distributions of preferences were a priori plausible, as well as to illustrate the consequences of Southern pivotality,

[62] Anthony J. Badger, "Whatever Happened to Roosevelt's New Generation of Southerners?," in *New Deal/New South* (Fayetteville: University of Arkansas Press, 2007), 58–71.
[63] Sammy L. Morgan, "Elite Dominance in the Arkansas Delta, from the New Deal to the New Millennium" (PhD dissertation, University of Mississippi, Department of History, 2005); quote from J. Justin Castro, "Mexican Braceros and Arkansas Cotton: Agricultural Labor and Civil Rights in the Post-World War II South," *Arkansas Historical Quarterly* 75, no. 1 (2016): 37.
[64] Brian E. Lee, "A Matter of National Concern: The Kennedy Administration and Prince Edward County, Virginia" (master's thesis, Virginia Commonwealth University, Department of History, 2009), 32. In the 80th Congress, Abbitt was in the 60th percentile of conservatism among Southern representatives, but over the next decade gradually migrated to the far-right end of the Southern caucus.

it is helpful to examine concrete cases in greater detail. To do so, I examine lawmaking episodes in three of the policy areas highlighted in the previous chapter: minimum wages, union security, and income taxation. Each of these episodes divided the Southern caucus, and in each case the policy outcome would have differed in consequential ways had the distribution of Southern ideal points differed.

4.5.1 Minimum Wages

In 1935 the Supreme Court invalidated the National Industrial Recovery Act, which among other things had provided for national regulation of wages and hours. In the wake of the Court's action, the 1936 Democratic platform called for standalone wages-and-hours legislation, which FDR named as one of his "must" bills for the 75th Congress (1937–38). On May 24, 1937, Senator Hugo Black (D-AL) and Representative William Connery (D-MA) introduced the administration-drafted Fair Labor Standards Act (FLSA) in their respective chambers. The FLSA's first major test came in July, when the Senate voted on a crucial motion to recommit that would likely have killed the bill.[65] Despite the support of 11 Southern and 14 non-Southern Democrats, the motion failed 39 to 51. As Figure 4.7 shows, support for the motion is quite well explained by general economic conservatism: the estimated discrimination of the roll call, $\beta = 2.6$, is higher than that of the typical economic vote in the Senate during this period. There were 18 mispredicted votes on the motion, however, 7 of which were yeas by Southern Democrats predicted to vote nay. All eight Southern opponents of the motion came from the liberal half of the Southern caucus. If, counterfactually, these eight liberals had been as conservative as the remaining Southern senators, the motion to recommit would almost certainly have passed and the bill would likely have died.

Instead, the Senate passed the FLSA and sent it on to the House of Representatives. There, despite the floor majority in favor, the bill experienced a rougher reception. It was reported out of committee in August 1937, but a nascent coalition of Republicans and conservative Southern Democrats on the Rules Committee refused to issue a rule for the bill, denying it a floor vote. Over the next 10 months, the bill followed a vicissitudinous path. A discharge petition received the 218 signatures required to get the bill onto the floor, only to be followed by successful floor vote to recommit. The initial bill was amended to assuage opposition from various corners, including the American Federation of Labor, retailers, and Southern and agricultural interests. In the end, three events turned the tide

---

[65] Douglas and Hackman, "Fair Labor Standards Act," 505.

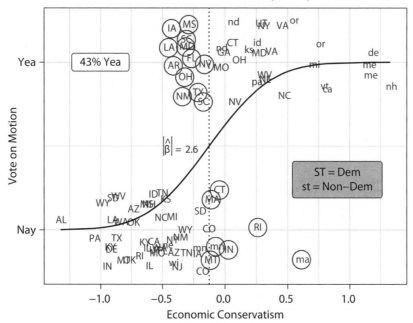

Figure 4.7. Senators' predicted and actual roll-call votes on the motion to recommit the FLSA (July 31, 1937). The motion failed, 39–51. The dotted vertical line indicates the midpoint separating predicted nay and yea votes. State abbreviations of Democratic senators are uppercase, and Republicans are lowercase. Circles indicate mispredicted votes.

for the bill: the Senate primary victories of Lister Hill (D-AL) and Claude Pepper (D-FL), both of whom campaigned as strong supporters of the bill, and the publication of a Gallup poll indicating widespread public support for the bill.[66] A second discharge petition succeeded in once again forcing the FLSA onto the floor, after which passage was ensured. In May 1938, the House approved the bill in a lopsided vote, opposition to which was better predicted by region than general economic conservatism.

Though almost half of Southern House members supported the FLSA on final passage, no more than a quarter gave it consistent support throughout the process.[67] Southern Democrats had good reason to be

---

[66] Douglas and Hackman, "Fair Labor Standards Act," 511–12; Mayhew, *Electoral Connection*, 71–72.

[67] Only 22 Southern Democrats signed the first discharge petition, and 18 signed the second; see data collected by Kathryn Pearson and Eric Schickler, "Discharge Petitions,

unenthusiastic about the bill. Despite the FLSA's exemption of (disproportionately black) agricultural and domestic laborers, setting a national minimum wage clearly hurt the interests of Southern employers, especially textile and other manufacturers for whom the region's low wages offered a major advantage over non-Southern competitors. Indeed, according to Bruce Schulman, the dramatic increase in Southern wages imposed by the FLSA could well have spelled "economic catastrophe for southern industry" had not it been followed shortly after by war mobilization and resulting tight labor markets.[68] Unlike the non-South, where both industrial workers and employers benefitted from regional equalization of wages, in the South the main effect of the FLSA was to redistribute income from low-wage employers to their employees.[69] In other words, the FLSA helped Southern industrial workers covered by the law, hurt Southern manufacturers, and brought few if any benefits to the large number of farmers and agricultural laborers in the region.

As we saw in Chapter 3, these differential costs and benefits across classes were reflected in large differences in support for minimum wages—as large as 50% in some polls—between upper- and lower-income Southern whites. Given the FLSA's negative effects on the competitiveness of Southern industry and the concentration of support for the law among lower-class whites, it is remarkable that the act received as much support from Southern MCs as it did. These characteristics also make the FLSA something of a "least likely" case for the argument that MCs were responsive to the preferences of the broader white public, as opposed to only those of economic elites.[70]

Were Southern Democrats pivotal to the passage of the FLSA? Perhaps, but probably not uniquely so. On the crucial Senate vote, almost all Southerners in the liberal half of the Democratic caucus voted against recommittal. Had these Southern FLSA supporters instead been relatively conservative Democrats—as would be true of nearly every Southern

---

Agenda Control, and the Congressional Committee System, 1929–76," *Journal of Politics* 71, no. 4 (2009): 1238–1256.

[68] Schulman, *Cotton Belt to Sunbelt*, 66, 72.

[69] Seltzer presents three "stylized facts" regarding the effects of the FLSA: (1) Demand for low-wage workers was inelastic enough that the FLSA would raise wages more than it would reduce employment, resulting in "net redistribution to workers"; (2) the FSLA hurt the profits of firms employing low-wage workers; (3) the FSLA benefitted high-wage firms (mainly outside the South) that competed with low-wage firms. See Andrew J. Seltzer, "Democratic Opposition to the Fair Labor Standards Act: A Comment on Fleck," *Journal of Economic History* 64, no. 1 (2004): 226–230.

[70] Harry Eckstein, "Case Studies and Theory in Political Science," in *Handbook of Political Science*, ed. Fred I. Greenstein and Nelson W. Polsby, Vol. 7 (Reading, MA: Addison-Wesley, 1975), 94–137.

senator only a few congresses later—the FLSA would likely not have passed, at least not in the same form. Similarly, in the House, groups of marginal Southern Democrats held the balance of power at key points. The bill's recommittal following the first discharge petition, for example, hinged on the surprise defection of the Louisiana delegation, who had previously "been enthusiastic in their promises to support the Wage-Hour bill [and whose] support was essential to victory."[71] But the same was true of other key groups in House, notably Democrats from rural districts outside the South and Republicans from the industrial Northeast, who at various points also switched their positions on the bill.[72] In sum, Southern Democrats were clearly influential in the establishment of a national minimum wage in the United States, and Southern support, uneven though it was, was critical to the FLSA's passage. But given that other marginal groups of MCs could also have turned victory into defeat, it would be hard to argue that Southern Democrats, individually or as a group, were *uniquely* pivotal in this case.

4.5.2 Taft–Hartley

The political context of the second case I examine, the Taft–Hartley Act of 1947, was quite different from that of the 1938 FLSA. Two important developments had occurred in the intervening decade: Southern MCs had shifted to the right on economic issues, and Republicans had made marked gains in Congress. In 1946, Republicans had finally recaptured majority control of the House and Senate. They were led by conservatives like Senator Robert Taft, who exhibited a "zealously sincere desire to dismantle the New Deal."[73] Among Republicans' foremost priorities in the 80th Congress (1947–48) was "rebalancing" union regulation in favor of business, a goal they ultimately achieved with the passage of Taft–Hartley over Truman's veto.[74] Taft–Hartley's most important provisions

---

[71] Joseph Alsop and Robert Kintner, "Louisiana Switch Sank Wages Bill," *New York Times*, December 22, 1937, 20.

[72] Additional indication of the pivotality of different groups can be gleaned from the identity of those who were the last to sign the first discharge petition for the FLSA, who presumably were the least enthusiastic supporters of the bill. Of the final 25 signatures, 5 came from the South (defined to include Kentucky), 9 from rural areas outside the South (including 3 from Oklahoma), and 8 from industrial districts in the Northeast; Douglas and Hackman, "Fair Labor Standards Act," 509 and passim.

[73] Patterson, *Mr. Republican*, 314. As Plotke emphasizes, the dismantlement of the New Deal in the 80th Congress was a real possibility, and the defeat of most conservative attempts to do so was thus a major liberal achievement in its own right; Plotke, *Building a Democratic Political Order*.

[74] Mason, *Republican Party*, 116. Though there is no indication that Truman seriously considered signing the bill, he did sympathize with some elements of the bill (notably its "national emergency" anti-strike provisions) and at least made a show of thoroughly

were its prohibition of the "closed shop," the strongest form of union security agreement, and its explicit sanctioning of state "right to work" laws banning weaker forms of union security.

Although pressure to reduce union power had been building for the past decade, anti-union conservatives had achieved little on this front aside from the passage of the relatively ineffective War Labor Disputes Act of 1943.[75] The reason for this was the opposition of Presidents Roosevelt and Truman, whose veto power made the pivotal voter in each chamber not the median, as it was in the case of the FLSA, but rather the veto pivot (i.e., the member in the 33rd percentile of conservatism). As Figure 4.6 indicates, in the 80th Congress about half of Southern Democrats in each chamber were more conservative than the veto pivot, implying that no bill could surmount a presidential veto without the support of the bulk of the Southern caucus.

The House having passed the bill easily, the closest call for Taft–Hartley came in the Senate vote to override Truman's veto. As Figure 4.8 shows, the division on this vote was quite well predicted by general conservatism ($\beta = 2.8$), even more so than the 1937 FLSA vote in Figure 4.7. Despite presidential pressure to oppose the bill, only four liberal Southern senators voted against overriding Truman's veto—one of whom, John Sparkman (D-AL), was supposedly "convinced" by Truman's veto message to switch his vote to nay.[76] The remaining 17 Southerners voted to override, however, and the bill passed with 72% support. Had just five senators switched their votes, Taft–Hartley would not have passed in the form that it did. From Figure 4.8, it is clear that Southern Democrats predominated in the ranks of near-indifferent senators, and so any additional votes against Taft–Hartley would have had to include several Southerners. The fact that so few Southern senators bowed to party loyalty on this issue was consistent with the relatively anti-union preferences of the Southern white public documented in Chapter 3.

The record of attempts to repeal Taft–Hartley after the 1948 elections offer an interesting postscript to the preceding account of the act's passage. The Democrats regained a large majority in the 81st Congress, and although supporters of the original act still constituted a majority of both chambers, the results of the intervening election convinced

canvasing Democratic leaders before ultimately vetoing it; Garson, *Democratic Party*, 218; Richard E. Neustadt, "The Fair Deal: A Legislative Balance Sheet," *Public Policy: A Yearbook of the Graduate School of Public Administration, Harvard University* 5 (1954): 362.

[75] James Wolfinger, "War Labor Disputes Act (Smith-Connally Act)," in *Historical Encyclopedia of American Labor*, Vol. 2 (Westport, CT: Greenwood, 2004), 537–538.

[76] Leslie H. Southwick, "John Sparkman," in *Presidential Also Rans and Running Mates, 1788–1980* (Jefferson, NC: McFarland, 1984), 639.

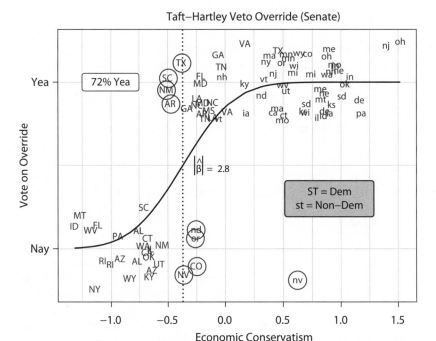

Figure 4.8. Senators' predicted and actual roll-call votes to override President Truman's veto of the Taft–Hartley Act (June 23, 1947). The dotted vertical line indicates the midpoint separating predicted nay and yea votes. State abbreviations of Democratic senators are uppercase, and Republicans are lowercase. Circles indicate mispredicted votes.

most observers that repeal was likely.[77] Since President Truman favored the proposed revision, the pivotal voter was the median legislator and Southern MCs were again the critical players, especially in the more conservative House. The administration's strategy was to covertly push a compromise repeal bill that eliminated the union security prohibitions but retained enough other provisions of Taft–Hartley to obtain Southern support. These included employer "free speech" provisions, non-Communist oaths, reporting requirements, and, most controversially, emergency anti-strike injunctions. Rep. Hugo Sims, a liberal freshman Democrat from South Carolina, was tasked with introducing the compromise repeal bill. "Though the Sims measure won some Southern support," *CQ* later reported, "it was soon evident that it was not acceptable to many strong

---

[77] Gerald Pomper, "Labor and Congress: The Repeal of Taft–Hartley," *Labor History* 2, no. 3 (1961): 323; Neustadt, "The Fair Deal," 368.

labor supporters," who preferred to hold out for a stronger bill.[78] As a result, the Sims bill was narrowly defeated, 211 to 183, as were similar efforts in the Senate.[79] In retrospect, labor's strategic reluctance to compromise seems to have cost it dearly, as the prospects for repealing Taft–Hartley were arguably never so good as in the 81st Congress.

The case for Southern pivotality on Taft–Hartley is clearer than for the FLSA. Notwithstanding the role of other groups of members, such as the pro-labor holdouts mentioned earlier, Southern Democrats—particularly in the liberal half of the caucus—were consistently the ones holding the balance of power. And, in a broader sense, Southern Democrats' dramatic antilabor shift between the 1930s and 1940s was arguably the decisive factor that enabled Republicans to retrench the New Deal labor regime.[80]

4.5.3 Postwar Tax Cuts

There were also important policy areas where Southern Democrats did not cooperate with Republicans' efforts to roll back the liberal achievements of the 1930s and 1940s. While scholars have focused mainly on Southerners' pivotal role in blocking liberal proposals and advancing conservative ones, Southerners were also pivotal to preserving many elements of the New Deal.[81] Southern Democrats' positive role in consolidating the New Deal order is exemplified by the issue of taxation, where Southern Democrats largely refused to cooperate with Republican efforts to dismantle the system of mass-based progressive taxation that emerged from World War II.[82]

---

[78] John Lewis's United Mine Workers and some left-wing CIO unions were particularly opposed to the compromise bill; "Taft–Hartley Repeal Attempts," in CQ Almanac 1949, 5th ed. (Washington, DC: Congressional Quarterly, 1950), 336, http://library.cqpress.com/cqalmanac/cqal49-1400386; Pomper, "Labor and Congress," 337.

[79] Pomper, "Labor and Congress," 336. The individual-level votes on the Sims compromise were not recorded, but a CQ poll revealed 13 Southern supporters among the 130 House members who responded to the poll: Laurie Battle (D-AL), Brooks Hays (D-AR), Charles Bennett (D-FL), Robert Sikes (D-FL), George Smathers (D-FL), Henderson Lanham (D-GA), Charles Deane (D-NC), Hugo Sims (D-SC), Joe Evins (D-TN), James Frazier (D-TN), James Sutton (D-TN), John Lyle (D-TX), and Wright Patman (D-TX). Eleven Southern Democrats reported opposing the Sims bill; "Congressional Quarterly Polls," in CQ Almanac 1949, 5th ed. (Washington, DC: Congressional Quarterly, 1950), 06-462–06-463, http://library.cqpress.com/cqalmanac/cqal49-1400486.

[80] Farhang and Katznelson, "Southern Imposition."

[81] For a compelling account of one Southerner's outsized role in creating a politically sustainable New Deal order, see Zelizer, Taxing America on Wilbur Mills.

[82] Mayhew identifies mass-based progressive taxation as one of the most important policy consequences of the war; David R. Mayhew, "Wars and American Politics," Perspectives on Politics 3, no. 3 (September 2005): 478.

Southern MCs had a long history of championing progressive taxation. During the Woodrow Wilson administration, Tennessee Democrat Cordell Hull had spearheaded the drive for a federal income tax, which other Southerners amended to also include a graduated surtax on large incomes.[83] As we saw in Chapter 3, the Southern white public was also disproportionately supportive of progressive taxation and opposed to tax cuts, both before and after World War II. The war itself represented a major break point between tax regimes. By the war's end, "mass taxation had replaced class taxation" as a basis for funding the American state.[84] In particular, the Revenue Act of 1942 dramatically expanded the number of income tax payers, which grew from 7.6 million Americans in 1939 to 43.7 million in 1943. Moreover, in contrast to the taxation system erected during World War I, the new system of mass taxation was not dismantled after World War II. Indeed, it proved to be remarkably stable: in almost every year since 1943, income tax revenues have constituted 7–9% of national income, a proportion far higher than before the war.[85] In addition to funding the postwar defense establishment, mass income taxation provided a critical foundation for postwar liberal policymaking and state-building, both as a source of funding for social welfare policies and as a tool of Keynesian macroeconomic management.[86]

Had Republicans gotten their way, however, high levels of mass taxation might never have survived the war. A 20% across-the-board cut in income tax was a central plank of Republicans' 1946 congressional campaign and, along with Wagner Act revision, one of their top two legislative priorities in the 80th Congress.[87] The Republicans sought tax cuts not only to ease the burden on individuals and business but also to, in the words of House Ways and Means Chair Harold Knutson (R-MN), "cut off much of the government's income ... and compel the government to retrench."[88] Given widespread concern about the tax burden and size of government, Republicans had reason to believe public opinion was on their side. In Congress, there was in fact broad consensus on the necessity of some income tax reduction. The main points of contention were how much taxes would be reduced, how regressive the cuts would be, and

---

[83] Perman, *Pursuit of Unity*, 215.

[84] W. Elliot Brownlee, "Tax Regimes, National Crises, and State-Building in America," in *Funding the Modern American State, 1941–1995*, ed. W. Elliot Brownlee (New York: Cambridge University Press, 1996), 37–104.

[85] Bill White, *America's Fiscal Constitution: Its Triumph and Collapse* (New York: PublicAffairs, 2014), 209.

[86] Zelizer, *Taxing America*, 265–267.

[87] Holmans, *United States Fiscal Policy*, 58–60; Mason, *Republican Party*, 116.

[88] Brown, *Race, Money*, 120.

how soon they would be implemented.[89] On these questions Southern Democrats once again held the balance of power.[90]

Like Taft–Hartley, tax cuts required the support of the veto pivot, which in both chambers was located in the center of the Southern caucus. Seeking supermajority support, Republicans on Ways and Means modified Knutson's 20% across-the-board cut, proposing instead to reduce marginal tax rates by 30% for low incomes, 20% for middle, and 10% for high.[91] Despite this concession, only a third of Southern Democrats in the House voted for the modified bill, leaving it two votes shy of a veto-proof majority.[92] A second iteration of the bill, which to mollify budget hawks delayed implementation of the cuts until 1948, surmounted the two-thirds threshold in the House, thanks in large part to switches by the Virginia and North Carolina delegations.[93] But, despite the support of several conservative Southerners who had opposed the first bill, it failed to achieve supermajority support in the Senate.[94] Many Southern senators, it was clear, would support only "very moderate" tax cuts that were both tilted toward lower incomes and more limited in their impact on revenue.[95] Thus, in their third and ultimately successful attempt at

---

[89] Holmans, *United States Fiscal Policy*, chapter 5.

[90] Brown, *Race, Money*, 120.

[91] The only Democrat on Ways and Means to support the modified bill was Rep. Milton West (D-TX), the second-most conservative member of the Southern caucus; "Tax Reduction," in *CQ Almanac 1947*, 3rd ed. (Washington, DC: Congressional Quarterly, 1948), 09-101–09-104, http://library.cqpress.com/cqalmanac/cqal47-1397733.

[92] Holmans, *United States Fiscal Policy*, 61, 79.

[93] Rep. Robert Doughton (D-NC), ranking member on House Ways and Means, spearheaded his state delegation's switch from opposition to support. As justification for his changed position, Doughton cited the change in implementation date, which delayed the cut's fiscal impact; "Second Income Tax Reduction Bill," in *CQ Almanac 1947*, 3rd ed. (Washington, DC: Congressional Quarterly, 1948), 09-507–09-509, http://library.cqpress.com/cqalmanac/cqal47-1398910. Doughton later voted against the third and final version of the tax reduction bill, again citing concern for fiscal impact; "Tax Reduction," in *CQ Almanac 1948*, 4th ed. (Washington, DC: Congressional Quarterly, 1949), 344–350, http://library.cqpress.com/cqalmanac/cqal48-1407007. Another factor behind some Southerners' change of heart may have been House Republicans' introduction of an anti-poll tax bill on the same day as the second iteration of the income tax bill (June 24, 1947). Rep. Gerald Landis (R-IN) explained the poll tax bill's unexpected introduction as revenge for Southern defections on income tax cuts: "Since some of the Southerners opposed us on taxes, the idea is to put 'em on the spot," he explained. "And if the Senate had overriden the labor bill veto we would have got out an anti-lynching bill"; AP, "Republicans to Push Poll Tax Fight to Avenge South's Vote on Income Levy," *New York Times*, June 24, 1947, 9.

[94] The marginal voters on the veto override seem to have been a mix of Southern and Border Democrats and liberal Republicans; Holmans, *United States Fiscal Policy*, 81.

[95] Quoting Sen. Walter George (D-GA); ibid., 94.

tax revision, Republicans were forced to accept not only Democratic-sponsored exemptions but also much more modest reductions in tax rates: a 12.6% rate reduction for income up to $2,000 and a 7.4% reduction for most income above that threshold.[96] These concessions finally succeeded in winning over a sufficient number of marginal Southern senators, and Truman's veto was easily overridden, 78 to 11.[97]

The roll call on the Revenue Act of 1948 was not a pure conservative coalition vote. A few Southern senators opposed even the final bill, while a number of non-Southern Democrats, sensitive to the appeal of election-year tax cuts, supported it.[98] Nevertheless, it was largely Southern Democrats whose votes were pivotal to tax legislation in the 80th Congress. In contrast to their position on labor legislation, Southerners used their pivotal status to stymie Republicans' ambitions to revise tax law in a dramatically conservative direction.[99] Southerners continued to play a similar role in the years that followed. After the Democrats recaptured Congress in 1948, Southern Democrats fully supported the Revenue Act of 1950, which reversed many of the 1948 act's cuts.[100] Over the longer term, key "activist fiscal conservatives" such as Rep. Robert Doughton (D-NC), Rep. Wilbur Mills (D-AR), and Sen. Russell Long (D-LA) used their positions atop key tax-writing committees to play a critical role in defending and consolidating a politically and fiscally sustainable New Deal state.[101] These chairmen in turn reflected the preferences of a large swath of Southern senators and representatives, who, despite their cooperation with Republicans on some issues, remained largely committed to preserving the political order they had helped construct.[102]

---

[96] "Tax Reduction."

[97] Of the 16 senators who voted for the third bill but not the previous two, 10 were Southerners; Holmans, *United States Fiscal Policy*, 94–95.

[98] Brown, *Race, Money*, 121.

[99] It should noted, too, that Republicans made tax cuts a top priority precisely because they believed that their political prospects were more favorable on this issue than on, say, retrenching Social Security or abolishing the minimum wage; see Mason, *Republican Party*, 116.

[100] "Revenue Act of 1950," in *CQ Almanac 1950*, 6th ed. (Washington, DC: Congressional Quarterly, 1951), 573–595, http://library.cqpress.com/cqalmanac/cqal50-1375509.

[101] Jacobs, "Policymaking as Political Constraint"; see also Zelizer, *Taxing America*.

[102] As Sundquist notes in his history of policymaking in the 1950s to mid-1960s, Southern committee chairmen like Mills frequently stood in for their fellow Southerners in the caucus. "[T]he Ways and Means Committee accurately reflected the makeup of the House itself. Chairman Wilbur Mills was representative not just of the second district of Arkansas but of his region"; James L. Sundquist, *Politics and Policy: The Eisenhower, Kennedy, and Johnson Years* (Washington, DC: The Brookings Institution, 1968), 477.

102 Chapter 4

4.6 CONCLUSION

As Orren and Skowronek have observed, left-leaning scholars diverge over whether the New Deal order that was consolidated in the 1940s should be viewed as a glass "half full or half empty."[103] On the more negative side are scholars such as Ira Katznelson, Nelson Lichtenstein, and Alan Brinkley, who lament the decade as a "lost opportunity" to reconstruct the American political economy in a more social-democratic mode.[104] On the more positive side lies work by such scholars as Alonzo Hamby, Alan Jacobs, David Plotke, and Julian Zelizer, who emphasize the impressiveness of liberals' achievements at time when the "most likely practical alternative" was not social democracy but rather "major political shifts well to the right."[105]

From either perspective, Southern senators and representatives played an outsized, if nuanced, part in shaping the regime that emerged. Southern MCs' collective shift to the right between the mid-1930s and mid-1940s—first on labor policies and then on economic issues more generally—set the basic parameters of domestic policymaking in the wake of the New Deal. By the end of World War II, when Southern Democrats settled in a position midway between that of non-Southern Democrats and Republicans, Southern support was usually both a necessary and sufficient condition for the passage of economic legislation. As illustrated by the postwar politics of income taxation, Southern Democrats used their pivotal position to stymie conservative policy shifts as well as enable them. But contrary to some stylized renderings, Southerners did not act as a bloc on economic issues. Rather, the *distribution* of Southern ideal points, along with the content and context of the proposal in question, determined what *kind* of Southerner was the pivotal player.

This chapter, in conjunction with the preceding one, has also suggested an explanation for Southern MCs' ideological evolution and continued ideological diversity: the preferences of their white constituents. Just as the Southern white public turned against the New Deal in the late 1930s, most intensely on labor but eventually on other issues, so too did Southern

---

[103] Orren and Skowronek, "Regimes and Regime Building," 697.

[104] Ira Katznelson, "Was the Great Society a Lost Opportunity?," in *The Rise and Fall of the New Deal Order, 1930–1980*, ed. Steve Fraser and Gary Gerstle (Princeton: Princeton University Press, 1989), 185–211; Lichtenstein, "Corporatism to Collective Bargaining"; Alan Brinkley, *The End of Reform: New Deal Liberalism in Recession and War* (New York: Vintage Books, 1995).

[105] Quote from Plotke, *Building a Democratic Political Order*, 191; see also Hamby, *Beyond the New Deal*; Jacobs, "Policymaking as Political Constraint"; Zelizer, *Taxing America*; Julian E. Zelizer, "Review of *Race, Money, and the American Welfare State*, by Michael K. Brown," *Journal of American History* 87, no. 2 (2000): 722.

MCs. Just as Southern whites remained supportive of many aspects of the New Deal order, so too did Southern MCs. And just as Southern whites remained ideologically diverse on economic issues, so did Southern MCs. These parallel patterns provide suggestive evidence of a much greater degree of representation of the white public than standard accounts of the one-party South imply. But given the very real differences between the South and the more inclusive and competitive non-South, is such a strong representational linkage between Southern whites and MCs plausible? For evidence that it was, we must look more closely at electoral politics in the one-party South, a topic I turn to in the following chapter.

4.A APPENDIX: DETAILS OF THE IDEAL-POINT MODEL

Most of the empirical findings are based on the Bayesian dynamic one-dimensional IRT model developed by Martin and Quinn and implemented in the R package MCMCpack.[106] A two-parameter probit IRT model is mathematically equivalent to a spatial voting model with quadratic utility function and normal errors.[107] A static one-dimensional version of this model can be written as

$$P(y_{ij} = 1) = \Phi(\beta_j \theta_i - \alpha_j) \tag{4.1}$$

where y_{ij} indicates a "yea" vote by legislator i on bill j, Φ is the standard normal CDF, θ_i represents i's ideal point, β_j is the "discrimination" of bill j, and α_j is the "difficulty" (i.e., unpopularity) of the bill.

The static IRT model assumes that legislator ideal points are constant over time. To loosen this assumption, one could, for example, allow the ideal points to change linearly over time, which would be the IRT equivalent of DW-NOMINATE. Alternatively, separate models could be estimated in each time period (e.g., each congress), implying a belief that legislators' ideal points are independent across periods. A more plausible and yet still flexible approach is to model each legislator's ideal point in period t as a random walk from her ideal point in period $t - 1$. This approach, which is that taken by Martin and Quinn, uses the ideal point posteriors in each period as priors for the next. More formally, the ideal point of legislator i in congress t is modeled as

$$\theta_{i,t} \sim N(\theta_{i,t-1}, \, \tau^2_{\theta_{i,t}}) \tag{4.2}$$

---

[106] Martin and Quinn, "Dynamic Ideal Point Estimation via Markov Chain Monte Carlo for the U.S. Supreme Court, 1953–1999"; Martin, Quinn, and Park, "MCMCpack."
[107] Clinton, Jackman, and Rivers, "The Statistical Analysis of Roll Call Data," 356.

where the evolution variance $\tau^2_{\theta_{i,t}}$ is provided by the analyst, as is the prior for ideal points in the first period.

In addition to allowing for a flexible yet plausible degree of ideological evolution in each period, this model also produces estimates that are comparable over time, given certain assumptions. One key assumption for comparing estimates over time is that for every legislator i and period t, the expected value of $\theta_{i,t}$ is $\theta_{i,t-1}$. For example, if no legislators retired between periods and all moved a constant amount to the right, the model would not detect any ideological change among legislators. More subtly, if a large bloc of legislators became more conservative while all others remained constant, the estimated movement of the bloc would be biased toward zero and that of the constant legislators biased away from zero. In other words, the model does not account for aggregate ideological movement, and the ideological change of individual legislators is identified only up to the assumption that each legislator is no more likely to move left of her previous ideal point than right of it.

Another key feature of the model used in this chapter is that it is one-dimensional, meaning that in each period t legislator i's ideal point $\theta_{i,t}$ takes on a single scalar value. Given that the period under study is one in which a second spatial dimension was unusually prominent (though still much less so than the first dimension),[108] the choice of a one-dimensional model requires some explanation. An advantage of a one-dimensional model is that it collapses a myriad of individual pieces of information into a single indicator of legislators' positions on the left–right ideological continuum. Only roll calls related to issues of social welfare and economic regulation—the issues historically most closely related to first-dimension conflict between the parties—were used to calculate the ideal points.[109] To evaluate the distinctiveness of roll calls related to organized labor, ideal points were estimated twice in each chamber, once including labor votes and once excluding them. In addition to fitting with the substantive concerns of the study (Southerners' evolving positions on New Deal liberalism), the exclusion of more explicitly sectional issues like civil rights enhances the plausibility of the unidimensional model. The resulting ideal point estimates are similar in interpretation to first-dimension DW-NOMINATE estimates.

---

[108] Poole and Rosenthal, *Ideology & Congress*, 39.

[109] Specifically, only roll calls classified in the "Government Management" and "Social Welfare" issue categories developed by Clausen, *How Congressmen Decide* were used to estimate legislator ideal points. Roll calls relating to agriculture, civil liberties, and foreign and defense policy, as well as unclassifiable or unidentifiable votes, were excluded from the dataset.

The estimation was carried out in R using the `MCMCdynamicIRT1d` function from the package `MCMCpack`.[110] A vague $N(0, 10)$ prior was specified for the bill difficulty (α) and discrimination (β) parameters, as well as for legislators' initial ideal points θ_1. The evolution variance (τ^2) of the ideal point random walk was set to 0.1. This value of τ^2 implies a "typical" ideological shift between congresses of around $\sqrt{0.1} \approx 0.32$, about a third of the standard deviation of ideal points. The model is identified by the proper priors on the bill parameters and by constraining the ideal points of legislators with extreme DW-NOMINATE scores to be either positive (extreme liberals) or negative (extreme conservatives). The starting values of the bill parameters were set to 0. Democrats' ideal points were started at 1, Republicans' at -1, and independents' at 0. After 1,000 burn-in simulations were run and discarded, a further 50,000 iterations were run, of which every tenth was saved for a total of 5,000 MCMC samples. Standard MCMC diagnostics[111] indicated that the chain had reached a stationary distribution and autocorrelation was not unduly severe, indicating that it approximates a random sample from the posterior distribution.

---

[110] Martin, Quinn, and Park, "`MCMCpack`."
[111] See Simon Jackman, *Bayesian Analysis for the Social Sciences* (Hoboken, NJ: Wiley, 2009), 252–255.

CHAPTER 5

Democratic Primaries and the Selectoral Connection

In the coming primaries. . . , there will be many clashes
between two schools of thought, generally classified as
liberal and conservative. . . . [T]he important question
which it seems to me the primary voter must ask is this:
"To which of these general schools of thought does the
candidate belong?"[1]

—*President Franklin Roosevelt*
Fireside Chat (1938)

I love being a senator. Now, how did I get to be a senator?
I was elected by the voters of Alabama. . . . If I were to
campaign in Alabama on a platform that is opposite to the
thinking of most Alabama voters, I'd never get elected. So
long as I'm in Alabama and so long as I want to be in the
Senate, I've got to do what the white voters in Alabama say
for me to do.[2]

—*Senator John Sparkman of Alabama (1952)*

IN THE SPRING OF 1936, Congressman George Huddleston found himself
in a fight for his political life. Since 1925 Huddleston had represented
Alabama's 9th congressional district, which was composed of the city

---

[1] Franklin D. Roosevelt, "Fireside Chat (June 24, 1938)," *The American Presidency
Project*, ed. Gerhard Peters and John T. Woolley, http://www.presidency.ucsb.edu/
ws/?pid=15662.
[2] As quoted by Lyman Johnson; Wade Hall, *The Rest of the Dream: The Black Odyssey of
Lyman Johnson* (Lexington: University Press of Kentucky, 1988), 174.

of Birmingham and surrounding Jefferson County. After years of little opposition, Huddleston had survived a stiff electoral challenge in 1934, and in 1936 he faced another formidable opponent in Luther Patrick, a young Birmingham attorney and radio personality. As was typical of Southern House races, Patrick's challenge came not in the general election, which would be a cakewalk for the Democratic candidate, but rather in the Democratic primary.

At the time, Birmingham politics was loosely organized around two Democratic factions: the so-called Big Mules, which represented business interests, and a working-class faction allied with local labor unions and a declining Ku Klux Klan.[3] By the mid-1930s, President Franklin Roosevelt's New Deal program had sharpened the ideological divisions between the factions, with the Big Mules largely opposed and the working-class faction, which controlled federal patronage, enthusiastically in favor. A Wilsonian progressive, Huddleston had been a friend to organized labor earlier in his career but had grown more conservative over time. His opposition to several key New Deal measures cost him support in the labor community, and in 1936 the working-class faction backed Patrick's bid for Huddleston's seat.[4]

Patrick's campaign emphasized the incumbent's tepid support for the New Deal, "singling out in particular Huddleston's fight against the 'death sentence' for utility holding companies" as well as his "negative votes on the Social Security and Guffey Coal Bills."[5] Huddleston responded with a defense of Jeffersonian individualism and, for the first time in his career, race-baiting attacks on Patrick, who was supported by Congress of Industrial Organizations (CIO) unions that were racially integrated. The campaign became so heated that when the candidates encountered each other at a restaurant, they fell into an altercation that culminated in Huddleston's smashing a ketchup bottle over his opponent's head.[6] Riding the wave of Roosevelt's popularity, Patrick finished just behind Huddleston in the six-candidate first primary. Patrick won the subsequent run-off

---

[3] J. Mills Thornton III, *Dividing Lines: Municipal Politics and the Struggle for Civil Rights in Montgomery, Birmingham, and Selma* (Tuscaloosa: University of Alabama Press, 2002), 141–158; Robert J. Norrell, "Labor at the Ballot Box: Alabama Politics from the New Deal to the Dixiecrat Movement," *Journal of Southern History* 57, no. 2 (1991): 221.

[4] Rogers et al., *Alabama*, 494. Huddleston did retain the support of some Birmingham labor unions affiliated with the American Federation of Labor, the more conservative rival to the Congress of Industrial Organizations, which backed Patrick; Norrell, "Labor at the Ballot Box," 213.

[5] AP, "New Deal Loyalty Issue in Alabama Vote Today," *New York Herald Tribune*, June 9, 1936, 5A; AP, "Huddleston Is Defeated: Alabamian's Negative Votes on New Deal Bills Figured in Campaign," *New York Times*, June 10, 1936, 24.

[6] George Packer, *Blood of the Liberals* (New York: Farrar, Straus and Giroux, 2000), 123–4.

handily with 20,488 of 34,549 votes cast, and he coasted to victory in the general election.

Once in Congress, Patrick became a Roosevelt loyalist, amassing a largely liberal and pro-labor voting record.[7] In 1938, for example, he broke with most other Southern Democrats to support the Fair Labor Standards Act (FLSA), which established minimum wages and maximum hours across the nation. By end of the decade, however, the pro–New Deal tide that had carried Patrick into office had already begun to recede amid a national conservative, antilabor backlash.[8] A rising sense that the New Deal posed a threat to Jim Crow intensified the reaction in the South and aided the conservative Big Mules in retaking control of Birmingham city government. Patrick, increasingly cross-pressured between his dependence on union support and the public's anti-union mood, responded by supporting such conservative initiatives as a congressional investigation into the wave of sit-down strikes that hit Detroit in 1936–37.

Patrick's dilemma came to a head in 1941 when he was confronted with a bill to prohibit strikes in war industries. Conservative Virginia Democrat Howard Smith sought to strengthen the bill with bans on the union and closed shops as well. Speaking on the floor of Congress, Patrick acknowledged that "Mr. and Mrs. America wants legislation to curb strikes," but he implored the House to reject Smith's conservative substitute.[9] Despite Patrick's opposition, the Smith amendment passed, and on final passage Patrick voted for the bill. "Surely you must have seen that America was fed up on strikes," he explained to a dismayed Birmingham labor leader, "and was going to see some legislation through."[10]

Patrick's vote for anti-strike legislation, however, could not save him from the conservative backlash among his constituents. After three terms in office, he was defeated for renomination in 1942 by John Newsome, an antilabor businessman backed by the Big Mules. Though Patrick regained his seat in 1944, he lost it for good to another opponent of the New Deal, Laurie Battle, in the conservative wave of 1946. In Congress, both Newsome and Battle partnered with Republicans to block liberal initiatives and advance conservative ones.[11]

* * *

---

[7] H. C. Nixon, "Politics of the Hills," *Journal of Politics* 8, no. 2 (1946): 125.

[8] Schickler and Caughey, "Public Opinion."

[9] 87 Cong. Rec. 9389 1941.

[10] Letter quoted in Norrell, "Labor at the Ballot Box," 222–223.

[11] Over his four terms in office, Patrick's economic conservatism scores ranged between −1.4 and −1.0. By comparison, the ideal points of his conservative opponents Huddleston, Newsome, and Battle were about a standard deviation more conservative, ranging between −0.5 and −0.1. Battle, though he voted for Taft–Hartley in the 80th Congress, also apparently supported a failed effort in the 81st Congress to revise the law in a more pro-union direction—a position that likely reflected the fact that unions remained important players in Birmingham politics; "Congressional Quarterly Polls," in

The story of Luther Patrick, though largely forgotten today, illustrates four themes central to my argument in this book.

First, Patrick's story highlights the opportunities that Democratic primaries created for ordinary Southern whites to participate in politics. Like most urban areas in the South, voter turnout in Birmingham was below the regional average: out of a white voting-age population (VAP) of 150,000, there were about 60,000 registered voters, half of whom turned out in a typical contested primary.[12] Yet even within this truncated and racially exclusive electorate, there was still substantial economic and political diversity. While the Birmingham electorate contained many silk-stocking opponents of the New Deal, it also included plenty of enthusiastic supporters, particularly among blue-collar workers advantaged by Roosevelt's pro-labor policies. And of course the relative balance of liberal and conservative sentiment in Birmingham changed over time, just as it did nationally.

Second, this political diversity resulted in structured and ideologically meaningful electoral competition. Although not partisan, political contestation in Birmingham did take place between coherent factions with durable class and organizational bases. The Big Mules, backed by industrial interests and allied in state politics with plantation owners, drew disproportionate support from the economically conservative upper classes. For its part, the working-class faction relied on the organizational support of labor unions and of the Klan, which in this period embraced economic reforms anathema to the conservative elite,[13] as well as on patronage from national Democrats. Further, these factional conflicts were expressed in issue-based primary contests between ideologically differentiated candidates for office. Candidates adopted and advertised distinct policy platforms, to which voters apparently responded.

Third, voters held congressional incumbents accountable for their behavior in office. Huddleston's opposition to certain New Deal measures left him vulnerable to the charge that he was "an enemy of President Roosevelt, perhaps the most damning accusation one could make" at the height of FDR's popularity.[14] The charge was sufficiently credible that Patrick was able to unseat the longtime incumbent. But as the white

---

CQ Almanac 1949, 5th ed. (Washington, DC: Congressional Quarterly, 1950), 06-462–06-463, http://library.cqpress.com/cqalmanac/cqal49-1400486.

[12] Author calculations; Norrell, "Labor at the Ballot Box," 207–209; on turnout in urban areas, see Key, Southern Politics, 510–511.

[13] Kenneth D. Wald, "The Visible Empire: The Ku Klux Klan as an Electoral Movement," Journal of Interdisciplinary History 11, no. 2 (1980): 217–234; J. Mills Thornton III, "Alabama Politics, J. Thomas Heflin, and the Expulsion Movement of 1929," Alabama Review 21 (1968): 83–112; Samuel L. Webb, "Hugo Black, Bibb Graves, and the Ku Klux Klan," Alabama Review, October 2004, 243–283.

[14] Norrell, "Labor at the Ballot Box," 213.

public's mood changed, the liberal Patrick found himself out of step with his increasingly conservative constituents. Anticipating voters' judgment of policy positions, Patrick trimmed to the right by, for example, voting for antilabor bills. But in the end, Patrick was removed in favor of representatives with sincerely conservative policy views.

Fourth, and finally, this narrative illustrates the one-party system's capacity for responsiveness. The threat of electoral sanction induced incumbents to respond anticipatorily to voters' (changing) preferences, as Patrick did with respect to labor legislation. When incumbents were not sufficiently responsive, voters made good on this threat and removed out-of-step members like Huddleston and eventually Patrick himself. But in replacing incumbents, voters did not choose randomly among potential challengers. Rather, they prospectively selected challengers who suited their ideological mood: in 1936, a liberal like Patrick; in 1942 and 1946, conservatives like Newsome and Battle. The overall result was shifts in representation that mirrored national partisan tides, which in 1936 washed out conservative Republicans and in 1942 and 1946 washed them back in again.

The politics of Jefferson County, Alabama, though not in all respects typical of Southern congressional districts, illustrates dynamics at play throughout the one-party South. The remainder of this chapter is devoted to exploring these dynamics in a more general way. Using a combination of qualitative and quantitative evidence, its main goal is establishing the plausibility of the claim that Democratic primaries created electoral incentives for Southern MCs to represent the white electorate—a "selectoral connection," to adapt Mayhew's famous phrase.[15]

Specifically, I argue that Democratic primaries, though racially exclusionary, provided forums for political participation by a broad swath of the white population. Not only did the electorate extend well beyond a narrow economic elite, but the *potential* electorate was even larger than the actual one, in part because whites' electoral participation depended on the competitiveness of the race. While primary competition was hardly universal, it was frequent and meaningful enough to provide a credible threat of opposition. Moreover, congressional primary campaigns and media coverage often included a good deal of issue content, particularly regarding incumbents' positions on salient policy controversies in Congress. This in turn helped give voters the information they required to select representative candidates and, in particular, to hold incumbents accountable for their actions in office. In addition to enabling voters to remove out-of-step incumbents, these accountability

---

[15] Mayhew, *Electoral Connection*; cf. Manion, "'Good Types'."

mechanisms induced sitting incumbents to change their positions to pre-empt electoral punishment. The end result, I argue, was a selectoral connection that, through turnover as well as adaptation, fostered responsiveness to the preferences of the white public, despite the absence of partisan electoral competition.

5.1 THE WHITE PRIMARY

I begin with a discussion of the institutional mechanisms for political competition that did exist in the one-party South: Democratic primary elections. Some scholars seem unaware of the very existence of Southern primaries as sites of electoral competition. One study by Besley, Persson, and Sturm, for example, conflates partisan and political competition so completely that it codes the region as totally uncompetitive until the 1965 Voting Rights Act, which "reintroduced political competition in the US South."[16] Similarly, Quadagno characterizes the one-party South as "an oligarchy ... [w]ith no competition for elective office."[17] Other scholars acknowledge the existence of Southern primaries but characterize them as meaningless charades. Domhoff and Webber, for example, argue that primaries "provid[ed] a semblance of political choice and electoral competition, thereby allowing the dominant planter class to continue to profess its allegiance to democratic principles." In the end, however, they served merely as a means by which "complete planter dominance through the Democratic Party was solidified."[18]

The reality was more complicated. Elite dominance is arguably an apt description of Democratic nominations in the nineteenth century, when nominees were selected by conventions dominated by party bosses. But by the end of the nineteenth century, state Democratic parties in the South had begun experimenting with opening up nominations to rank-and-file voters. In 1892, Mississippi passed the nation's first statewide primary law, and other Southern states followed suit in the next two decades. In the wake of the successful "redemption" campaigns of the late nineteenth and early twentieth century, party primaries proved critical to Democrats' consolidation of their temporary dominance into long-term hegemony.[19] This was thanks in part to two refinements: the "white primary" and the run-off primary. The first refers to Southern Democrats' limitation of participation in party primaries to whites only, a practice that until

---

[16] Besley, Persson, and Sturm, "Political Competition."
[17] Quadagno, *Color of Welfare*, 21.
[18] Domhoff and Webber, *Class and Power*, 59.
[19] Perman, *Pursuit of Unity*, 179–181.

1944 was not deemed to violate the Fifteenth Amendment.[20] The efficacy of the white primary was further enhanced by the institution of run-off primaries for the top two finishers in the first round, which ensured that the ultimate nominee was acceptable to a majority of Democratic voters.[21]

The white primary had paradoxical consequences. On one hand, it proved crucial to institutionalizing white Democratic supremacy following the disenfranchising reforms of the late nineteenth and early twentieth centuries. To maintain their hegemony, Southern Democratic parties had to forestall opposition-party challenges from disaffected whites, who might be tempted to mobilize blacks. "[W]ithout the legal primary," wrote one turn-of-the-century editor, "divisions among white men might result in bringing about a return to the deplorable conditions when one faction of white men call upon the Negroes to help defeat another faction."[22] By providing a formal, legal mechanism for whites to settle their differences before the general election, primary elections helped the Democratic Party co-opt protest movements and monopolize political talent and ambition.[23] The "finality of the primary" was further ensured by loyalty oaths and other devices.[24] In short, the white primary was a key pillar of Southern disenfranchisement and one-party rule.[25]

At the same time, however, the direct primary was also a democratizing reform for ordinary whites. Unlike the old convention system, "the direct primary forced politicians to cultivate a popular following rather than simply appealing to local party elites."[26] In many states, the adoption of the primary led to major political shifts. In Mississippi, for example, it broke Delta planters' control of Democratic nominations and fueled the rise of racist but economically progressive demagogues, such as James Vardaman and Theodore Bilbo.[27] Throughout the South, Democratic primaries thus became a mechanism "through which the interests of

---

[20] The white primary was "probably the most efficacious method of denying the vote to African Americans"; Keyssar, *Right to Vote*, 249.

[21] J. Morgan Kousser, "Origins of the Run-Off Primary," *The Black Scholar* 15, no. 5 (1984): 23–26.

[22] Quoted by ibid., 25.

[23] Leon D. Epstein, *Political Parties in the American Mold* (Madison: University of Wisconsin Press, 1986), 129–130; Gary W. Cox, *Making Votes Count: Strategic Coordination in the World's Electoral Systems* (New York: Cambridge University Press, 1997), 166.

[24] Key, *Southern Politics*, 424–442.

[25] Mickey, "Beginning of the End."

[26] Earl Black and Merle Black, *Politics and Society in the South* (Cambridge, MA: Harvard University Press, 1987), 5–6.

[27] Morgan, *Redneck Liberal*, 12–13.

low-income whites could be pressed," at least potentially.[28] Whether this potential was realized, however, hinged on further questions: whether the primary electorate was broad enough to extend beyond a narrow elite, and whether political competition was frequent and substantive enough to be meaningful. I next explore each of these questions in turn.

5.2 THE SELECTORATE

As Bruce Bueno de Mesquita and his coathors observe, political regimes can be distinguished not only by the mechanisms they use to choose political leaders, but also by the size of their "selectorate"—the subset of the population permitted to participate in the selection of leaders.[29] Some regimes, such as feudal elective monarchies, select leaders "democratically" in a Schumpeterian sense, but the selectorate is limited to a very small subset of the population.[30] In regimes with such restrictive selectorates, elections are but forums for resolving conflicts between competing factions of a narrow elite. Was the selectorate in the one-party South so small as to include only a narrow economic elite? Or did the selectorate encompass an economically diverse swath of the white population?

The answer, I argue, is that the selectorate, while racially restricted, extended well beyond the economic elite. This is not to deny that the South's suffrage restrictions and lack of party competition markedly reduced political participation, especially among blacks but also among whites.[31] Between 1892 and 1908, presidential turnout in the average Southern state fell from 54% to 29%, as compared to a drop from 76% to 72% in the average non-Southern state.[32] By the end of the first decade of the twentieth century, only about half of white men, and less than a tenth of black men, were turning out to vote in Southern

---

[28] Elizabeth Sanders, *Roots of Reform: Farmers, Workers, and the American State, 1877–1917* (Chicago: University of Chicago Press, 1999), 153.

[29] Bueno de Mesquita et al., *The Logic of Political Survival*. According to these authors, the other key characteristic distinguishing regimes is the size of the "winning coalition," the subset of the selectorate whose support determines who prevails in leadership struggles. The size of the winning coalition relative to the selectorate is closely related to the formal mechanisms of leadership selection, among other factors.

[30] Schumpeter, *Capitalism, Socialism and Democracy*.

[31] J. Morgan Kousser, *The Shaping of Southern Politics: Suffrage Restriction and the Establishment of the One-Party South* (New Haven, CT: Yale University Press, 1974).

[32] Curtis Gans, ed., *Voter Turnout in the United States 1788–2009* (CQ Press, 2011), chapter 6, Table "Presidential Turnout, 1892–1908," http://dx.doi.org/10.4135/9781608712700.

general elections.[33] Once Democratic hegemony was established, turnout in Democratic primaries increased, often exceeding that in general elections, but it remained relatively low. By the 1930s–40s, turnout in contested primaries for Congress averaged around 20% of VAP, and turnout in gubernatorial primaries averaged around 25%.[34] These turnout levels compare unfavorably to those in general elections in non-Southern states, such as in New York, where during this period about 60% of adults voted in statewide races.

Regional differences are less stark, however, if one compares turnout among *whites*.[35] V. O. Key reports that in Senate primaries between 1920 and 1946, white turnout ranged from an average of 20% in Tennessee to 46% in South Carolina.[36] Data on contested House primaries indicate similar overall turnout levels.[37] Between 1930 and 1944, white primary turnout hovered around 30% in both chambers. After a dip during World War II, when deployment overseas inhibited many GIs from voting, turnout in Southern congressional primaries increased to around 35% of white VAP and remained at that level into the early 1960s (see Figure 5.1, top panels).

Turnout in congressional primaries is an imperfect measure of the selectorate, for two reasons. First, it is available only for primaries that were contested, which as I discuss in the text that follows was only about half of all races. For the other half of races, data on primary turnout are missing. Second, even turnout in contested primaries depended on the competitiveness of the race. If the outcome was predictable, many potential voters were likely to stay home. Indeed, turnout in the typical district ranged about 10 percentage points over the course of a decade.[38] Primary

---

[33] Carles Boix, *Democracy and Redistribution* (New York: Cambridge University Press, 2003), 122.

[34] In Senate primaries between 1920 and 1946, for example, VAP turnout ranged from an average of 16% in Tennessee to 27% in Texas and South Carolina; Key, *Southern Politics*, 504–5. Owing to the lack of contested Senate primaries, Key does not report figures for Virginia, but the state's average turnout in gubernatorial primaries was the lowest in the South, at 11.6%.

[35] Before the Supreme Court's 1944 decision in *Smith v. Allwright*, the Southern electorate, especially for Democratic primaries, included almost no African Americans. Even after the decision, the number of black voters remained very small. We can thus derive rough estimates of the turnout rates of Southern whites by dividing votes cast by the size of the white VAP, keeping in mind that for years after 1944 this will slightly overestimate white turnout (and underestimate black turnout).

[36] Key, *Southern Politics*, 505.

[37] Ansolabehere et al., "More Democracy."

[38] More precisely, the difference between the highest and lowest white turnout in a given district-decade dyad averaged around 11 percentage points.

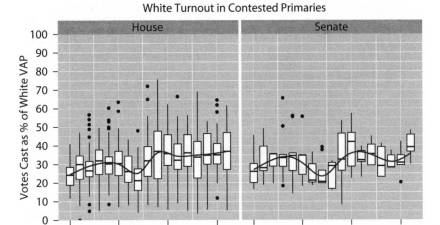

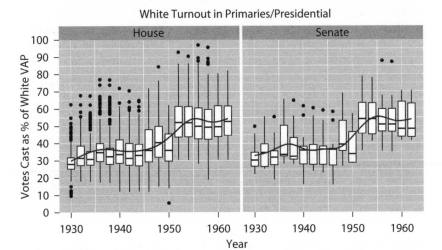

Figure 5.1. Year-specific box plots of white turnout in congressional primaries (top) and in primaries or presidential elections, whichever is greater (bottom). Calculated based on data from Ansolabehere et al., David Leip, and the U.S. Census.

turnout is thus likely to underestimate the *potential* electorate—the set of citizens who could, if mobilized, decide to vote.

The plots in the bottom panels of Figure 5.1 are based on a more expansive definition of the potential congressional electorate: the maximum of the number of voters in that year's House or Senate primary (if any) and the number of voters in the most recent presidential election (that year or two years previous).[39] Turnout is defined with respect to the white VAP in the relevant state or congressional district. By this measure, turnout in both states and congressional districts averaged around 36–37% in the period 1930–51 and was quite stable across years. The return of partisan presidential competition to the South in 1952 stimulated a marked rise in turnout, to more than half of the white VAP.

While the voting participation of Southern whites compares unfavorably to turnout in the non-South during the same period of time, it is not so markedly different from turnout in contemporary American elections. In presidential elections between 1968 and 2000, for example, turnout in the South exceeded half the VAP only twice: in 1968 (50.7%) and in 1992 (50.5%). Southern turnout in midterm elections has never been higher than 35% of the VAP.[40] VAP turnout in the non-South was once considerably higher but in recent years has largely converged with the South. In short, the active electorate in the one-party South constituted about the same fraction of the white population as the contemporary American electorate's fraction of the U.S. population.

Of course, voters in the one-party South were not fully representative of Southern whites generally, let alone the region's population as a whole. In addition to its profound racial skew, the Southern electorate also contained an upper-class bias. This was (and remains) true in the non-South as well, but the bias was stronger in the South. In opinion polls fielded 1936–52, 69% of Southern whites reported voting in the last presidential election.[41] These self-reported Southern voters were 16 percentage points more likely than nonvoters to have a professional occupation, 12 points more likely to own a phone, and 12 points more likely to have graduated high school. The analogous gaps among non-Southern voters and nonvoters were smaller: 11 points for professional, 9 points for phone, and

---

[39] Data on presidential elections are derived from David Leip, "Dave Leip's Atlas of U.S. Presidential Elections," 2013, http://www.uselectionatlas.org. While uncompetitive before 1952, Southern presidential elections nevertheless brought many voters to the polls, and usually presidential turnout was higher than turnout in congressional elections (4 percentage points on average). The difference between presidential and primary turnout among whites shot up to 20 percentage points in 1952, when Eisenhower won several Southern states, and it remained at that level through the 1960 elections. While these figures of course include many presidential Republicans, this does not mean that they should be excluded from the potential electorate. Southerners who voted Republican for president—which included a great many who firmly identified as Democrats—could and often did participate in Democratic primaries, which were usually the only meaningful elections for local, state, and congressional offices.

[40] Michael P. McDonald and Samuel L. Popkin, "The Myth of the Vanishing Voter," *American Political Science Review* 95, no. 4 (2001): 969, table 3.

[41] This and the figures that follow are based on unweighted analysis of the raw poll samples. Weighting the data reduces the estimated voting rate, but as in contemporary surveys, a strong tendency to overreport voting remains.

5 points for high school. Similarly, turnout among Southern whites of at least "average" class status was about 15 points higher than those rated "poor," as compared to a gap of 9 points outside the South.[42] Thus, although class bias in turnout was more severe among Southern whites than among residents of the non-South, regional differences in this respect were not huge.

Moreover, because the South was so much poorer than the rest of the country,[43] the material and class status of the Southern white electorate barely differed from that of the non-South electorate. "Even the [one-party South's] shrunken electorates," note Earl and Merle Black, "probably contained more have-littles and have-nots than middle-class whites."[44] White voters in the South were actually somewhat *less* likely than non-Southern voters to have a phone or a high-school education, and no more likely to be a professional. Fully 45% of self-reported white voters in Southern poll samples were classified as "poor" or "on relief," as compared to 47% of non-Southern voters. In both regions, 17% of voters were classified by their interviewer as "average plus" or "wealthy."

Given the imperfect representativeness of the polls' quota samples, as well as the imperfect reliability of self-reported turnout, these figures must be treated with caution. But, overall, the evidence suggests that active electorate in the South extended far beyond the economic elite. Further, Southern voters were only modestly less representative of the Southern white public than non-Southern voters were of the non-Southern public. Thus, if it is plausible to define the selectorate in the non-South as the entire public, then it is only slightly more of a stretch to define the selectorate in the South as the white public.

5.3 ELECTORAL COMPETITION

Membership in the selectorate is of little value in the absence of meaningful political choice and competition. As noted earlier, scholars sometimes assume that because general elections were uncompetitive in the one-party South, political competition was entirely lacking from the region. This of course ignores the existence of Democratic primaries, which provided at

---

[42] Interviewers used their own judgment to classify white respondents into one of six categories: "on relief," "poor," "poor plus," "average," "average plus," and "wealthy." These categories were defined, somewhat arbitrarily, with reference to the community where the interview occurred. See Adam J. Berinsky, "American Public Opinion in the 1930s and 1940s: The Analysis of Quota-Controlled Sample Survey Data," *Public Opinion Quarterly* 70, no. 4 (2006): 503.

[43] The South's per capita income was around half that of the rest of the United States; Schulman, *Cotton Belt to Sunbelt*, 3.

[44] Black and Black, *Politics and Society in the South*, 6.

least the potential for political contestation within the one-party system. Whether this potential was realized, however, is a separate question.

Until recently, scholars lacked comprehensive information on primaries in the one-party South. This problem has been largely rectified thanks to the work of Ansolabehere, Hansen, Hirano, and Snyder, who have collected data on primary candidates and results in the United States over many decades.[45] These data show that Democratic primaries compensated to a substantial degree for the South's lack of general-election competition, at least in numerical terms. This was especially true in the heyday of the one-party system. In 1930s and 1940s, around two-thirds of Southern Democratic primaries for state and federal offices were contested, with nearly two-fifths of winning candidates garnering less than 60% of the total vote.[46] In the 1950s primary competition, especially for non-open seats, declined nationwide, but primaries remained the most important site of electoral competition in the South.

As Figure 5.2 shows, competition was widespread in Southern House and Senate primaries, though in both chambers it declined in the 1950s. In primaries between 1930 and 1948, almost half of Southern Democratic primaries for the U.S. House and nearly two-thirds of Senate primaries featured at least two candidates (Figure 5.2, left panel). After 1950, the competition rate declined by 8 points for the House and 14 points for the Senate. In the typical contested primary, the runner-up ran 30–40 percentage points behind the winner (Figure 5.2, right panel). Since contested primaries often featured more than two candidates (46% in the House and 62% in the Senate), the winner's share of the total vote was often quite a bit lower than their margin would suggest.

Primary competition was typically fiercer in races with no incumbent candidate, particularly after the 1940s. But incumbents running for reelection were by no means guaranteed renomination. Not counting any defeats they experienced, one third of Southern MCs experienced at least two contested primaries over the course of their career. Even established and powerful members, such as long-serving Texans Sam Rayburn (the top House Democrat between 1940 and 1961) and Wright Patman rarely saw an election year pass without a contested primary, forcing each into a "permanent campaign which found him constantly on the watch for challengers."[47] Across all state and congressional offices, 7% of Southern

[45] Details on these data, which were generously shared by the authors, can be found in Ansolabehere et al., "More Democracy."
[46] Ibid., 197, figure 2.
[47] Nancy Beck Young, "Change and Continuity in the Politics of Running for Congress: Wright Patman and the Campaigns of 1928, 1938, 1962, and 1972," *East Texas Historical Journal* 34, no. 2 (1996): 55; on Rayburn's campaigns, see D. B. Hardeman and

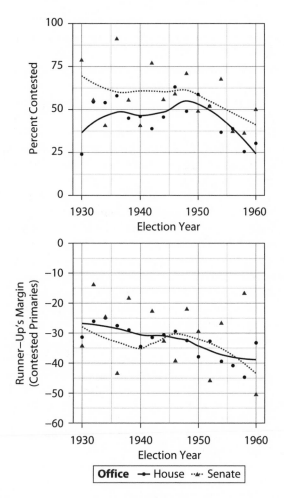

Figure 5.2. Competition in Southern Democratic primaries

Democratic incumbents who ran for renomination in the 1930s were defeated. In the 1940s, the figure declined to 3.5%, and to 2% in the 1950s.[48] House incumbents who sought renomination lost about 5% of the time in the 1930s–40s and 3% in the 1950s. In the Senate, the

Donald C. Bacon, *Rayburn: A Biography* (Austin: Texas Monthly Press, 1987), 58, 102, 204–206, 297, 338–339.
[48] Ansolabehere et al., "More Democracy," 197, figure 2. Incumbents' advantage in primary elections seems to have been larger in Southern states without strong intraparty factions; Stephen Ansolabehere et al., "The Incumbency Advantage in U.S. Primary Elections," *Electoral Studies* 26, no. 3 (2007): 665.

incumbent defeat rate was much higher, closer to 30%. Between 1920 and 1954, a total of 18 Southern Democratic senators were defeated for renomination.[49]

How does the competitiveness of Southern primaries compare to two-party competition? Clearly, uncontested elections are much less likely where there is two-party competition. For example, between 1930 and 1960 around 95% of non-Southern general elections for the U.S. House were contested—twice the rate of Southern House primaries.[50] But many of the contested races in the non-South took place in one-sided districts where one party was all but guaranteed victory and the minority candidate was merely a sacrificial lamb. In Southern primaries, contestation was probably more endogenous to the vulnerability of the incumbent.

For this reason, Southern primaries compare more favorably to those of the non-South on the metric of incumbent defeat rates than they do on contestation per se. This is especially true for Southern senators, who were at least as, if not more, likely to be denied renomination as their non-Southern counterparts were to be defeated in the general election.[51] Southern members of the House were, by contrast, less than half as likely to be defeated as contemporaneous non-Southerners. But given the declining competitiveness of congressional elections since the 1950s, even Southern House members' 5% defeat rate is about on par with today's Congress, where the defeat rate of incumbent House candidates is about the same.[52]

Overall, then, the data on Southern primaries suggest that intraparty competition, while not as universal as in two-party settings, was widespread enough to provide genuine choice in open-seat races. It also posed a genuine, if often potential, electoral threat to incumbents who fell out of step with their constituencies.

---

[49] The figures for the Senate include Oklahoma and exclude senators appointed to office; V. O. Key Jr., *Politics, Parties & Pressure Groups* (New York: Crowell, 1964), 441.

[50] J. Mark Wrighton and Peverill Squire, "Uncontested Seats and Electoral Competition for the U.S. House of Representatives over Time," *Journal of Politics* 59, no. 2 (1997): 453–456.

[51] In non-Southern general elections between 1932 and 1970, 22% of incumbent senators who stood for reelection were defeated; Donald Gross and David Breaux, "Historical Trends in U.S. Senate Elections, 1912–1988," *American Politics Quarterly* 19, no. 3 (1991): 300, table 5.

[52] In general elections between 2000 and 2010, only 6% of House incumbents running for reelection were defeated; Harold W. Stanley and Richard G. Niemi, "House and Senate Incumbents Retired, Defeated, or Reelected, 1946–2010," in *Vital Statistics on American Politics 2011–2012*, ed. Harold W. Stanley and Richard G. Niemi (Washington, DC: CQ Press, 2011), http://library.cqpress.com/elections/vsap11%5C_tab1-18. See also David R. Mayhew, "Congressional Elections: The Case of the Vanishing Marginals," *Polity* 6, no. 3 (1974): 295–317.

5.4 IDEOLOGICAL CHOICE

Just because primary competition was prevalent in the South, however, doesn't imply that it was meaningful. Indeed, many studies of Southern politics emphasize that primary campaigns tended to revolve around flamboyant personalities, geographic loyalties, social networks, and symbolic appeals rather than real policy issues.[53] Party primaries encouraged a "stylistic division" of Southern politicians between "respectability and audacity," in which relatively staid candidates backed by local power brokers or well-heeled economic interests faced off against populist demagogues hoping to use "a colorful and dramatic personal campaign to arouse the electorate."[54] But these differences did not map neatly onto policy differences, as attested by the many demagogues who once in office betrayed the economic interests of their poor white supporters. Moreover, these stylistic alignments competed with more or less transient factional affiliations, "friends and neighbors" networks, and other patterns that further obscured policy-based cleavages.[55] The result, according to many scholars, was a politics characterized by "[d]emagogues whipping up the coarsest emotions of 'common whites,' an obsession with race, feckless reformers, wealthy elites directing government policy, and voters incapable of recognizing their economic interests."[56]

Despite the great deal of truth to these claims, Southern primaries' lack of issue-based competition relative to partisan general elections should not be exaggerated. First of all, even in partisan settings Democratic and Republican candidates often focus their campaigns on nonpolicy considerations.[57] But more to the point, ideological competition, whether

---

[53] For the classic exposition, see Key, *Southern Politics*; for a study of a specific MC that echoes Key's perspective, see John C. Weaver, "Lawyers, Lodges, and Kinfolk: The Workings of a South Carolina Political Organization, 1920–1936," *The South Carolina Historical Magazine* 78, no. 4 (1977): 272–285.

[54] Dewey W. Grantham, *The Life and Death of the Solid South: A Political History* (Lexington: University Press of Kentucky, 1988), 29; Anthony J. Badger, "Huey Long and the New Deal," in *New Deal/New South* (Fayetteville: University of Arkansas Press, 2007), 1.

[55] On friends and neighbors specifically, see Key, *Southern Politics*, 38–41.

[56] Samuel L. Webb, "Southern Politics in the Age of Populism and Progressivism: A Historiographical Essay," in *A Companion to the American South*, ed. John B. Boles (Malden, MA: Blackwell, 2007), 324, http://dx.doi.org/10.1002/9780470996300.ch19.

[57] See, e.g., Stokes's classic discussion of "valence-issues"; Donald E. Stokes, "Spatial Models of Party Competition," *American Political Science Review* 57, no. 2 (1963): 373–374; for evidence that congressional campaigns became more issue-focused after the 1970s, see John Arthur Henderson, "Downs' Revenge: Elections, Responsibility and the Rise of Congressional Polarization" (PhD dissertation, University of California–Berkeley, Department of Political Science, 2013).

explicit or implicit, was in fact a salient feature of many Southern primary campaigns. As Chapter 4 showed, Southern Democrats in Congress ranged greatly in their policy positions, particularly on economics. As was discussed in Chapter 3, so too did the Southern white public. And as the career of Luther Patrick suggests, these elite and mass-level ideological differences found expression in issue-based conflict between candidates of the same party.

To a substantial if imperfect degree, the one-party system established around the turn of the century absorbed into the Democratic Party dissident movements among whites that had previously been expressed as third-party protests.[58] As noted earlier, the Democratic Party's ability to do so hinged on the development of party primaries, which offered dissident whites both a mechanism for expressing their opposition to the Democrats' hitherto conservative leadership and a reason to remain within instead of outside the party. As Dewey Grantham notes, throughout much of the South there emerged a "Bourbon–agrarian reform bifactionalism" characterized by conflicts between richer and poorer farmers, which in time was supplemented by the emergence of an urban middle class interested in progress, growth, and reform.[59] In the 1930s, the New Deal sharpened and intensified the ideological cleavages within the one-party South, just as it did in national politics. After 1933, contests between pro– and anti–New Deal candidates became an endemic feature of intraparty conflict in the South. As Key himself later acknowledged, Southern congressional primaries began "to take on the tone of contests between Democrats and Republicans elsewhere."[60]

A few Southern states featured electoral conflict between two durable and ideologically distinct Democratic factions. The most prominent example is Louisiana after the rise of Governor and later Senator Huey Long, who forged a remarkably cohesive (and corrupt) factional organization committed to real programmatic action on behalf of poorer whites. Long/anti-Long bifactionalism in Louisiana survived Long's assassination in 1935, and despite its founder's antagonism toward Roosevelt, the Long faction continued to provide firm backing of New Deal–style policies at the national level.[61] More than in any other Southern state, factional labels in Louisiana served as a direct functional substitute for parties,

---

[58] C. Vann Woodward, *Origins of the New South, 1877–1913* (Baton Rouge: Louisiana State University Press, 1951); Perman, *Pursuit of Unity*, 151–163.

[59] Grantham, *Life and Death of the Solid South*, 34.

[60] Key, *Politics, Parties & Pressure Groups*, 441.

[61] Key, *Southern Politics*, 156–182; T. Harry Williams, *Huey Long* (New York: Vintage, 1969); Badger, "Huey Long and the New Deal."

especially with respect to informing voters about candidates' policy positions and relationship to the governing coalition.[62]

As Key emphasizes, Louisiana's durable bifactionalism was an outlier among Southern states, most of which exhibited much more fluid and individualized intra-party competition.[63] But even in atomized states without clear factional divisions, voters had access to a variety of other sources of information to infer candidates' policy commitments. One direct source of ideological information was the common practice of crafting and disseminating policy platforms describing candidates' stances on the issues. In his successful 1934 campaign against the conservative Sen. Hubert Stephens (D-MS), for example, Theodore Bilbo released a 27-point program detailing his liberal positions on economic redistribution, unemployment insurance, federal aid to education, and numerous other issues.[64] Kentucky Democrat Earle Clements did the same in his successful 1944 primary challenge to incumbent Rep. Beverly Vincent, enumerating his support for veterans' benefits, a soldier vote bill, rural electrification, farm-to-market roads, high education spending, and free trade.[65] Less successfully, Rep. Laurie Battle expounded a lengthy list of policy positions in his failed 1954 challenge to Sen. John Sparkman (D-AL), offering a stark conservative contrast to the incumbent on the Tennessee Valley Authority (TVA), housing, Tidelands Oil, and labor issues.[66] A platform distributed by 1957 House candidate Bobby Lee Cook of Georgia was similarly detailed, describing his stance on issues ranging from TVA and social security (in favor) to civil rights and foreign aid (opposed).[67]

Unsurprisingly, candidates' platforms were not always completely forthright, often ignoring or misrepresenting electorally unpopular

[62] John Mark Hansen, Shigeo Hirano, and James M. Snyder Jr., "Parties within Parties: Parties, Factions, and Coordinated Politics, 1900–1980," in *Governing in a Polarized Age: Elections, Parties, and Political Representation in America*, ed. Alan S. Gerber and Eric Schickler (New York: Cambridge University Press, 2017), 174–183.
[63] Virginia, dominated by the oligarchical and conservative Byrd Organization, presents a partial exception to this lack of structure, but its politics were much less competitive than Louisiana's; Key, *Southern Politics*, chapter 2.
[64] Martha H. Swain, "Hubert D. Stephens: Mississippi's 'Quiet Man' in the Senate, 1923–1935," *Journal of Mississippi History* 63, no. 4 (2001): 278.
[65] Thomas Hamilton Syvertsen, "Earle Chester Clements and the Democratic Party, 1920–1950" (PhD thesis, Department of History, University of Kentucky, 1982), 140–141.
[66] Thomas Jasper Gilliam Sr., "The Second Folsom Administration: The Destruction of Alabama Liberalism, 1954–1958" (PhD dissertation, Auburn University, 1975), 75–76.
[67] Bobby Lee Cook, "Let's Send Bobby Lee Cook to U.S. Congress: Platform," Box 6, Folder 27 (Georgia, 1957), Committee on Political Education Research Department Collection, George Meany Memorial AFL-CIO Archives, University of Maryland, College Park, MD (cited hereafter as "COPE Collection"), 1957.

positions. In his losing campaign against Bilbo, for example, Sen. Stephens sought vainly to evade the poisonous anti-Roosevelt label by making "Stand by the President and his program" his sole campaign plank.[68] As Stephens and other out-of-step incumbents discovered, however, voters found insincere campaign positions less credible when contradicted by candidates' previous records in office. The very public and salient nature of congressional roll-call voting made obfuscation particularly difficult for incumbent MCs. For this reason, challengers put great effort into identifying and publicizing incumbents' out-of-step positions. Wright Patman, for example, prepared for his 1928 primary challenge to seven-term representative Eugene Black (D-TX) by scouring the *Congressional Record* and other sources for "opposition research" on the incumbent's record in office. Rep. Black's votes against agricultural relief measures had left him vulnerable to the charge that he had "lost touch with his rural constituents"—a weakness that Patman successfully exploited in a campaign, publicized through "mass mailings and numerous public appearances," that "at every turn...attacked some part of Black's record."[69] Outside groups sometimes supplemented candidates' efforts to publicize their own and their opponents' records. In 1950, for example, labor unions backing incumbent Senator Claude Pepper against his challenger Rep. George Smathers prepared a document entitled "Let the Record Speak for Itself," which contrasted the candidates' positions on social security, minimum wage, unions, public housing, taxes, and other issues.[70]

Interest groups also conveyed policy information in less direct ways, through their endorsement of or public affiliation with candidates. Conservative candidates typically relied on financial and organizational support from groups that represented better-off agricultural and business interests. Agents of the American Farm Bureau, for example, often worked on behalf of conservative candidates who supported the interests of the larger landowners represented by the Bureau.[71] Business interests, such as power companies, oil firms, and real-estate agents, also tended to be key supporters of conservative causes. When, for example, James Simpson, a state senator associated with Birmingham's Big Mule faction,

---

[68] Swain, "Hubert D. Stephens," 278.

[69] Young, "Change and Continuity," 52–54. Rep. Black "refuted Patman's assaults on his record in newspaper advertisements and in the *Congressional Record*, but Patman stood his ground: 'You have accused me of being unfair in my speeches...If I am unfair, the Congressional Record is unfair as I am quoting from that record.'"

[70] "Let the Record Speak for Itself," 1950, Box 5, Folder 29 (Florida: 1950, Primary), COPE Collection.

[71] On the Farm Bureau's general conservatism, see Saloutos, "American Farm Bureau." On its role in Southern politics, see, e.g., Rogers et al., *Alabama*, 455.

challenged liberal Alabama senator Lister Hill, he was publicly supported by the Alabama Chamber of Commerce, Associated Industries of Alabama, the Farm Bureau, the Alabama Cooperative Extension Service, and other organizations representing employers and large-scale farmers. Given Simpson's salient association with these conservative groups, there was little ambiguity about his general ideological orientation, and the race was widely perceived as a liberal–conservative showdown.[72]

Liberal candidates relied on an analogous, if less well-heeled, set of groups. Earlier in the period, the coalitions of economically progressive candidates sometimes brought together strange bedfellows, as in the Alabama Klan's alliance with labor unions and other liberal groups in the 1920s and 1930s.[73] But by the 1940s, New Dealish candidates were being elected by lower-class coalitions that looked much more similar to the Democratic coalition in the North.[74] Typically, these coalitions consisted of an amalgam of blue-collar workers, small farmers, government beneficiaries and employees, and any blacks eligible to vote, plus the candidate's personal network. For example, the potential support coalition of one progressive House candidate in late-1950s Arkansas was described as "Labor, the Negroes, REA [Rural Electrification Administration cooperatives], Farmers Union [a liberal farm organization], a majority of the school teachers, and the Garland County political organization."[75]

---

[72] Ibid., 531.
[73] Thornton, "Alabama Politics"; Webb, "Hugo Black."
[74] Anthony J. Badger, "The Rise and Fall of Biracial Politics in the South," in *The Southern State of Mind*, ed. Jan Nordby Gretlund (Columbia: University of South Carolina Press, 1999), 23–35.
[75] The candidate in question was former governor Sid McMath, who ultimately decided not to run for Congress; Daniel A. Powell to James L. McDevitt, March 13, 1957, Box 2, Folder 5 (Arkansas, 1957–1959), COPE Collection. Liberal Alabama senator Lister Hill relied on a similar coalition, which one scholar describes as follows:

> As a long-tenured senator, Hill had had the opportunity to establish a strong "factional machine"—a "network" of people throughout Alabama who considered themselves "big Hill men." Some observers even thought that his was the "best" political organization in the state in the 1940s. At that time teachers and municipal officials and their respective organizations, the Alabama Education Association and the Alabama League of Municipalities, were two of the state's strongest organized political groups and the real cogs in the Hill organization. Also to be counted upon were numerous federal officials, many of whom in some way owed their jobs to Hill.... Hill had inherited these groups from Sen. Hugo Black (Birmingham-centered liberals, strength in Tennessee Valley, young progressive-minded officeholders) and from Gov. Bibb Graves (office-holders, educators, and teachers). He supplemented this initial base through hard work as a young congressman and senator.

Over time, particularly in the 1940s, organized labor played an increasingly central role in backing liberal candidates and generally fostering
programmatic politics in the region. Union inroads in places like steel-
making Birmingham and textile-producing North Georgia added both
votes and organization on the side of pro–New Deal candidates.[76] Labor's
importance expanded after the 1942 formation of the CIO's Political
Action Committee (CIO-PAC), which contributed to victories by a number of Southern liberals in 1944 and 1946.[77] Labor's support was a decid-
edly mixed blessing for Southern liberals. Southern politicians, recalled
CIO-PAC's Southern director, "wanted PAC support, but they wanted
it as quietly as possible.... Occasionally some unscrupulous candidate,
while seeking PAC covert support, would suggest that we publicly endorse
his opponent." And indeed, conservative candidates often attacked their
PAC-supported candidates as the "lackey" or "captive candidate" of the
CIO, whose support for black civil rights made it especially unpopular in
the South.[78]

Candidates' relations with the national party could convey ideological information as well. As we have already seen, many pro–New Deal
candidates (and, less successfully, some conservative ones) sought to por-
tray themselves as Roosevelt's preferred candidate in the race, as a means
of both harnessing the president's personal popularity and signaling their
ideological colors. Such claims were of course most credible when FDR
explicitly endorsed a candidate, as he did in a number of primaries in
1938.[79] Chastened by the relative (though not complete) lack of success

See Julia Marks Young, "A Republican Challenge to Democratic Progressivism in the
Deep South: Alabama's 1962 United States Senatorial Contest" (master's thesis, Auburn
University, 1978), 93 and footnote 11.

[76] Norrell, "Labor at the Ballot Box"; Michelle Brattain, "Making Friends and Enemies:
Textile Workers and Political Action in Post-World War II Georgia," *Journal of Southern
History* 63, no. 1 (1997): 91–138.

[77] Norrell, "Labor at the Ballot Box," 228; Sullivan, *Days of Hope*, 8–9.

[78] On the desire for covert PAC support, see Daniel A. Powell, "PAC to COPE," 247; on
attacks on PAC-supported candidates, see, e.g., Ralph J. Christian, "The Folger-Chatham
Congressional Primary of 1946," *North Carolina Historical Review* 53, no. 1 (1976): 33;
Morris B. Abram to Jack Kroll, "Analysis of the Fifth District Democratic Congressional
Primary," September 29, 1954, Box 6, Folder 24 (Georgia, 1954), COPE Collection. The
latter is a post-mortem report on a labor-backed candidate's narrow 1954 primary loss to
a conservative Georgia House member.

[79] Even when Roosevelt tried to avoid involvement in Democratic primaries, as he did in
Texas in 1938, the press sought "to interpret every word and nod" as a sign of the
president's favor or disfavor; L. Patrick Hughes, "West Texas Swing: Roosevelt Purge in
the Land of the Lone Star?," in *The West Texas Historical Association Year Book*, Vol. 75
(Abilene, TX: West Texas Historical Association, 1999), 42.

of his so-called purge,[80] Roosevelt subsequently confined himself to subtler means of fostering what he called "a new generation of leaders" in the South.[81] For example, though generally cautious in his use of patronage to punish Southern conservatives, Roosevelt sometimes used it as a way to build up a New Deal faction in a state, as he attempted in Virginia in the late 1930s.[82]

As Roosevelt's popularity ebbed, association with him brought dangers as well. The Texas Regulars, a right-wing Democratic faction that opposed Roosevelt's reelection in 1944, also backed conservative challengers to Speaker Rayburn and other "Texas congressmen they considered too liberal, too cozy with the President."[83] In a similar fashion, the battles between pro- and anti-Truman forces that played out in Alabama, Louisiana, and other states in the wake of the 1948 Dixiecrat Revolt helped clarify ideological lines within the party in the early 1950s.[84] Primary contenders who associated too closely with national Democrats risked being tarred, as one Georgia liberal was, as the candidate of the "radical northern wing of the Democratic party."[85] Partisan disloyalty carried risks of its own. In 1954, the relatively conservative Sen.

---

[80] Several Roosevelt-favored candidates did prevail in the 1938 Southern primaries, including senators Alben Barkley (D-KY), Lister Hill (D-AL), and Claude Pepper (D-FL), the latter two in open-seat races.

[81] Badger, "Whatever Happened." Southern liberals also enjoyed "an unprecedented entree in Washington"; Tindall, *Emergence of the New South*, 633. Moreover, Southern MCs who supported the administration line found comparatively easy paths to key committees, congressional leadership, and presidential tickets. Between 1935 and 1961, the House Speakership was occupied by three loyal Southern Democrats: Joseph Byrns (D-TN), William Bankhead (D-AL), and Sam Rayburn (D-TX). During that same period, three Southerners (along with two non-Southerners) served as Democratic Leader in the Senate: Joseph Robinson (D-AR), Alben Barkley (D-KY), and Lyndon Johnson (D-TX). Other Southern liberals who served in congressional leadership include Lister Hill (D-AL), John Sparkman (D-AL), Robert Ramspeck (D-GA), Percy Priest (D-TN), and Carl Albert (D-OK). In addition, every Democratic presidential ticket between 1948 and 1964 included a liberal Southerner.

[82] A. Cash Koeniger, "The New Deal and the States: Roosevelt versus the Byrd Organization in Virginia," *Journal of American History* 68, no. 4 (1982): 876–896.

[83] Hardeman and Bacon, *Rayburn*, 338–339.

[84] Rogers et al., *Alabama*, 536. In 1952, for example, the conservative Robert Kennon ran a successful race for governor of Louisiana in which he "campaigned on an anti-Truman, anti-Long platform" that called for "civil service for the state administration and a reduction in state taxes"; COPE Research Department, "Louisiana Election, 1952," January 28, 1952, Box 11, Folder 9 (Louisiana, 1948–1952), COPE Collection.

[85] Morris B. Abram to Jack Kroll, "Analysis of the Fifth District Democratic Congressional Primary," September 29, 1954, Box 6, Folder 24 (Georgia, 1954), COPE Collection. One of Rep. Laurie Battle's main attacks in his 1954 campaign against Sen. John Sparkman was that Sparkman's acceptance of the 1952 Democratic nomination for

John McClellan (D-AR) faced a strong challenge from progressive former governor Sid McMath, who "attacked McClellan primarily on the point that he has voted more often with the Republicans than the Democrats," calling the incumbent "Arkansas' 'Republican' Senator."[86]

Like the national party, association with government programs also signaled ideological information. Lyndon Johnson's stint as Texas National Youth Administration director no doubt rendered more credible his claim to be "Roosevelt's man" in his first House race.[87] "Big Jim" Folsom, later a progressive governor of Alabama, was a supervisor in the Alabama Relief Administration and worked for the Works Progress Administration in Washington before his first run for office, a 1936 race in which he challenged House Banking and Currency Chair Henry Steagall from the left.[88] Estes Kefauver, a liberal representative and later senator from Tennessee, first became involved in politics through his work on a TVA-related planning commission in Chattanooga.[89] The TVA in particular exemplifies the ways that New Deal programs provided bases of support for "TVA liberals" and provided a rallying point for their ideological battles with conservative candidates.[90] As suggested earlier, the Rural Electrification Administration and the local cooperatives it spawned played a similar role in Arkansas and other non-TVA states. New Deal policies such as these not only created local networks of vested interests dependent on federal spending, but also provided concrete, visible symbols of a beneficent national government to counter whites' increasing fear of external interference.

---

vice president rendered him suspect on civil rights and other issues; Gilliam, "Second Folsom Administration," 77.

[86] "Arkansas: 1954 Primary Elections," 1954, Box 2, Folder 2 (Arkansas, 1951–1955), COPE Collection. In response to McMath's attacks, McClellan "widely circulated the reproduced letters from 42 Democratic Senators, including the most liberal Democrats, praising his performance during the Army-McCarthy investigations. (McClellan and his staff had insistently solicited these letters which he used to 'prove' his standing as a Democrat in the Senate.)"

[87] Caro, The Path to Power, 395.

[88] William D. Barnard, Dixiecrats and Democrats: Alabama Politics, 1942–1950 (Tuscaloosa: University of Alabama Press, 1974), 16; Joseph B. Treaster, "James E. Folsom, Colorful Politician and Twice Governor of Alabama, Is Dead at 79," New York Times, November 22, 1987, http://www.nytimes.com/1987/11/22/obituaries/james-e-folsom-colorful-politician-and-twice-governor-of-alabama-is-dead-at-79.html.

[89] Charles L. Fontenay, Estes Kefauver: A Biography (Knoxville: University of Tennessee Press, 1980), 61.

[90] Schulman, Cotton Belt to Sunbelt, 35; Badger, "Whatever Happened." For more on the political effects of the TVA, see Devin Caughey and Sara Chatfield, "Creating a Constituency for New Deal Liberalism: The Policy Feedback Effects of the Tennessee Valley Authority" (Paper presented at the APSA Annual Meeting, Philadelphia, September 1, 2016).

Finally, even the localistic political alignments highlighted by Key were not devoid of ideological meaning. As Key himself notes, several states, including South Carolina, Mississippi, and Alabama, exhibited a persistent sectional cleavage between the more populist upcountry and relatively conservative plantation belt.[91] Knowledge of such geographic affiliations was easily obtained by voters and often provided a useful cue regarding candidates' ideological leanings. Even in states Key categorizes as lacking both factions and sectional cleavages, such as "atomized" Florida, consistent geographic patterns emerged when candidates took divergent issues positions along liberal–conservative lines.[92] Most liberal candidates in Alabama, for example, hailed from TVA-dependent, largely white north Alabama, whereas conservatives tended to come from Birmingham, Mobile, or the plantation belt. Significantly, candidates who broke this pattern, such as the Montgomery-born progressive Lister Hill, drew as much or more support from the liberal northern part of the state as he did from his "friends and neighbors" in the black belt. As one of Hill's advisors reported, "Anybody [sic] but a fool would have expected the [TVA-dependent] Eighth Congressional District to do other than to stand by Mr. Hill, the President, and the National Democratic Administration."[93]

Of course, many Southern primary campaigns, even if issue-based, did not feature substantial ideological divergence between the candidates. On numerous issues, even those that were controversial nationally, there was really only one position a mainstream candidate could take in a Southern Democratic primary. Almost all racial issues fell in this category, but so did a number of other issues, often on a more local basis. John Sparkman, for example, recalled that in his first House race both he and his opponent had been "strong for TVA," and both had tried to paint the other as the candidate of private utility companies.[94] In the 8th District, where the TVA's benefits were highly salient, there was really no

[91] Key, *Southern Politics*, 302; see also Nixon, "Politics of the Hills."
[92] Herbert J. Doherty Jr., "Liberal and Conservative Voting Patterns in Florida," *Journal of Politics* 14, no. 3 (1952): 403–417.
[93] Roy Nolen, "Confidential Memoranda for Senator Lister Hill," January 15, 1938, Box 267, Folder 1, Lister Hill Senatorial Collection, W. S. Hoole Library, University of Alabama, 4. In his initial election to the Senate in 1938, then-representative Hill drew strongest support (70.8%) from his own 2nd District, centered in Montgomery, and from North Alabama's 8th District (62.7%).
[94] Marguerite Johnston, "Alabama's Congr. John Sparkman Is One of Three Top Men in House," *Birmingham News Age-Herald*, March 10, 1946, Sparkman parried the accusation that he was tied to power companies by revealing that his opponent's brother had gone to college on a power company scholarship.

other position to take. Such "me-tooism" was probably more common in Southern primaries than it was in two-party settings, where the constraints of party reputations and the centrifugal pull of partisan core constituencies limited candidates' ability to converge in general elections. Nevertheless, closely contested liberal–conservative showdowns were a frequent and endemic occurrence in Southern primaries, particularly in the wake of the New Deal.

Examples in Senate primaries are particularly easy to identify. In 1934, for instance, Hubert Stephens, "a colorless two-term conservative" from Mississippi, was defeated for renomination by the "redneck liberal" Theodore Bilbo.[95] In 1936, North Carolina's Josiah Bailey, also an early opponent of Roosevelt's policies, fended off a stiff challenge from Richard Fountain, an "ardent New Dealer."[96] In the same year, Richard Russell of Georgia, at that point a Roosevelt loyalist, survived a bitter anti–New Deal challenge from Governor Eugene Talmadge, who "promised to uphold the constitution, oppose the income tax, reduce the budget, take the government out of business, and refuse dictation from boards and bureaus that had Negro members."[97] The elections of 1938, the year of FDR's "purge," brought a spate of pro- versus anti–New Deal Senate primaries in Alabama, Arkansas, Florida, Georgia, Kentucky, and South Carolina.[98]

Ideological showdowns continued in the 1940s. In 1940, Bilbo faced off against a business-oriented former governor, who attacked the incumbent for his support of poll tax repeal while Bilbo "praised the New Deal and pointed to his consistent support for Roosevelt's policies."[99] In 1941, the very conservative Gov. Lee O'Daniel of Texas squeaked into the Senate over the much more liberal Rep. Lyndon Johnson. In 1942, Bilbo's fellow Mississippi liberal Wall Doxey was unseated by the arch-conservative James Eastland, while in South Carolina the pro–New Deal Burnet Maybank barely survived a challenge from the race-baiting Eugene Blease.[100] In 1944, the "Jim Crow New Dealer" Olin Johnston of South Carolina finally succeeded in knocking off the reactionary

[95] Swain, "Hubert D. Stephens," 261; Morgan, *Redneck Liberal*.
[96] Ronald E. Marcello, "The Politics of Relief: The North Carolina WPA and the Tar Heel Elections of 1936," *North Carolina Historical Review* 68, no. 1 (1991): 27.
[97] Tindall, *Emergence of the New South*, 617; Howard N. Mead, "Russell vs. Talmadge: Southern Politics and the New Deal," *Georgia Historical Quarterly* 65, no. 1 (1981): 28–45.
[98] Susan Dunn, *Roosevelt's Purge: How FDR Fought to Change the Democratic Party* (New York: Cambridge University Press, 2010).
[99] Morgan, *Redneck Liberal*, 228.
[100] Ibid., 212.

E. D. Smith, whom he had failed to beat in 1938.[101] That same year, Alabama's Lister Hill fended off a strong challenge from State Senator James Simpson, a forthright critic of the New Deal. In 1947, Hill was joined in the Senate by his fellow "administration stalwart" Rep. John Sparkman, who had dispatched both Simpson and another conservative, Rep. Frank Boykin.[102] In 1948 LBJ fought a close Senate race against another conservative governor, Coke Stevenson, this time eking out a victory.[103] In 1950, now-senator Olin Johnston survived his own challenge from Strom Thurmond, who attacked his support for federal aid to education, foreign aid, and labor unions.[104] Johnston's liberal colleagues Claude Pepper (D-FL) and Frank Graham (D-NC) were not so lucky, and in that same year both were unseated in primary campaigns that mixed red-baiting and race-baiting.[105]

As these Senate primaries (to which many examples from the House could be added) illustrate, ideologically divergent competition between candidates was quite common in Southern congressional primaries. Moreover, voters possessed a number of direct and indirect sources of information from which to infer candidates' issue positions: factional affiliation, policy platforms, interest group endorsements, relations with the national party, association with New Deal programs, and even geographic roots. Though by no means foolproof, these cues helped voters make meaningful policy-based choices between candidates, even in the absence of party labels. Indirect evidence that voters absorbed this information is provided by the fact that voters appear to have been able to coordinate strategically on the optimal number of candidates at the county level.[106] Taken together, this evidence suggests that Southern primaries provided a functioning mechanism by which voters could select representative candidates into office. But prospective selection is but one mechanism by which representation can be induced. I now turn to a second mechanism: the retrospective sanctioning of out-of-step incumbents.

---

[101] Roger P. Leemhuis, "Olin Johnston Runs for the Senate," *Proceedings of the South Carolina Historical Association*, 1986, 57–58, 60.

[102] Rogers et al., *Alabama*, 531; Quote from United Press, "Multi-Billion Job Measure Ready Today," *Washington Post*, January 10, 1949, 1.

[103] Robert A. Caro, *Means of Ascent* (New York: Vintage Books, 1990), 303–313.

[104] Leemhuis, "Olin Johnston."

[105] Frederickson, *The Dixiecrat Revolt and the End of the Solid South*, 9; Jonathan W. Bell, "Conceptualising Southern Liberalism: Ideology and the Pepper–Smathers 1950 Primary in Florida," *Journal of American Studies* 37, no. 1 (2003): 17–45.

[106] Jeffrey D. Grynaviski, "The Impact of Electoral Rules on Factional Competition in the Democratic South, 1919–48," *Party Politics* 10, no. 5 (2004): 499–519.

5.5 ACCOUNTABILITY

Elections allow voters not only to select representative candidates ex ante, but also to sanction incumbents ex post. Retrospective sanctioning can induce responsiveness even if voters have no information at all about challengers, because in order to stay in office incumbents must at least be as representative as a randomly chosen challenger would be.[107] Sanctioning induces responsiveness in two ways: by screening out unrepresentative types of officeholders and by incentivizing incumbents to respond preemptively to voters' preferences—what Stimson, MacKuen, and Erikson refer to as *turnover* and *anticipation*.[108] For sanctioning to be effective, voters must be able to identify out-of-step incumbents and hold them electorally accountable. While there is evidence of such accountability in contemporary congressional elections,[109] many scholars assume that "[b]ecause of the South's one-party politics, . . . Southern Democrats, once elected, were nearly assured of reelection."[110] Having already shown that primary elections subjected Southern MCs to electoral competition and the credible threat of defeat, I now present evidence that voters specifically recognized and punished incumbents who took positions out of step with their constituencies.

One barrier to demonstrating the effectiveness of accountability is that strategic politicians should rarely if ever be far out of step with their constituents. This is most obvious on the issue of civil rights for blacks, to which Southern whites were overwhelming opposed and on which Southern MCs exhibited almost no variation.[111] On such issues, note Miller and Stokes, "most of the time the electorate's sanctions are potential rather than actual," but are swiftly realized on the rare occasions when representatives do step out of line.[112] Miller and Stokes cite the example of Arkansas's Brooks Hays, who in 1958 was defeated for renomination by a militantly segregationist write-in candidate after revealing himself to be a racial moderate. A similar fate befell North Carolina representative Charles Deane, who barely faced opposition in

---

[107] John Duggan, "Repeated Elections with Asymmetric Information," *Economics & Politics* 12, no. 2 (2000): 109–135.

[108] Stimson, MacKuen, and Erikson, "Dynamic Representation."

[109] Brandice Canes-Wrone, David W. Brady, and John F. Cogan, "Out of Step, Out of Office: Electoral Accountability and House Members' Voting," *American Political Science Review* 96, no. 1 (2002): 127–140.

[110] Lieberman, *Shifting the Color Line*, 36.

[111] But see Werner, "Congressmen of the Silent South."

[112] Warren E. Miller and Donald E. Stokes, "Constituency Influence in Congress," *American Political Science Review* 57, no. 1 (1963): 55.

1952 and 1954 but was soundly defeated in 1956 after refusing to sign the Southern Manifesto pledging resistance to *Brown v. Board*.[113]

Southern voters' preferences on economic issues were rarely as one-sided as on racial ones, but incumbents could be sanctioned for their economic positions as well. In some cases, the mobilization of new constituencies led to the defeat of unresponsive incumbents. In 1937, for example, the liberal representative Claude Pepper helped engineer the abolition of Florida's poll tax, and he rode the ensuring expansion of the electorate into the Senate the following year. Similarly, newly organized workers mobilized by their unions helped to unseat antilabor incumbents like Alabama representative Joseph Starnes in 1944 and Georgia representative Malcom Tarver in 1946.[114] And after the war, returning veterans undermined political machines such as that of Memphis's E. H. Crump, whose favored candidate in Tennessee's 1948 Senate race was defeated by the liberal reformer Estes Kefauver.[115]

More common than such sudden changes in the composition of the electorate were incumbents who found themselves out of step because of changes in the mood of the existing electorate. "In a period of conservatism," noted one contemporary observer, the two-party non-South responds by replacing liberal Democrats with Republicans, but "the one-party South responds by electing conservative Democrats."[116] In the early to mid-1930s, when Roosevelt's popularity was at its height, electoral punishment fell mostly on Southern Democrats who opposed the New Deal. In the 1934 primaries in Mississippi, for example, not only was Senator Stephens unseated by Bilbo, but two of the state's representatives "also lost to more radical challengers."[117] In 1936, outspoken Roosevelt critic Thomas Gore of Oklahoma, despite two decades of service as his state's senator, did not even finish among the top three candidates in the Democratic primary and was replaced by sound New Dealer Joshua Lee.[118] The *New York Times* described these liberal

---

[113] Badger, "Southerners Who Refused to Sign the Southern Manifesto," 528–530.

[114] Joseph Rosenfarb, "Labor's Role in the Election," *Public Opinion Quarterly* 8, no. 3 (1944): 376; Brattain, "Making Friends and Enemies."

[115] James C. Cobb, *The South and America since World War II* (New York: Oxford University Press, 2010), 67. In general, World War II veterans proved to be a destabilizing force in Southern politics, but as often in a conservative direction as in a liberal one; Jennifer E. Brooks, "Winning the Peace: Georgia Veterans and the Struggle to Define the Political Legacy of World War II," *Journal of Southern History* 66, no. 3 (2000): 563–604.

[116] Carleton, "The Southern Politician," 226.

[117] Morgan, *Redneck Liberal*; Swain, "Hubert D. Stephens," 280.

[118] Royden J. Dangerfield and Richard H. Flynn, "Voter Motivation in the 1936 Oklahoma Democratic Primary," *Southwestern Social Science Quarterly* 17, no. 2 (1936): 97–105; Patterson, *Congressional Conservatism*, 22–24.

insurgents as "riding the crest of a popular uprising in the South against Democrats of the type of Senator Stephens, who, prior to the birth of the New Deal, was regarded as a liberal but is [now] looked upon as a conservative if not a reactionary."[119] On the other hand, formidable conservative challenges, such as popular Georgia governor Eugene Talmadge's race-baiting 1936 bid for the Senate seat of New Deal supporter Richard Russell, failed in the face of the popularity of Roosevelt and his program.[120] Even in Virginia, where the conservative Byrd Organization exerted tighter political control than existed in any other state, the Organization's hostility toward the New Deal "provided independent Democrats with a potent issue." Seizing the moment, newspaper publisher Norman Hamilton, "campaign[ing] as an unqualified New Dealer and enemy of the machine," unseated Rep. Colgate Darden, "an organization stalwart who had bolted the Roosevelt administration on numerous votes."[121]

Later, as Southern opinion swung against the New Deal, it was more often liberal incumbents who found themselves out of step. The 1938 midterms, when Republicans began their comeback in national politics, also brought reversals for liberal Southern Democrats. In Virginia, Colgate Darden recaptured his House seat from Norman Hamilton.[122] In Texas, Maury Maverick, outspoken leader of the "liberal bloc" in the House, and William McFarlane—two of the few Southern representatives to back the FLSA—were turned out as well.[123] The frequency of liberal defeats increased over the next decade. In addition to being the year of Luther Patrick's first defeat, 1942 saw the unseating of such congressional liberals as Mississippi senator Wall Doxey and Louisiana representatives Newt Mills and Jared Sanders.[124] Another Republican year, 1950, was also a bad one for Southern liberals. The only two Southern senators unseated that year were Florida's Claude Pepper, who was so far left that

---

[119] Quoted by Robert J. Bailey, "Theodore G. Bilbo and the Senatorial Election of 1934," *Southern Quarterly* 10 (October 1971): 102.

[120] Mead, "Russell vs. Talmadge."

[121] Koeniger, "New Deal," 877–878.

[122] Koeniger, "New Deal," 887.

[123] Frantz, "Opening a Curtain," 11; Stuart L. Weiss, "Maury Maverick and the Liberal Bloc," *Journal of American History* 57, no. 4 (1971): 880–895.

[124] Sanders, who represented Baton Rouge 1933–37 and 1941–43, was associated with Louisiana's anti-Long faction and is generally considered to have been a conservative. Sanders's voting record in the 77th Congress, however, was among the most liberal of those of Southern Democrats and was much more so than that of his successor James Morrison, though the latter did become markedly more liberal over the twelve terms he served in Congress.

even President Truman supported his opponent, and fellow liberal Frank Graham of North Carolina.[125]

The story of South Carolina representative Hugo Sims, another liberal defeated in 1950, helps to illustrate how accountability can induce responsiveness, even in the absence of explicitly issue-based campaigns. In 1948 Sims, a young lawyer, veteran, and newspaper editor, challenged John J. Riley, a two-term representative from South Carolina's 2nd District. Riley was a business-friendly conservative who had worked closely with Republicans,[126] but Sims largely avoided challenging Riley on policy grounds, aside from claiming to represent "the laboring man." In fact, when his father asked him what his issues were, Sims replied, "No issues. The man who gets elected will be the one who knows and is liked by the most people."[127] Sims's energetic campaign surprised Riley,[128] who had never faced primary opposition, and Sims prevailed in the first primary 32,059 to 26,811. Notwithstanding his "issueless" campaign, Sims did receive strong support from the state CIO as well as from the overwhelmingly nonunion industrial workforce in his rural district.[129]

---

[125] For an indication of how out of step Pepper was, consider the fact that his support for national health insurance was shared by less than a quarter of Floridians; Joe Abram, "Florida Political Survey and Poll," April 24, 1950, Box 5, Folder 29 (Florida: 1950, Primary), COPE Collection, Jacksonville, FL.

[126] Liberal columnist Drew Pearson described Riley, who had a background in real estate, as a congressman "who came to Washington with his votes already lined up for the real-estate lobby" and who "voted for the real-estate cabal and against the veterans every time"; Drew Pearson, "The Daily Washington Merry-Go-Round," *Southeast Missourian* (Cape Girardeau, MO), September 25, 1948, 4.

[127] George McMillan, "Three Southern Portraits: Liberal Congressman," *The Reporter*, March 28, 1950, 14. Like all South Carolina House members except one (Rep. Joseph Bryson), Sims also affirmed his support for South Carolina governor Strom Thurmond's "States Rights" presidential bid in 1948; "Bryson Says Nobody Questioning Him on How He Stands on Political Bolt," *Florence Morning News* (Florence, SC), October 17, 1948, 12–A.

[128] "It was with . . . stealth and surprise that Sims won his race for Congress"; Frank van den Linden, "'Baby' Of Next Congress, Ex-Paratrooper, Plans to Be Real Working Representative," *Olean Times Herald* (Olean, NY), October 14, 1948, 19.

[129] According to McMillan, Sims received 7,126 votes to Riley's 2,340 in Horse Creek Valley, the main industrial area of the 2nd District, where "not one of the approximately ten thousand men and women . . . is, as far as is known, a member of a union"; McMillan, "Liberal Congressman," 15. The CIO's records indicate that it had about 4,500 members, mostly textile workers, in the district, whose total adult population was around 230,000; "South Carolina," Box 21, Folder 21 (South Carolina, 1948–1950), COPE Collection. Before the primary, CIO organizer Franz Daniel reported, "Our Columbia organizations are going all-out for Sims." Afterwards, he claimed that "Sims defeated John Riley because of our labor votes," and also that the small black vote in Columbia had gone to Riley because black leaders "selected the people they thought would win"; Franz E. Daniel to Al Barkan, July 8, 1948, Box 21, Folder 21 (South Carolina, 1948–1950), COPE Collection;

Even Sims's labor supporters were surprised, if pleasantly so, by the congressman's performance in office, when he showed his true ideological colors. Sims became a key pro-administration vote on the House Education and Labor Committee, whence he provided crucial Southern support for a minimum wage increase, Taft–Hartley repeal, federal aid to education, and other elements of Truman's agenda.[130] Sims also voted to weaken the obstructionist powers of the House Rules Committee, explaining to his constituents that he did so "because the future of the South and South Carolina depends on the passage of many pieces of liberal legislation."[131] "I'm trying," Sims declared, "to work out a liberal program a Southerner can run on and get elected." If this was his goal, Sims did not achieve it. Sims's support for the Fair Deal met a chilly reception from many of his constituents. "We call it the Raw Deal down here," said one local farmer.[132] Upon returning to his district to campaign for reelection, Sims found that "his voting record ha[d] disturbed many among even those constituents who were most deeply buried in reverie."[133] These concerns came home to roost in the 1950 primary, when Sims faced a rematch with Riley and lost 60% to 40% in the run-off.

As Sims's story makes clear, challengers who obfuscated their policy positions in their initial campaign found it much more difficult to do so as incumbents. Once in office, Southern MCs were forced to take public positions on almost every issue that made it to a floor vote in Congress. These positions then provided fodder for challengers, who brought them to the attention of voters. Such attacks in turn forced incumbent MCs to explain and justify these positions to voters—the sort of "explanation of Washington activity" Richard Fenno identifies as central to MCs' relationships with their constituencies.[134] This is not to say that Southern MCs spent all or even most of their time talking about policy rather than, say, connecting with constituents on a more personal, nonpolitical level.[135] But the fact that they had to do so to at least some degree—and especially so if they voted out of line with their constituents—was

Franz E. Daniel to Al Barkan, August 13, 1948, Box 21, Folder 21 (South Carolina, 1948–1950), COPE Collection.

[130] Thomas Stokes, "Government and Politics," *Reno Evening Gazette*, March 19, 1949, 4; McMillan, "Liberal Congressman," 14; Pomper, "Labor and Congress," 334.

[131] McMillan, "Liberal Congressman," 14.

[132] "At Home on Wheels," *Time*, November 14, 1949, no. 20, 27.

[133] McMillan, "Liberal Congressman," 14–15.

[134] Richard F. Fenno Jr., "U.S. House Members in Their Constituencies: An Exploration," *American Political Science Review* 71, no. 3 (1977): 883–917.

[135] A "person-intensive" rather than policy-centered strategy was probably the typical representational style of Southern MCs in this period; see Richard F. Fenno Jr., *Congress at the Grassroots: Representational Change in the South, 1970–1998* (Chapel Hill: University of North Carolina Press, 2000), 21–32.

crucial to the Southern selectorate's capacity to hold incumbent MCs accountable.

5.6 RESPONSIVENESS

Electoral sanctions, in addition to holding unrepresentative officials accountable after the fact, also incentivize incumbents to anticipate the voters' judgment and respond accordingly. The anticipation of electoral sanction, while a dominant feature of congressional behavior,[136] does not necessarily lead to responsiveness to the median voter in a two-party setting if MCs fear the judgment of primary voters instead.[137] Indeed, the centrifugal pull of the partisan subconstituencies may explain why most MCs do not "adapt to changing constituent preferences" but rather "die with their ideological boots on."[138] In this respect, the fact that in the one-party South the party *was* the electorate may have enhanced Southern MCs' freedom to respond to the changing mood of the median voter. Consistent with this supposition, the ideal-point model described in Chapter 4 estimates that the between-congress ideological changes of continuing MCs tended to be substantially larger among Southern Democrats than among other members.

In any case, there is abundant evidence Southern MCs were at least as attentive to constituency opinion as their non-Southern counterparts. Before the wide availability of public opinion polls, politicians derived assessments of constituents' preferences from a variety of indirect measures, including election results, the reports of political allies, letters from constituents, and interactions with citizens while out on the hustings.[139] Elections are perhaps the crudest but most vivid source of information on voters' preferences. "Nothing is more important in Capitol Hill politics," writes David Mayhew, "than the shared conviction that election returns have proven a point."[140] Even a close electoral shave can do the trick. One union-connected Mobile politico, reflecting on his

---

[136] Arnold, *The Logic of Congressional Action.*

[137] For example, Joshua D. Clinton, "Representation in Congress: Constituents and Roll Calls in the 106th House," *Journal of Politics* 68, no. 2 (2006): 397–409.

[138] Poole and Rosenthal, *Ideology & Congress,* 28.

[139] John G. Geer, *From Tea Leaves to Opinion Polls* (New York: Columbia University Press, 1996), 51. Geer contends that these traditional methods were highly imperfect and that the advent of polling enhanced politicians' information about their constituents' views. David Karol disagrees, arguing that the rise of polling did not in fact improve representation; see David Karol, "Has Polling Enhanced Representation? Unearthing Evidence from the Literary Digest Issue Polls," *Studies in American Political Development* 21 (Spring 2007): 16–29.

[140] Mayhew, *Electoral Connection,* 71.

conservative representative's narrow renomination in 1954, concluded that labor's preferred candidate "gave him a good scare and I believe that in the next two years Frank Boykin will not be so anti-Labor as he has been in the past."[141]

Conservatives faced many such scares in the early to mid-1930s, for in these years "to oppose Roosevelt was to court political suicide."[142] Bilbo's 1934 primary victory over Stephens was an indication of the sort of challenge on the left that kept otherwise wary Southerners loyal to FDR in the mid-1930s.[143] Reacting to such defeats, Bilbo's fellow Mississippian Pat Harrison and other personally conservative Southerners delayed their break with the New Deal until they had been safely reelected in 1936.[144] As late as the spring of 1938, the primary victories of FLSA supporters Hill and Pepper helped convince MCs of the popularity of wages-and-hours legislation (and of Roosevelt generally), leading to a successful petition to discharge the bill from the House Rules Committee.[145] Even in machine-dominated Virginia, incumbents felt constrained to swim with the liberal tide. "There is strong sentiment for Roosevelt . . . in nearly all . . . sections of the state," one Byrd lieutenant warned in 1935. "Unless the situation is treated in the proper way, the future success of the state organization will be placed in jeopardy." Sensing the shift, Rep. John Flanagan severed ties with the Byrd Organization and declared himself a New Dealer, while Sen. Byrd himself, fearing electoral defeat for the Organization, acquiesced to the nomination of a pro–New Deal governor in 1936.[146]

When, in the late 1930s, the electoral tides began to turn against Southern liberals, many responded by trimming their ideological sails. "Whereas constituency pressures before 1936 demanded support for the New Deal," notes Anthony Badger, "after 1936 that pressure counseled caution."[147] Lyndon Johnson, an erstwhile New Dealer who as a young man worked on Maury Maverick's initial campaign for Congress,[148] interpreted his fellow Texan's 1938 defeat as a warning to tack to the right. "I can go so far in Texas . . . my people won't take it," Johnson explained

---

[141] Layton Overstreet to Joseph Curran, May 5, 1954, Box 1, Folder 1 (Alabama, 1950–54), COPE Collection.

[142] Tindall, *Emergence of the New South*, 618.

[143] Morgan, *Redneck Liberal*, 64.

[144] Patterson, "Conservative Coalition Forms," 764.

[145] Kirke L. Simpson, "Capital Watching Primary in Florida as Political Straw," *Atlanta Constitution*, May 1, 1938, Douglas and Hackman, "Fair Labor Standards Act," 511–512.

[146] Koeniger, "New Deal," 878–879; James R. Sweeney, "'Sheep without a Shepherd': The New Deal Faction in the Virginia Democratic Party," *Presidential Studies Quarterly* 29, no. 2 (1999): 438–458.

[147] Badger, "Whatever Happened," 59.

[148] Caro, *The Path to Power*, 276.

to a liberal ally. "Maury forgot that and he is not here.... There's nothing more useless than a dead liberal."[149] Many other Southern Democrats appear to have learned the same lesson. The typical Southern senator who remained in office between 1935 and 1947 became about a quarter standard deviation more conservative over these years; in the House, the typical rightward shift was more than half a standard deviation.[150]

Southern MCs also assessed public opinion by means more direct than interpreting election outcomes. Many relied on allied political operatives and newspaper editors to keep them apprised of sentiment back home. Senator Lister Hill, for example, depended heavily on Montgomery postmaster Roy Nolen for intelligence about political developments back in Alabama.[151] He also paid close attention to letters from his constituents. Whereas on a personal level Hill was a strong supporter of a greater federal role in health care, he was also sensitive to the communications he received from his constituents, most of which strongly opposed "socialized medicine." Only after his last election in 1962 did Hill feel free to embrace Medicare.[152] More reelection-minded incumbents could rarely afford to buck constituency sentiment in this way. In 1947, for example, New Orleans representative Hale Boggs voted against an early version of what later became the Taft–Hartley Act. After a surprisingly virulent reaction from his constituents, however, Boggs reversed his position and supported the bill on subsequent roll calls.[153]

Like MCs elsewhere, Southern senators and representatives also received valuable information from campaigns, both through the issues raised by challengers and through their interactions with constituents.[154] Campaigning in traditional Southern politics often took place through local elite intermediaries.[155] In the 1930s and 1940s, however, ambitious politicians increasingly found ways to bypass local elites, taking "their

---

[149] Rowe, "Interview by Joe B. Frantz," 15. It is interesting to note that a version of this quote forms the epigraph of the most influential article on electoral accountability in the House of Representatives: Canes-Wrone, Brady, and Cogan's "Out of Step, Out of Office."
[150] These comparisons are based on the ideal points described in Chapter 4, whose standard deviation in the typical congress was around 1. As was noted in that chapter, over-time comparisons such as these are best interpreted in relative terms, that is, as how much Southern MCs changed relative to other continuing members.
[151] Hamilton, *Lister Hill*, 78–79.
[152] Markley, "Senators Hill and Sparkman."
[153] Patrick J. Maney, "Hale Boggs, Organized Labor, and the Politics of Race in South Louisiana," in *Southern Labor in Transition, 1940–1995* (Knoxville: University of Tennessee Press, 1997), 232.
[154] On the role of challengers, see Tracy Sulkin, *Issue Politics in Congress* (New York: Cambridge University Press, 2005).
[155] On "Old South" homestyle, see Fenno, *Congress at the Grassroots*.

electoral case directly to the people."[156] Once in Congress, an incumbent would often organize constituent interactions "for his own education." Hugo Sims, for example, toured his district with a "mobile office" attached to a pickup truck, announcing over the loudspeaker, "Congressman Sims brings his office to you to report, to talk over your problems."[157]

Finally, some incumbents responded to shifts in public mood not by changing their votes, but by retiring from Congress. Often, these retirements occurred in response to near defeats. The biographer of conservative Georgia representative Bryant Castellow, for example, describes his 1936 decision to retire as follows:

> tired of public office, wary of facing a campaign against a serious contender he had defeated by only 2,000 votes two years before, apparently having lost whatever earlier enthusiasm his voting record suggests that he had for the New Deal, and unable to stop the march of the new order, Castellow declined to run for re-election.[158]

A decade later, the liberal Rep. John Folger of North Carolina made a similar choice. Having earned "the enmity of the district's business community" for his pro-labor votes, Folger barely survived a close race in 1946 in which his association with the CIO was the most salient issue. Taking his narrow victory as a sign of a rightward shift in his district, Folger declined to run for reelection in 1948 and was replaced by his conservative challenger from two years prior.[159] It is difficult to say how many such preemptive retirements occurred in this period, but it is clear that they served as yet another mechanism by which the threat of electoral punishment induced responsiveness in congressional representation.

5.7 CONCLUSION

This chapter has argued for the existence of a selectoral connection between Southern MCs and the white potential electorate. I presented evidence that the white primary, in addition to being a crucial prop of one-party rule, also provided a forum for political competition within the Democratic Party. The selectorate eligible to participate in these primaries

[156] On bypassing local elites, see the initial House campaigns of Lyndon Johnson, Lindley Beckworth, William Fulbright, and Big Jim Folsom; Badger, "Whatever Happened," 64–66; Barnard, *Dixiecrats and Democrats*, 20.
[157] Julien D. Martin, "Topics of the Week: Sims to Have Mobile Office," *Aiken Standard and Review* (Aiken, SC), February 16, 1949, 4; *Time*, "At Home on Wheels."
[158] Thomas H. Coode, "Bryant Thomas Castellow of Georgia," *Georgia Advocate* 8, no. Fall (1971): 19.
[159] Christian, "Folger-Chatham," 26, 40, 53.

was large and diverse enough to contain class and thus ideological differences. Electoral competition was common and vigorous enough to provide a genuine threat of opposition, and it was issue-based enough to offer voters meaningful ideological choice on economic issues. Voters were able to hold incumbents accountable for their behavior in Congress, and the threat of electoral defeat caused incumbents to respond anticipatorily to constituency opinion. In short, primaries made MCs agents not just of a narrow elite, but of a broad swath of the white population. This chapter has thus established the plausibility of a selectoral connection in the one-party South. But it has not directly assessed the character of representation in the one-party South, nor compared it with representation in the two-party North. It is to these issues that I now turn.

CHAPTER 6

Representation in the One-Party South

If I represented the city of Birmingham, I'd probably vote that way too.[1]

—*Representative Carter Manasco of Alabama, referring to Representative Luther Patrick (1946)*

This measure was drafted by the committee, but it was written in the hearts and minds of the American people. Read the polls of the past year, taken of public opinion. Talk to the man on the street, in the filling station, on the farm. This is the composite voice of the American people.[2]

—*Representative O. C. Fisher of Texas, referring to the Taft–Hartley Act (1947)*

Though the South is often assumed to be conservative on matters of domestic economic policy, its appearance of conservatism results from imperfect representation of its views rather than from a peculiar mass opinion.... In fact, southern opinion on these matters ... closely resembles that of the rest of the country.... How can the similarity in opinions between the South and the rest of the country be reconciled with the conservative outlook of many southern Senators and Representatives?[3]

—*V. O. Key (1961)*

---

[1] Stephen Kemp Bailey, *Congress Makes a Law: The Story behind the Employment Act of 1946* (New York: Columbia University Press, 1950), 202.
[2] National Labor Relations Board, *Legislative History of the Labor Management Relations Act, 1947*, Reprint of the 1959 edition, Vol. I (Washington, DC: U.S. Government Printing Office, 1985), 676.
[3] Key, *Public Opinion and American Democracy*, 102–105.

EACH PRECEDING CHAPTER has brought a different aspect of Southern politics into focus. The analysis of public opinion in Chapter 3 showed that between the mid-1930s and mid-1940s, the Southern white public turned dramatically—though incompletely—against New Deal liberalism, while still remaining internally diverse on questions of economic policymaking. Chapter 4 uncovered similar patterns in Congress, where Southern Democrats collectively shifted from core supporters of the New Deal to economic centrists holding the balance of power between non-Southern Democrats and Republicans. Chapter 5 documented the ways that Democratic primaries induced a selectoral connection between Southern MCs and their white constituents, creating mechanisms of electoral accountability and incentivizing incumbents to cater to nonelite whites. Overall, the evidence presented thus far suggests a political system that was responsive not to a narrow elite only, but to a broad swath of the white public. This chapter subjects this suggestive impression to more direct and rigorous examination through an analysis of the empirical relationship between mass and elite politics, both within and outside the South. In marked contrast to the conventional wisdom, it not only shows that Southern MCs were responsive to their white constituents, but also finds little indication that congressional responsiveness was weaker in the one-party South than in the two-party North, though the mechanisms and character of responsiveness did differ between regions.

6.1 RUPTURED LINKAGES AND SUBNATIONAL EMBEDDEDNESS

Before proceeding, it bears revisiting V. O. Key's seminal argument against one-party politics, as laid out most fully in chapter 14 of his *Southern Politics*. In an important contrast to the book's overall theme of "state and nation," Key's chapter 14 focuses exclusively on the consequences of the one-party system for "the running of state governments."[4] It stresses that, notwithstanding the varieties of factionalism across Southern states and the frequent vigor of intraparty conflict, factional competition was no substitute for two-party politics. Southern factions, Key argues, were kaleidoscopic, personalistic, and transient, confusing the electorate and inhibiting issue-based political conflict—especially "genuine" or "rational" conflict along class rather than racial lines.[5] Even the simple division between "ins" and "outs" in state government, Key

---

[4] Key, *Southern Politics*, 298.
[5] See Harold W. Stanley, "Reflections on Reading V. O. Key Jr.'s *Southern Politics*," in *Unlocking V. O. Key, Jr.: Southern Politics for the Twenty-First Century* (Fayetteville: University of Arkansas Press, 2011), 105–125.

notes, was frequently impossible to discern. As a result, state politics in the South revolved not around policy and performance, but rather around personalities, demagoguery, localism, and favoritism.

According to Key and those who have extended his arguments to other contexts, "no-party" politics has two main consequences for the character of representation. The first is to attenuate policy responsiveness to voters' preferences. Nonpartisan politics, in the words of one prominent scholar of state and local government, "ruptures" the representational linkages between citizens and politicians and thus "diminishes the connection between constituency preferences and [the] policy behaviors" of government officials.[6] Second, this lack of responsiveness is not neutral in its distributional consequences. Rather, by raising the barriers to concerted government action, it benefits those advantaged by the policy status quo. "Over the long run," Key claims, "the have-nots lose in a disorganized politics."[7] Thus, in his view, a second representational consequence of nonpartisan politics is a conservative bias toward the economic interests of upper-income citizens.[8] These putative effects of nonpartisan elections, it should be emphasized, are conceptually distinct from (though in practice linked with) the effects of disenfranchisement and other limitations on the scope of political participation. That is, Key's argument pertains to representation *of the selectorate*, which in the one-party South included many poor whites but almost no African Americans.

In short, Key's argument is that the South's one-party system inhibited responsiveness to the white public and biased politics in an economically conservative direction. Lacking systematic measures of mass preferences, Key was forced to rely mainly on qualitative and circumstantial evidence to support these conjectures. The new data and measures described in Chapter 3, however, offer the prospect of evaluating these hypotheses more explicitly. Specifically, we can estimate the relationship between the conservatism of the state selectorates and the conservatism of political outcomes and compare this relationship across regions. If Key is correct, then we should find political outcomes outside the one-party South to be both more strongly related to mass preferences and more liberal on average than political outcomes in the South.

---

[6] Wright, "Charles Adrian," 15.

[7] Key, *Southern Politics*, 307. Interestingly, Key appears to have abandoned this claim in his later work; see David R. Mayhew, "Why Did V. O. Key Draw Back from His 'Have-Nots' Claim?," in *Parties and Policies: How the American Government Works* (New Haven, CT: Yale University Press, 2008), 73–93.

[8] See also Schattschneider's claim that "one-party politics tends strongly to vest political power in the hands of people who already have economic power"; E. E. Schattschneider, *The Semi-Sovereign People* (New York: Hold, Rinehart, Winston, 1960), 80.

Following Key, I begin by examining state politics. To operationalize the outputs of the state representational process, I rely on a summary measure of the conservatism of state economic policies, including tax rates, spending on social programs, and labor regulations.[9] I average the estimates for each state within congressional terms, yielding a biennial measure of state economic policy conservatism between 1936 and 1952. Figure 6.1a plots the relationship between these biennial estimates and analogously averaged estimates of the conservatism of state selectorates, distinguishing between Southern and non-Southern states. As this figure shows, the relationship between the economic conservatism of state selectorates (x-axis) and state policies (y-axis) is remarkably consistent with Key's hypotheses.[10] In the non-South, the conservatism of state economic policies is strongly correlated with the conservatism of the state selectorate (defined as all adults). Liberal states like New York tended to have relatively liberal economic policies, whereas conservative states like South Dakota had relatively conservative ones. This is what we should expect in a functioning democracy that is responsive to citizens' preferences.

By contrast, the opinion–policy relationship in Southern states is almost completely flat, suggesting that state policies in the region were entirely unresponsive to the preferences of the selectorate (defined as all white adults). Moreover, economic policies in Southern states were also markedly more conservative than in comparably conservative non-Southern states. Even in the late 1930s, when there was still substantial mass-level ideological overlap between regions, the economic policies of non-Southern states with relatively moderate state publics, such as Ohio or Colorado, tended to be one or two standard deviations more liberal than those of Southern states with similarly moderate selectorates, such as Arkansas or Virginia. If we, along with Key, presume that conservative economic policies like low tax rates, meager spending, and limited economic regulation generally serve the interests of the upper classes, then Southern state policies were indeed biased toward "the haves" relative to comparable non-Southern states.

In sum, this simple comparison of state policy representation in the South and non-South offers striking corroboration for Key's argument

---

[9] This measure is a domain-specific analog to that created by Devin Caughey and Christopher Warshaw, "The Dynamics of State Policy Liberalism, 1936–2014," *American Journal of Political Science* 60, no. 4 (2016): 899–913. The difference is that instead of using data on all state policies, it uses data on economic policies only. See also Devin Caughey and Christopher Warshaw, "Policy Preferences and Policy Change: Dynamic Responsiveness in the American States, 1936–2014," *American Political Science Review*, 2017, doi:10.1017/S0003055417000533.
[10] The patterns are the same if we examine the cross-sectional relationship in each congressional term.

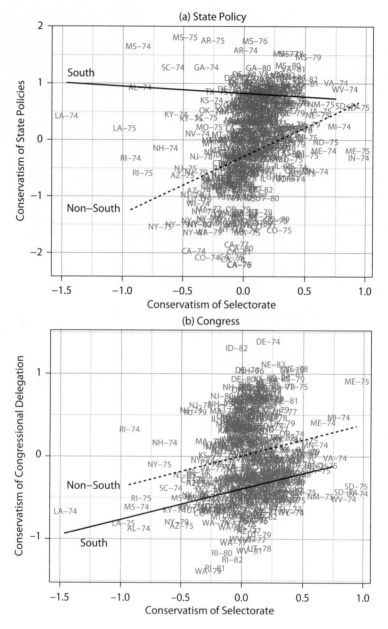

Figure 6.1. Representation on economic issues by region and political domain, 1936–52. Each observation is the within-state average across the two years in a given congressional term. The selectorate is defined as the whole public in non-Southern states and the white public in Southern states. *Source for poll data*: Roper Center for Public Opinion Research.

that the South's one-party system gave state politics a conservative bias and rendered it unresponsive to mass preferences, even in the white public. As such, this evidence seems to support the more general conventional wisdom that without partisan political competition, elections alone are insufficient to induce governments to represent the selectorate. But as earlier chapters in this book have already suggested, there are reasons to expect that this conventional wisdom does not hold for congressional politics in the one-party South.

As Key notes, a critical factor undermining state-level representation in the one-party South was the "isolation of state politics from national politics," which "removes the opportunity for the easy projection into the state arena of national issues and national political organization."[11] This isolation inhibited the emergence of organized and stable cleavages in the electorate, and it undermined voters' capacity to identify candidates' ideological commitments and hold them responsible for their policy choices. As I noted in Chapter 2, however, a distinguishing feature of congressional as opposed to state politics in the South is that the former were much more fully embedded in the national political system. In particular, Southern MCs were elected in intraparty primaries but, once in office, operated in a policy setting structured by interparty conflict. As I documented in Chapter 5, partisan conflict in turn filtered down into Southern congressional primaries, which, in Key's words, "tend[ed] to take on the tone of contests between Democrats and Republicans elsewhere."[12] Such partisan "spill over" from higher levels of government mitigated the informational problems endemic to nonpartisan elections and made Democratic congressional primaries more effective mechanisms of popular control than state and local primaries.[13]

Figure 6.1b provides preliminary evidence consistent with this argument. As in the top panel of the same figure, the horizontal axis of this plot indicates the economic conservatism of state selectorates in a given congressional term (e.g., white Louisianans in the 75th Congress). In this case, however, the vertical axis plots the economic conservatism not of state policies but of state congressional delegations, based on the average item response theory (IRT) scores of representatives and senators from the same state in a given term. The solid and dashed lines summarize the relationship in the South and non-South, respectively.

Figures 6.1a and 6.1b could hardly be more different. Unlike Southern state *policies*, Southern congressional *delegations* were clearly more conservative where and when the state selectorate was more conservative.

---

[11] Key, *Southern Politics*, 310–311.
[12] Key, *Politics, Parties & Pressure Groups*, 441–442.
[13] Compare Ware, *Citizens, Parties, and the State*, 61–62.

Indeed, the relationship between congressional and mass conservatism was just as strong in the South as in the non-South. Even more strikingly, the regression line for the South runs parallel to but below the line for the non-South, indicating that Southern MCs were substantially *less* conservative than non-Southerners who represented ideologically equivalent state publics. In short, regional patterns of representation in Congress are precisely contrary to the conventional wisdom: Southern congressional delegations appear to have been no less responsive, and substantially less conservative, than their non-Southern counterparts.

The remainder of this chapter provides a more systematic analysis of congressional representation in the South. I begin with Southern MCs' collective representation of the Southern white public, after which I compare cross-sectional and dynamic responsiveness between regions. I then examine Southern MCs' responsiveness to their white constituents' economic interests (as opposed to their preferences). Overall, I find the same pattern: Southern MCs were responsive to their selectorates, and were not obviously less responsive than their non-Southern counterparts.

6.2 COLLECTIVE REPRESENTATION

Chapter 3 showed that between the mid-1930s and mid-1940s, Southern whites turned against many aspects of the New Deal—first on policies related to labor and then on economic issues more generally. This shift to the right brought Southern whites' economic views more closely in line with their already-conservative racial ones, but it was not accompanied by major partisan shifts, as the vast majority of Southern whites continued to identify as Democrats. In Chapter 4, we saw that similar developments played out in Congress. Southern Democrats, having overwhelmingly supported the early New Deal, too shifted markedly to the right after the mid-1930s and began voting with Republicans on many issues.

The similarity between trends at the mass and elite levels can be seen clearly in Figure 6.2, which compares ideological trends in the white public, U.S. Senate, and U.S. House between 1937 and 1952. Within each venue, the figure distinguishes among Southern Democrats, non-Southern Democrats, and non-Southern Republicans, with mass-level partisanship defined in terms of retrospective presidential vote. Comparing these three partisan groups highlights Southern Democrats' changing position relative to the two parties in the non-South, whose conflict over economic issues defined the main ideological cleavage of this period.[14]

---

[14] I defined mass-level partisanship in terms of retrospective presidential vote because this is the most frequently available indicator. Although blacks could vote in the North, they

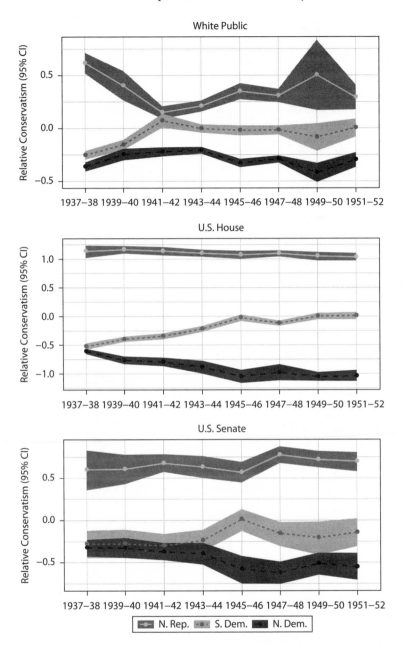

Figure 6.2. Trends in the economic conservatism of the white public (top), U.S. House (middle), and U.S. Senate (bottom), by region and party, 1937–52. The estimates have been demeaned within each congress so that the average of the three groups is zero. *Source for poll data*: Roper Center for Public Opinion Research.

Two major patterns emerge from the plots in Figure 6.2. The first is the partisan depolarization in the mass public—though not in Congress— that occurred in 1941–42. As Chapter 3 noted, this depolarization in the early years of World War II is evident also across class lines and in public approval of President Roosevelt.[15] By the end of the war, however, partisan polarization had returned to near its former levels.

More relevant to my argument is a second pattern: the similarities between Southern Democrats' trajectories across the three venues. The first complete congress for which survey data are available is the 75th (1937–38), which is also when the first glimmers of the conservative coalition appeared. By then, Southern white Roosevelt supporters, who constituted all but a tiny minority of Southern voters, were already slightly more conservative than their non-Southern counterparts. Still, this regional gap among Democrats paled compared to the massive gulf between the parties, and as Chapter 3 showed, white Southerners remained more liberal than the national average. Over the next few years, however, Southern white Democrats became markedly more conservative, and by 1943–44 they had stabilized in a position halfway between the average non-Southern Democrat and non-Southern Republican.

As is apparent from the figure, the trajectories of Southern Democrats in Congress were broadly similar to those in the mass public. In both the House and Senate, the average ideal point of Southern Democrats was almost identical to that of non-Southern Democrats. By the mid-1940s, the Southern caucus in each chamber had migrated to an ideological position midway between non-Southern Democrats and Republicans. In the House, Southern Democrats' transition was almost perfectly linear, and it took almost half a decade longer than the corresponding shift at the mass level. In the Senate, the Southern shift to the right was about as rapid as the Southern white public's but began about two congresses later.

Given that the ideal point estimates in the three venues are not estimated on the same scale, we must interpret them with caution. In particular, we cannot tell whether the congressional ideal points are collectively shifted to the right or left relative to citizens', or whether the

---

are excluded for consistency's sake from the mass-level estimates in the North as well as the South. Including Northern blacks in the analysis slightly increases the relative conservatism of Southern white Democrats. The same is true if Southern white Republicans, who in most years comprise fewer than 20% of self-reported voters in the poll samples, are included in the analysis.

[15] One possible contributing factor was the Republicans' 1940 nomination of Wendell Willkie, an erstwhile Democrat who was perhaps the most liberal Republican presidential nominee in history.

gap between Democrats and Republicans in Congress is larger or smaller than that at the mass level.[16] But under the assumption that non-Southern Democrats and Republicans in Congress were collectively in step with their citizen copartisans, the evolving positions of Southern MCs appear to have been roughly congruent with the economic preferences of white Democrats in the Southern public.

To the extent that Southern MCs were out of step, it was because their shift to the right, especially in the Senate, lagged behind that of their constituents. The lag in the congressional response is itself informative, because it suggests that Southern whites were not simply following the changing views of their congressional representatives.[17] The possibility that both shifts were driven by some third factor, such as the changing views of the Southern elite, cannot be ruled out. But on the whole, these patterns provide evidence consistent with dynamic responsiveness on the part of Southern MCs, who appear to have altered their positions on economic issues in response to changes in the policy preferences of their selectorate.

6.3 RESPONSIVENESS

The Southern caucus as a whole may have been broadly in step with the Southern white public, but were Southern MCs responsive to ideological variation within the region as well? To formalize this question, I make use of a regression model of dyadic representation, which models MCs' conservatism (y_i) as a linear function of the average conservatism of their selectorate (x_i), plus residual variation (ϵ_i):

$$y_i = \alpha + \beta x_i + \epsilon_i. \tag{6.1}$$

In this equation, β captures MCs' responsiveness—the expected difference in their conservatism associated with a given difference in the conservatism of their selectorate. The intercept α is related to the bias in a representational system: in an unbiased system $\alpha = 0$ and $\beta = 1$,

---

[16] Such comparisons across contexts can be dubious even when ideal points are jointly scaled; Jeffrey B. Lewis and Chris Tausanovitch, "When Does Joint Scaling Allow for Direct Comparisons of Preferences?" (Paper presented at the Conference on Ideal Point Models, Massachusetts Institute of Technology, Cambridge, MA, May 1, 2015), http://idealpoint.tahk.us/papers/lewisTausanovitch.pdf; Stephen A. Jessee, "(How) Can We Estimate the Ideology of Citizens and Political Elites on the Same Scale?," *American Journal of Political Science* 60, no. 4 (2016): 1108–1124.
[17] Cf. Lenz, *Follow the Leader?*

assuming that y_i and x_i are measured on the same scale.[18] While this joint-scaling assumption is generally implausible in practice, it is not necessary for my purposes because I do not need to estimate the true values of α and β. Rather, I mainly need to compare their magnitudes across regions, which depends on the more plausible assumption that the mass and congressional conservatism scales do not differ across regions.[19]

Ideally, I would analyze dyadic representation at the level of the relevant constituency: states for the Senate, districts for the House. Unfortunately, the most precise geographic variable contained in the poll data from this period is *State*, requiring that I analyze dyadic representation of constituency preferences at the state level. To construct state-level measures of congressional behavior, I average the estimated ideal points of all MCs who represented a given state in a given congressional term, doing so separately for senators and House members. This approximation to members' constituencies is clearly worse for the House, where districts in this period were not even equal in population. Later I offer a partial remedy to this problem by using income, which is available at the district level, to proxy for the economic interests of the median voter in the constituency.

6.3.1 Cross-Sectional Representation

Dyadic representation can be evaluated empirically by estimating covariation either across constituencies at a given point in time (cross-sectional responsiveness) or within the same constituency over time (dynamic responsiveness). I begin with the former. Figure 6.3 plots the cross-sectional relationship between mass and congressional conservatism in each congressional term between 1936 and 1952. Like Figure 6.1b, it does so separately by region, averaging the conservatism of each state's House and Senate delegations. The responsiveness slope in the South (solid line) is positive in every term, and in about half of congresses is at least as positive as the slope for non-Southern states. In addition, with the near exception of the overwhelmingly Democratic 75th Congress (1937–38), the non-Southern regression line is well above the South's. This means

---

[18] For more details, see Christopher H. Achen, "Measuring Representation," *American Journal of Political Science* 22, no. 3 (1978): 475–510.

[19] Specifically, if the elite conservatism scale is an unknown linear transformation of mass conservatism scale (i.e., $x^* = \gamma + \delta x$, where x^* is the desired level of elite conservatism implied by x), then the true responsiveness of y_i to x_i^* will be $\beta^* = \beta/\delta$. Thus, if we assume that δ is positive and does not differ across regions, then the difference in β between regions must have the same sign as the difference in β^*. For details, see Michael G. Hagen, Edward L. Lascher Jr., and John F. Camobreco, "Response to Matsusaka: Estimating the Effect of Ballot Initiatives on Policy Responsiveness," *Journal of Politics* 63, no. 4 (2001): 1259–1260.

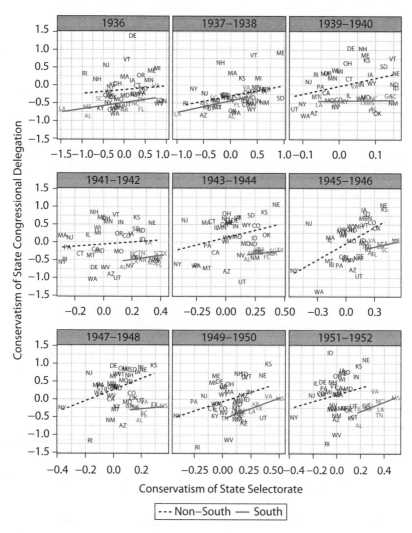

Figure 6.3. Cross-sectional responsiveness by congress and region, 1936–52. *Source for poll data*: Roper Center for Public Opinion Research.

that a state like North Carolina, which after 1940 had a selectorate that was about as economically conservative as Indiana's, received congressional representation that was at least half a standard deviation more liberal than Indiana.[20]

---

[20] In the House, the economic conservatism of the average non-Southern delegation was about 0.5 points higher than the average Southern delegation. In the Senate, the difference

To examine cross-sectional responsiveness more formally, I fit a regression model that estimates the responsiveness slope separately in each region and congressional term.[21] I then average the nine term-specific β estimates for each region, which provides an estimate of responsiveness in the typical year over this period. The results of this analysis are reported in the first four rows of Table 6.1. When we look at both chambers averaged together, we find that the responsiveness slope is significantly positive in both the South (row 1) and the non-South (row 2). The estimated slope is smaller in the South, though not quite significantly so (row 3), and Southern delegations are less conservatively biased than non-Southern ones (row 4).

The remaining rows of Table 6.1 replicate the same analysis separately by chamber. They reveal that the strength of responsiveness is more similar between regions when we look at the Senate (rows 5–8) than the House (rows 9–12). Indeed, in the House the estimated slope in the South is significantly smaller than in the North and, though positive, is not distinguishable from 0. On the other hand, in both chambers the gap between Southern and non-Southern delegations is about equally large. In short, based on these results it appears that the cross-sectional responsiveness of Southern state congressional delegations to the white public is driven mainly by the Senate.

6.3.1.1 Responsiveness to Economic Interests

An important limitation of the preceding analysis, however, is that both mass and congressional conservatism is measured at the level of the state rather than the House district. This is problematic because House districts in the South were not random subsets of the state, or even equal in population within states. Indeed, legislative malapportionment was severe in

---

was 0.4. Compare that to the within-congress standard deviation of ideal points of about 1.0 in the House and 0.7 in the Senate, and to the within-congress SD of state delegations of 0.6 and 0.5, respectively.

[21] Since the conservatism estimates are measured with error, I use a technique called "multiple overimputation," which involves randomly simulating multiple copies of poorly measured variables and averaging inferences across the simulated datasets. I overimputed using draws from a normal distribution centered at the point estimate and with a standard deviation equal to the estimated standard error. Since all the conservatism estimates are averages of ideal point estimates, either within states or within congresses, the standard errors derived from the posterior distributions of the relevant ideal point estimates were adjusted accordingly. For details on this method, see Matthew Blackwell, James Honaker, and Gary King, "A Unified Approach to Measurement Error and Missing Data: Overview and Applications," *Sociological Methods & Research* 46, no. 3 (2017): 303–341.

TABLE 6.1.
Cross-sectional responsiveness by region and chamber, 1936–52

Chamber	Quantity	Est	SE	p
Both	Slope in South	**0.31**	0.17	0.07
Both	Slope in North	**0.81**	0.29	0.01
Both	Slope, South − North	−0.49	0.34	0.15
Both	Bias, South − North	**−0.40**	0.10	0.00
Senate	Slope in South	**0.48**	0.28	0.09
Senate	Slope in North	**0.70**	0.29	0.01
Senate	Slope, South − North	−0.23	0.40	0.58
Senate	Bias, South − North	**−0.40**	0.11	0.00
House	Slope in South	0.15	0.16	0.33
House	Slope in North	**0.91**	0.33	0.01
House	Slope, South − North	**−0.76**	0.37	0.04
House	Bias, South − North	**−0.52**	0.10	0.00

Note: Standard errors are clustered by state, and measurement error is accounted for with multiple overimputation. Estimates in bold are statistically significant at the 10% level.

many Southern (as well as non-Southern) states in this period.[22] As a consequence, the relationship between average conservatism of state publics and the average conservatism of their House members is likely to have been imperfect at best, and thus the preceding analysis may understate the responsiveness of Southern House members.

To address this problem, I analyze responsiveness using an alternative measure: the median income in the selectorate (due to data limitations, this analysis examines Southern states only). The logic for doing so stems from the well-known predictions of median-voter models of redistribution.[23] According to these models, as the median income in the

[22] Stephen Ansolabehere and James M. Snyder Jr., *The End of Inequality: One Person, One Vote and the Transformation of American Politics* (New York: Norton, 2008); Mickey, *Paths out of Dixie*.
[23] Allan H. Meltzer and Scott F. Richard, "A Rational Theory of the Size of Government," *Journal of Political Economy* 89, no. 5 (1981): 914–927; John Londregan, "Political Income Distribution," in *The Oxford Handbook of Political Economy*, ed. Barry R. Weingast and Donald A. Wittman (New York: Oxford University Press, 2006), 84–101.

electorate increases relative to total income, the pivotal voter's demand for redistribution of income should decrease, leading to less-redistributive government policies. Thus, to the extent that Southern MCs were responsive to their selectorates, those with relatively conservative selectorates should have been less supportive of New Deal policies, which generally redistributed resources from rich to poor.[24]

Examining responsiveness to median income has two advantages. First, as suggested earlier, income data are available at the level of the congressional district as well as the state. This enables me to examine House members' responsiveness to the selectorate in their own district as opposed to in the state as a whole. A second advantage of using income rather than survey data is that the former are measures of objective interests rather than subjective preferences. As such, they assuage the concern that constituents' stated preferences may be influenced by the behavior of representatives or, more generally, be misguided or ill-informed.

Estimating the distribution of income in each congressional district requires a complex procedure, the details of which are described in Appendix 6.A. Based on these distributions, I derive estimates of the median income in the white public and in the active electorate, defined as those who voted in presidential elections.[25] Median voter income varied

---

Many empirical studies have found little cross-sectional correlation between the extent of redistribution and income inequality; see, for example, Peter H. Lindert, *Growing Public: Social Spending and Economic Growth since the Eighteenth Century* (New York: Cambridge University Press, 2004); Noam Lupu and Jonas Pontusson, "The Structure of Inequality and the Politics of Redistribution," *American Political Science Review* 105, no. 2 (2011): 316–336. There is more evidence, however, for the comparative statics of the median-voter model. Husted and Kenny, for example, find that the elimination of suffrage restrictions in U.S. states led to higher turnout, a poorer median voter, and higher state spending on social welfare; Thomas A. Husted and Lawrence W. Kenny, "The Effect of the Expansion of the Voting Franchise on the Size of Government," *Journal of Political Economy* 105, no. 1 (1997): 54–82. Fowler reports similar results in an examination of compulsory voting in Australian provinces; Anthony Fowler, "Electoral and Policy Consequences of Voter Turnout: Evidence from Compulsory Voting in Australia," *Quarterly Journal of Political Science* 8, no. 2 (2013): 159–182. In the study most relevant to the one-party South, Fleck analyzes voting patterns on the 1938 Fair Labor Standards Act, using general-election voter turnout as a proxy for the political influence of low-wage workers. Fleck finds that representatives from congressional districts where electoral turnout in 1932 was higher were more likely to support the FLSA; Fleck, "Democratic Opposition."

[24] Richard Oestreicher, "The Rules of the Game: Class Politics in Twentieth-Century America," in *Organized Labor and American Politics, 1894–1994: The Labor-Liberal Alliance*, ed. Kevin Boyle (Albany: SUNY Press, 1998), 19–50.

[25] The presidential electorate is a better measure of the selectorate than the primary electorate because the size of the latter depended heavily on the competitiveness of congressional primaries.

TABLE 6.2.
Cross-sectional responsiveness to the imputed median income of the selectorate, 1931–62 (South only)

Selectorate Definition	Responsiveness Coef.	Est	SE	p
Pres. electorate	House	**0.09**	0.03	0.00
Pres. electorate	Senate	0.11	0.15	0.48
Pres. electorate	Senate − House	0.01	0.16	0.93
White public	House	**0.19**	0.10	0.04
White public	Senate	0.50	0.32	0.12
White public	Senate − House	0.31	0.32	0.34

Note: All models include controls for constituency percent rural (interacted with congressional term).

across constituencies for three main reasons. First, some areas of the South, particularly urban areas, were more economically developed than others and thus had a higher median income. Second, income inequality varied across districts. And third, whether defined as white adults or presidential voters, the size of the selectorate relative to the population varied across districts. Thus, the districts with the poorest populations were often rural districts with large African American populations, such as Mississippi's 3rd, where the median household income was around 70% of national per capita income (NPCI). But the districts with the poorest *selectorates* were rural white districts where the population was poor but largely enfranchised, such as Arkansas's 2nd (represented by House Ways and Means Chair Wilbur Mills). The richest selectorates were in highly developed and largely white urban areas such as Dallas and northern Virginia, where median income was at least three times higher than in the Mississippi Delta. Across constituencies, the standard deviation of median white income is around 30% of NPCI; the SD of voter median income is about twice as large.

My analysis of the relationship between median income and congressional conservatism reveals clear evidence that Southern House members were also responsive to their selectorates. The results are summarized in Table 6.2, which reports the results of regressing the average conservatism of MCs representing a given constituency on the estimated median income in two alternative definitions of the selectorate: presidential voters and the white public. Both regressions control for constituency percent rural (interacted with year) to account for rural areas' disproportionate hostility to New Deal liberalism, particularly after the mid-1930s.[26] Regardless of whether the selectorate in the South is defined as the presidential electorate or as all whites, there is clear evidence that districts where the median voter was richer tended to be represented by more conservative representatives. Indeed, by this measure the relationship is significant only for the House, though the point estimates for the Senate are larger. Taken together, then, the analyses of responsiveness to white preferences and economic interests suggest that while responsiveness may have been stronger among Southern senators, members of both chambers seem to have been responsive to their selectorates.

6.3.2 Dynamic Responsiveness

Until this point, I have considered only cross-sectional responsiveness: the relationship between mass preferences and congressional behavior across constituencies at a given point in time. As Stimson, MacKuen, and Erikson note, however, representation is a dynamic process, and so an arguably superior way to evaluate responsiveness is to examine mass–elite covariation over time.[27] That is, in addition to being correlated cross-sectionally, *changes* in a state selectorate's preferences over time should produce changes in congressional representation. We have already seen suggestions of dynamic responsiveness in Figure 6.2, which showed that Southern MCs collectively tracked shifts in white opinion in their region. Here, I conduct a more formal analysis of dynamic responsiveness, both within the South and compared to the North.

I employ two basic approaches to estimating dynamic responsiveness: a two-way fixed effect (FE) model and a lagged dependent variable (LDV) model. The FE model includes separate intercepts for each state and congressional term, thus controlling for persistent differences across states as well as trends common to all states. Intuitively, the FE model can be thought of as estimating the within-state, cross-year correlation between mass and congressional conservatism. If this relationship is positive, then years when a state's selectorate was relatively conservative tended to be years when its congressional delegation was also relatively conservative. The LDV model is similar in spirit, except that instead of state and term intercepts it controls for each state delegation's conservatism in the previous term. It can thus be roughly interpreted as estimating the relationship

---

[26] As before, I multiply imputed income as well as MCs' conservatism and combined across imputations to account for uncertainty in the measures. Standard errors are clustered by constituency.

[27] Stimson, MacKuen, and Erikson refer to this as "dynamic representation," but I follow Przeworski, Stokes, and Manin in calling it "dynamic responsiveness." See Stimson, MacKuen, and Erikson, "Dynamic Representation"; Przeworski, Stokes, and Manin, "Introduction."

TABLE 6.3.
Dynamic responsiveness by region and chamber, 1936–52

Model	Chamber	Quantity	Est	SE	p
FEs	Senate	Slope in South	**0.14**	0.07	0.04
FEs	Senate	Slope in North	−0.04	0.12	0.75
FEs	Senate	Slope, South − North	0.18	0.14	0.21
FEs	House	Slope in South	**0.26**	0.11	0.02
FEs	House	Slope in North	−0.14	0.14	0.34
FEs	House	Slope, South − North	**0.40**	0.18	0.02
LDVs	Senate	Slope in South	**0.29**	0.10	0.00
LDVs	Senate	Slope in North	0.18	0.12	0.12
LDVs	Senate	Slope, South − North	0.11	0.15	0.45
LDVs	House	Slope in South	**0.20**	0.08	0.01
LDVs	House	Slope in North	**0.28**	0.15	0.05
LDVs	House	Slope, South − North	−0.09	0.17	0.62

Note: Estimates in bold are statistically significant at the 10% level.

between mass conservatism and changes in congressional conservatism. As before, in both models the responsiveness coefficient β is allowed to vary between regions. Standard errors are again clustered by state and measurement error corrected with multiple overimputation.

Table 6.3 summarizes the results of the FE and LDV models for each chamber and region. The results for the South are very similar across the two models. Under either specification, Southern state delegations in both chambers are estimated to be dynamically responsive to white opinion in their state (see rows labeled "Slope in South"). By contrast, the evidence for dynamic responsiveness in the North is generally weaker, as the rows labeled "Slope in North" indicate. Indeed, under the FE specification, Southern House members are estimated to be significantly more responsive than their non-Southern counterparts. This, of course, is precisely contrary to the conventional wisdom that lack of partisan competition dampens responsiveness to voters' preferences.

Let us take stock of what we have learned from the foregoing statistical analyses. In Section 6.3.1, we saw that the economic conservatism of Southern state congressional delegations was correlated cross-sectionally with the conservatism of the white public, and that the cross-sectional responsiveness of Southern senators was not obviously weaker than that of non-Southern senators (Table 6.1). Moreover, Southern state congressional delegations were substantially less conservative on economic issues than non-Southern delegations representing equivalently conservative publics. Proxying for constituency conservatism using median voter income provided further evidence, in both chambers, of cross-sectional responsiveness to the economic *interests* of Southern whites as well as their preferences (Table 6.2). Finally, the over-time analysis in Section 6.3.2 revealed that *dynamic* responsiveness was, if anything, more robust among House and Senate delegations in the South than in the non-South. In short, though the details vary across analyses, the general pattern that emerges is that Southern MCs were not only responsive to their selectorates, but also no less responsive than non-Southern MCs were. Thus, overall, these analyses support the hypothesis that in the case of congressional politics, lack of partisan competition did not inhibit Southern MCs' representation of the white selectorate.

6.4 REPRESENTATIONAL DIFFERENCES BETWEEN REGIONS

The apparently similar strength of congressional responsiveness between regions does not, however, rule out important differences in the mechanisms and character of representation. Even if intraparty competition induced responsiveness, it mattered that MCs from the one-party South were all Democrats whereas non-Southern MCs were split between the parties. One way that it did so is through the trade-offs that Southern and non-Southern MCs faced between satisfying the median voter in their constituency and pursuing other goals. Among the goals competing with reelection were MCs' need to satisfy their primary constituency, whose support was necessary for renomination, as well as their desire to achieve positions of political power and to implement their own preferred policies.[28] The typical non-Southern Republican, for example, faced a trade-off between satisfying the relatively conservative Republican leadership and primary electorate in their constituency, on one hand, and the median general-election voter on the other.[29] Once in Congress, they faced further pressure to toe the party line. Non-Southern Democrats

---

[28] On MCs' multiple goals and constituencies, see Richard F. Fenno Jr., *Congressmen in Committees* (Boston: Little, Brown, 1973); Fenno, "U.S. House Members."
[29] For an explanation of the strategic logic underlying this dynamic, see Bernard Grofman, "Downs and Two-Party Convergence," *Annual Review of Political Science* 7 (2004): 28–30.

faced similar cross-pressures. In both cases, non-Southern MCs' partisan constituencies and loyalties inhibited them from fully converging on the median voter.

Such centrifugal forces were comparatively muted in Southern congressional politics. For one thing, since the Democratic nomination was tantamount to election, there was essentially no distinction between the median voter in the primary and in the general election. This is not to say that Southern MCs did not have core constituencies to please, as is illustrated by the pains Luther Patrick took to satisfy his labor supporters (see Chapter 5). Nor does it mean that they lacked strategic incentives to stake out extreme policy positions, as Lyndon Johnson did to distinguish himself as "Roosevelt's man" in his crowded initial election (Chapter 1).[30] But it does mean that there were fewer systematic pressures pushing Southern MCs to diverge from the ideological center of their selectorate. Although candidates were supported by different coalitions of voters, the fluid and personalized nature of Southern politics lowered the costs of constructing a new coalition in response to changes in the ideological winds. Relative to non-Southern MCs, Southerners thus probably enjoyed greater freedom to cater to—and shift with—the preferences of the median voter. To the extent that Southern MCs were pulled away from their selectorate, it was generally toward the positions of the national Democratic Party, whose national majority was a key to Southern MCs' power and which monopolized avenues of upward advancement.[31] Thus the main trade-off that Southern MCs faced was between their loyalty to the Democratic Party and the preferences of their selectorate.[32]

---

[30] Citizen-candidate models of elections, though I regard them as unrealistically rigid in their dismissal of strategic (as opposed to sincere) position-taking, are nonetheless helpful for understanding the strategic logic in Southern primary elections. Such models predict that if there is only one candidate, she will be the median voter. But if there are two or more, they will in general diverge from the median and from each other. See Besley and Coate, "An Economic Model of Representative Democracy."

[31] Katznelson, Geiger, and Kryder, "Limiting Liberalism." Committee chairmanships in Congress were awarded by strict seniority, meaning that there was little obstacle to Southern Democrats well to the right of the national party (e.g., House Rules Chair Howard Smith of Virginia) becoming chairs. But achieving the Speakership and other congressional leadership positions, not to mention judicial appointments and presidential and vice presidential nominations, required that Southern Democrats be ideologically acceptable to their non-Southern counterparts. Ambition for higher office was a particularly salient concern among Southern senators, who included a number of presidential and vice-presidential aspirants in these years: Alben Barkley, John Sparkman, Albert Gore, Sr., Estes Kefauver, and Lyndon Johnson.

[32] At times, this pressure to conform to the national party line proved too burdensome. In 1946, for example, Alabama senator Lister Hill resigned his position as Democratic whip, telling a staff member that he could not reconcile "the conflict of interest" between his

These differences had two main consequences for congressional representation in the South. First, the tug of party loyalty pulled Southern Democrats' systematically to the left relative to the position dictated by purely electoral calculations. This leftward pressure is almost certainly the main explanation for Southern MCs' "liberal bias" relative to non-Southerners representing similarly conservative states. Given that this bias was a somewhat arbitrary function of which national party Southern Democrats were affiliated with, we should not make too much of its broader implications for one-party politics. But it was nonetheless of great historical significance that about a quarter of the membership of Congress was substantially less conservative on economic issues than one would predict based on their selectorates' preferences.

A second important consequence of these differences is that in the non-South, the main mechanism of responsiveness to voter preferences was through partisan turnover. In the South, by contrast, this mechanism was unavailable. At the same time, because Southern MCs were not anchored by partisan subconstituencies, they had greater freedom to respond pre-emptively to shifts in voter sentiment. Individual Southern MCs could and did exhibit substantial ideological movement relative to the rest of Congress, as, for example, Theodore Bilbo did over his tenure as senator from Mississippi (see Chapter 4). Non-Southern MCs were much less adaptable. Thus, whereas non-Southern voters could merely "select" from among two partisan choices, Southern voters had greater room to "affect" their representatives' behavior.[33] In other words, congressional representation in the non-South changes occurred overwhelmingly through replacement of incumbents, but in the South adaptation of incumbents was equally if not more important as a mechanism of responsiveness.

The relative prominence of adaptation in the South had important implications for both dyadic and collective representation in Congress. At the dyadic level, congressional representation was much more variable outside the South, in the sense that similar (or the same) constituencies might be represented very differently over time depending on whether a Democrat or a Republican had won the last election. This led to what Bafumi and Herron, referring to contemporary American politics, have called "leapfrog" representation, in which alternation between two polarized parties results in congressional behavior that may be responsive to, but is rarely congruent with, voters' preferences.[34] Among Southern

---

constituents' wishes and his duty as whip to "be the president's man." See Hamilton, *Lister Hill*, 149.

[33] Compare Lee, Moretti, and Butler, "Do Voters Affect or Elect."

[34] Joseph Bafumi and Michael C. Herron, "Leapfrog Representation and Extremism: A Study of American Voters and Their Members in Congress," *American Political Science Review* 104, no. 3 (2010): 519–542; see also Keith T. Poole and Howard Rosenthal, "The Polarization of American Politics," *Journal of Politics* 46, no. 4 (1984): 1061–1079.

MCs, turnover was not only less common, but when it did occur the differences between successive MCs were much smaller. Thus, whether through adaptation or replacement, congressional representation in the South changed in more incremental fashion than outside the South. One indication of this is that the variation in congressional representation, whether measured as variance within a state over time or as residual variance not explained by mass preferences, was much lower in the South.[35] Thus, even if non-Southern MCs were less biased than Southern MCs— a claim that cannot be evaluated with the data and measures at my disposal—Southern MCs may nevertheless have been more *proximate* to their voting constituents, and in this sense represented them better.[36]

The implications for collective representation were arguably even more significant.[37] This was especially true following Southern MCs' shift to the center on economics, after which, as Chapter 4 showed, the distribution of Southern preferences largely determined the location of pivotal voters in Congress. As a result, the incremental character of dyadic responsiveness in the South translated into incremental changes in the location of congressional medians. This contrasts with contemporary American politics, where leapfrog representation at the dyadic level results in representational shifts that "overshoot" the mass public.[38] Southern Democrats thus acted as a kind of ballast in midcentury national politics, dampening the magnitude of ideological swings to the left and right. Moreover, because economic policy preferences in different regions moved roughly (though not completely) in tandem, Southern MCs' incremental responsiveness to

---

[35] The residual standard deviation of delegations' conservatism, controlling for mass conservatism, was 1.7 times larger in the Senate and 4.3 times larger in the House. On average, the SD of state delegations' conservatism across congressional terms was about 1.8 times larger in the non-South.

[36] Following Achen, define the proximity of a given representative as the mean squared error (MSE) between the representative's position and her constituents'. The MSE is equal to the within-district variance in constituents plus the squared distance between the representative and the mean constituent. For a region, proximity is the average MSE, which is equal to the average within-district variance plus the average district-level squared distance. Under the plausible assumption that the within-district variances in opinion were no larger in the South than in the non-South, the difference in proximity between regions thus boils down to the difference in the average squared distance between representatives and their district mean. In order for Southerners to be less proximate than non-Southerners, the much smaller (conditional) variance in their positions would have to be offset by a much larger squared bias. For the seminal discussion of proximity, see Achen, "Measuring Representation," 481–487.

[37] On collective representation, see Robert Weissberg, "Collective vs. Dyadic Representation in Congress," *American Political Science Review* 72, no. 2 (1978): 535–547.

[38] Bafumi and Herron, "Leapfrog Representation"; Robert S. Erikson, Michael B. MacKuen, and James A. Stimson, *The Macro Polity* (New York: Cambridge University Press, 2002), 373.

their selectorates resulted in a sort of vicarious incremental responsiveness to the national median voter. In short, the South's one-party system did not preclude congressional representation, but it changed its character in ways that had implications for national as well as regional politics.

6.5 RESOLVING THE PUZZLE OF SOUTHERN CONSERVATISM

For many observers, one of the great puzzles—and tragedies—of Southern politics has been its economic conservatism. "The vast majority of southerners have been poor," laments the historian Robert Norrell, "and their economic interests have surely belonged with liberal or radical political movements." Why then have "political movements among the lower classes... failed to overcome the South's political conservatism"?[39] One answer is obvious: the exclusion of Southern blacks and many poorer whites from the electorate.[40] Clearly, the disfranchisement of the social groups likely to benefit most from government aid undermined elected officials' incentives to implement liberal policies. Yet, for many scholars, this answer is not fully satisfactory. As Earl and Merle Black note, even the electorate in the South "contained more have-littles and have-nots than middle-class whites"[41] and thus should have favored government action to improve their economic circumstances.

For this reason, scholars of Southern politics, exemplified and inspired by V. O. Key, have been drawn recurrently to the one-party system itself as a culprit for the persistent conservatism (and general dysfunction) of the region's politics. On this view, the one-party system was not merely a reflection of the homogeneity of the electorate's preferences, as might be said of, say, Republican-dominated Vermont.[42] Rather, it was a set of partly exogenous institutions that independently shaped and distorted the translation of those preferences into political outcomes. I am not entirely unsympathetic to this account, for as I discuss in the following chapter, I agree that there is a qualitative difference between the one-party dominance that arises as the consequence of distinctive constituency preferences and one that is enforced by legal and extralegal mechanisms.[43] Nevertheless, this book has shown that the "puzzle" that motivates this

---

[39] Norrell, "Labor at the Ballot Box," 201.
[40] Scholars have also stressed the conservatism of organized interests in the South; see, e.g., Boynton, "Southern Conservatism," 259.
[41] Black and Black, *Politics and Society in the South*, 6.
[42] For an account of one-party politics in Vermont, see Frank M. Bryan, *Yankee Politics in Rural Vermont* (Hanover, NH: University Press of New England, 1974).
[43] On the legal and extra-legal mechanisms that enforced one-party hegemony in the South, see Mickey, *Paths out of Dixie*.

account—the conservatism of Southern politics in light of the liberalism of Southern people—rests on shaky empirical foundations. Without those foundations, the puzzle largely dissolves.

First, as I showed in Chapter 3, white Southerners' attitudes toward the New Deal, hitherto relatively favorable, shifted markedly to the right in the late 1930s. While nowhere near as uniformly conservative on economics as they were on race, by the 1940s the typical white public in the South was about a standard deviation below the average state public in the nation. Thus, while it is true that Southern state publics as a whole (that is, including African Americans) were only slightly to the right of the average state nationally,[44] the Southern *selectorate*, expansively defined to include all whites, was clearly relatively conservative from 1940 on. In other words, regardless of their true interests (more on that later), there is little evidence that liberal, let alone radical, economic preferences predominated among Southern whites.

The one-party South's supposed representational disconnect is also premised on an exaggerated caricature of Southern members of Congress. Chapter 4 confirmed what careful observers have long understood: far from being uniformly conservative, Southern MCs were often highly supportive of liberal economic policies. This was particularly true in the 1930s, when the white publics they represented were relatively liberal as well. But even after their turn to the right, Southern Democrats were economic centrists, not conservatives. In fact, at no point between 1931 and 1958 was the median Southern Democrat more economically conservative than the median member of Congress. Of course, as Chapter 4 also emphasizes, Southern Democrats were ideologically diverse, and when it came to economic issues a number of them would have been perfectly comfortable in the Republican caucus. But as Chapter 6 makes clear, relative conservatives in the Southern caucus tended to represent constituencies where the selectorate was relatively conservative—a pattern of responsiveness that may plausibly be attributed to their incentives to cater to Democratic primary electorates (Chapter 5). To the extent Southern MCs' positions on economic issues did deviate from their selectorates', they seem to have been "too liberal," at least relative to MCs from ideologically comparable constituencies outside the South.

In short, when we actually measure white Southerners' preferences over economic policies, the puzzle of Southern conservatism largely dissolves, at least when we consider congressional representation. Relative to the rest of the country, the Southern white public was economically

---

[44] See Breaux and Shaffer, "Southern Political Attitudes."

liberal in the 1930s but conservative thereafter. Analogously, most Southern MCs were New Dealers in the 1930s and economic centrists thereafter. As this chapter has suggested, the existence of a representational disconnect seems to have more bite in state politics, where policy outcomes bore little relationship to Southern whites' attitudes toward New Deal liberalism.[45] But in Congress, Southern MCs seem to have been no more conservative than their white constituents wanted them to be, and perhaps quite a bit less so.

This conclusion begs the question of whether Southern whites' economic preferences were consistent with their material *interests*. Liberal and radical observers of the South have long argued that poorer Southern whites were more conservative than they "ought" to be, owing in large part to their racism against blacks, their "natural" class allies. On this view, Southern whites' racial preferences, or at least the extreme weight that they placed on subjugating blacks, were a form of false consciousness that prevented them from supporting candidates and policies that would serve their material interests.[46] Gerald Friedman, for example, argues that labor organization in the South was profoundly inhibited by whites' racism and consequential allegiance to the one-party system, which allowed "southern politicians to ignore labor's demands" and "advance an economic program otherwise unacceptable to many southerners."[47] A corollary of this general view is the notion that the dismantlement of Jim Crow would liberate whites from racism as well as blacks, thus benefitting Southerners of both races.[48]

There is no doubt that Southern whites' attitudes toward economic policies were colored by their attachment to white supremacy. In addition to fostering a general suspicion of a powerful national state, Southern whites' racism increased their resistance to otherwise-appealing policies that gave blacks and whites equal benefits or in other ways undermined

---

[45] Even this finding should be interpreted cautiously, given that states' liberalism with respect to *national* policy need not coincide exactly with their liberalism with respect to state politics.

[46] Indeed, Marx himself used the competition between whites and blacks in the South as an analogy for the debilitating ethnic divisions in the British working class. "The average English worker," he wrote, "hates the Irish worker as a competitor who lowers wages and the standard of life.... He regards him practically in the same way the poor whites in the southern states of North America regard the black slaves. This antagonism between the proletarians in England is artificially nourished and kept alive by the bourgeoisie. It knows that this split is the true secret of maintaining its power"; Marx, Karl to Dr. Ludwig Kugelmann, "Confidential Communication on Bakunin," March 28, 1870, https://www.marxists.org/archive/marx/works/1870/03/28.htm.

[47] Friedman, "Political Economy of Early Southern Unionism," 384–385.

[48] For an argument that this is in fact what happened, see Gavin Wright, *Sharing the Prize: The Economics of the Civil Rights Revolution in the American South* (Cambridge, MA: Harvard University Press, 2013).

racial hierarchy in the South. But extreme racial conservatism did not prevent a great many white Southerners from endorsing liberal economic policies during the New Deal and after. Moreover, the New Deal state that Southern MCs helped construct offered many concrete benefits to poor white Southerners. This was due only partly to the racially discriminatory design of many New Deal and Fair Deal programs, for Southern blacks too benefitted from the welfare spending and economic modernization brought by federal programs.[49] For many whites, especially relatively poor ones, such violations of the traditional "Herrenvolk, white-only nature of state action in the South" were tolerable in light of the value of federal aid, at least as long as it did not fundamentally threaten the Jim Crow system.[50] In sum, poor Southern whites' racism did not prevent them from being represented at the federal level in ways that furthered their material interests in important ways.

The fact that South's exclusionary one-party regime was reasonably responsive to Southern whites' racial *and* economic preferences helps us understand why it lasted so long. Like many durable authoritarian regimes, the one-party system endured in large part because of the acquiescence, and in many respects active support, of a large portion of the mass public. This is not to say that ordinary Southern whites favored or spontaneously defended all aspects of the regime. Indeed, conservative Southern elites often fretted about the white public's initially apathetic response to challenges like the *Brown* decision. Nevertheless, once Southern blacks began to mount a frontal challenge through direct action and legal assaults, conservative elites successfully rallied the white public in defense of the regime. Indeed, it was the fear of broad-based white backlash that helped convince the Supreme Court to adopt a gradualist court of "all deliberate speed" on desegregation. In the end, it was not lower-class whites whose defection was key to Southern acquiescence to *Brown*, but rather business-oriented modernizers who came to see

---

[49] Brown, *Race, Money*, 78–80; Price V. Fishback, Michael R. Haines, and Shawn Kantor, "The Impact of the New Deal on Black and White Infant Mortality in the South," *Explorations in Economic History* 38, no. 1 (2001): 93–122; Wright, "The New Deal and the Modernization of the South," 70–71. This appears to have been less true of state government expenditures, which after black disfranchisement were profoundly skewed toward whites; see, e.g., J. Morgan Kousser, "Progressivism—For Middle-Class Whites Only: North Carolina Education, 1880–1910," *Journal of Southern History* 46, no. 2 (1980): 169–194; Robert A. Margo, *Race and Schooling in the South, 1880–1950: An Economic History* (Chicago: University of Chicago Press, 1990); Elizabeth U. Cascio and Ebonya Washington, "Valuing the Vote: The Redistribution of Voting Rights and State Funds Following the Voting Rights Act of 1965," *Quarterly Journal of Economics* 129, no. 1 (2014): 379–433; GavinWright, Sharing the Prize: The Economics of the Civil Rights Revolution in the American South (Cambridge, MA: Harvard University Press, 2013).

[50] Schulman, *Cotton Belt to Sunbelt*, 47.

massive resistance (and, for many, the one-party system) as a barrier to economic progress.[51]

The responsiveness of the one-party system also helps explain why its dismantlement did not release the South's latent liberalism, as Key and many others expected. Rather, the South remained relatively conservative in its state-level politics and moderate in its congressional representation through the end of the twentieth century. This is particularly puzzling given the enfranchisement of millions of African Americans, who were and remain much more liberal than Southern whites. The key to this puzzle is the fact that black enfranchisement in the 1950s–60s was accompanied by (and perhaps spurred) the electoral mobilization of whites, mainly poorer ones.[52] In fact, in terms of absolute numbers, more Southern whites registered to vote between 1960 and 1980 than Southern blacks. Had these newly enfranchised whites been poorly represented by the previous regime, their enfranchisement alongside Southern blacks should have dramatically liberalized the electorate. Although the voting rights revolution did eventually create new opportunities for left-of-center biracial coalitions in the South, it did not fundamentally alter the region's political position relative to the nation. The region's policies remained relatively conservative and its congressional representation relatively moderate. Put simply, the Second Reconstruction's democratization of the South did not release the latent economic liberalism of white Southerners because the latter were neither particularly liberal nor poorly represented by the previous regime. The implications of this conclusion—and of my other findings in this book—are discussed in the concluding chapter that follows.

6.A APPENDIX: ESTIMATION AND IMPUTATION OF INCOME

The analysis of Southern MCs' responsiveness to the economic interests of their electorates relies on proxies for the median income in the electorate. This section describes how these proxies were estimated and multiply imputed.

[51] Anthony J. Badger, "*Brown* and Backlash," in *Massive Resistance*, ed. Clive Webb (Oxford: Oxford University Press, 2005), 39–55.
[52] Harold W. Stanley, *Voter Mobilization and the Politics of Race: The South and Universal Suffrage, 1952–1984* (New York: Praeger, 1987); James E. Alt, "The Impact of the Voting Rights Act on Black and White Voter Registration in the South," in *Quiet Revolution in the South: The Impact of the Voting Rights Act, 1965–1990*, ed. Chandler Davidson and Bernard Grofman (Princeton: Princeton University Press, 1994), 351–377.

Like all demographic characteristics of congressional districts in the dataset for this chapter, districts' estimated income distribution must be derived from data at the county level. Before 1962, all but a handful of Southern congressional districts were composed of whole counties.[53] Based on information provided by Martis et al.,[54] I assigned each county in the 17-state South to its House district in each congressional election 1930–62. Using this mapping, it is possible to calculate the district-level value of any quantity that is a function of data available at the county level. For example, to calculate the proportion of district residents who are white, I take the weighted average of the proportion white in the counties that composed the district, where the weights are given by the number of residents of each county.

The calculation of the districts' income distribution is not so straight-forward, for several reasons. First, county-level income data are not available before 1950, when the U.S. Census began collecting county-level data on median household income (which is missing for some counties) as well as on the proportions of households with yearly income below $2,000 and $5,000. Second, estimating the income of the median voter requires the whole income distribution, not just a single statistic such as the mean. I deal with these problems with a combination of multiple imputation and assumptions about the shape of the income distribution.

Let's start with 1950, when income data are observed. I can derive each district's proportions of household with income below $2,000 and $5,000 by taking a weighted average of the corresponding quantities for counties in that district.[55] Since I ultimately care not about absolute income but income relative to the national average, it is helpful to divide $2,000 and $5,000 by national per capita income in 1950, which was $1,516.[56] Let $p_{c,1950}^{1.3}$ and $p_{c,1950}^{3.3}$ respectively denote the proportion of county c's households with relative income below 1.3 ($\$2,000/\$1,516$) and 3.3 ($\$5,000/\$1,516$) in 1950. Denote the analogous district-level quantities as $p_{d,1950}^{1.3}$ and $p_{d,1950}^{3.3}$, which are population-weighted averages of the counties that compose district d. Together, $p_{d,1950}^{1.3}$ and $p_{d,1950}^{3.3}$ provide information on how rich district d is as well as how unequal it is.

---

[53] In the 13-state South, the exceptions are districts in New Orleans, Houston, and Miami. Split counties were more common in the non-South.

[54] Kenneth C. Martis et al., *The Historical Atlas of United States Congressional Districts, 1789–1983* (New York: Free Press, 1982).

[55] Strictly speaking, the counties should be weighted by their number of households, but I instead use number of residents, which is almost exactly proportional to the number of households.

[56] I divide by per capita national income rather than per household because only the former is available in every year.

The distribution of income is usually considered to be log-normal (i.e., the natural log of income is normally distributed), a regularity known as "Gibrat's law." Assuming Gibrat's law held within Southern congressional districts, $p_{d,1950}^{1.3}$ and $p_{d,1950}^{3.3}$ are sufficient to pin down the entire income distribution.[57] Specifically, the mean of (normally distributed) log relative income in district d is

$$\mu_{d,1950}^{\log} = \frac{\log(1.3) \times \Phi(p_{d,1950}^{3.3}) - \log(3.3) \times \Phi(p_{d,1950}^{1.3})}{\Phi(p_{d,1950}^{3.3}) - \Phi(p_{d,1950}^{1.3})}, \quad (6.2)$$

and its standard deviation is

$$\sigma_{d,1950}^{\log} = \frac{\log(3.3) - \log(1.3)}{\Phi(p_{d,1950}^{3.3}) - \Phi(p_{d,1950}^{1.3})}, \quad (6.3)$$

where Φ indicates the standard normal cumulative distribution function.

Given $\hat{\mu}_{d,1950}^{\log}$ and $\hat{\sigma}_{d,1950}^{\log}$ and the assumption that log relative income is normally distributed within districts, I can derive the median income in any subset of the income distribution. To estimate the median log income the electorate, I must assume that everyone in the electorate has a higher income than everyone outside the electorate—that is, the class bias is as extreme as possible, given the size of the electorate. Under this assumption, the median log income (= log median income) in the electorate is

$$\log(m_{d,1950}) = 1 - \Phi\left(\frac{0.5 \times e_{d,1950} - \hat{\mu}_{d,1950}^{\log}}{\hat{\sigma}_{d,1950}^{\log}}\right), \quad (6.4)$$

where $m_{d,1950}$ is 1950 median income in d's electorate and $e_{d,1950}$ is the size of the 1950 electorate as a proportion of the population.

To estimate median voter income in years other than 1950, I must (multiply) impute the county-level quantities $p_{c,1950}^{1.3}$ and $p_{c,1950}^{3.3}$. This requires county-level data on quantities that are strong predictors of county-level income in 1950 and are available in the 1930, 1940, and 1960 censuses as well. The following variables fit these criteria:

- *Population*
- *Proportion Urban*

---

[57] Battistin, Blundell, and Lewbel provide evidence that Gibrat's law is approximately true in the United States, and almost exactly so for the top 75% of the income distribution; see Erich Battistin, Richard Blundell, and Arthur Lewbel, "Why Is Consumption More Log Normal than Income? Gibrat's Law Revisited," *Journal of Political Economy* 117, no. 6 (2009): 1140–1154.

- *Proportion White*
- *State Per Capita Income*
- *Proportion Enrolled in School* (among 14–17-year-olds)

Since I wish to predict relative income, these variables must be demeaned within years so as to eliminate over-time changes common to all units.

The imputation model specification (with demeaned variables marked with an asterisk),

$$p_{ct}^x \sim N(Population_{ct}^* + Proportion\ Urban_{ct}^* + (Proportion\ Urban_{ct}^*)^2$$
$$+\ Proportion\ White_{ct}^* + (Proportion\ White_{ct}^*)^2$$
$$+\ Proportion\ Urban_{ct}^* \times Proportion\ White_{ct}^*$$
$$+\ State\ Per\ Capita\ Income_{ct}^* + \log(State\ Per\ Capita\ Income_{ct}^*)$$
$$+\ Proportion\ Enrolled\ in\ School_{ct}^*),\ x \in \{1.3,\ 3.3\} \qquad (6.5)$$

explains 69% of the variance of $p_{c,1950}^{1.3}$ and 51% of the variance of $p_{c,1950}^{3.3}$. To reflect our belief that a county's relative income distribution is stable over time, I add an informative Gaussian prior for p_{ct}^x centered on county c's value of $p_{c,1950}^x$. The standard deviation of the prior, $0.02 \times \sqrt{|1950 - t|}$, implies a belief that the typical yearly change in p_{ct}^x was 0.02.

The imputation model was estimated using the R package `Amelia`.[58] Ten imputed county-level datasets were created for $t \in \{1930, 1940, 1960\}$. In each imputed dataset, values of $p_{ct}^{1.3}$ and $p_{ct}^{3.3}$ for noncensus years were linearly interpolated from the census estimates. The estimates for each year and each imputed dataset were used to calculate the district-level income distribution using the same method described earlier. This yielded 10 imputed district-level datasets with estimates of $\mu_{dt}^{\log}, \sigma_{dt}^{\log}$, and m_{dt}.

[58] James Honaker, Gary King, and Matthew Blackwell, "Amelia II: A Program for Missing Data," *Journal of Statistical Software* 45, no. 7 (2011): 1–47, http://www.jstatsoft.org/v45/i07/.

CHAPTER 7

Conclusion

As he neared the end of his 35th year in office, the septuagenarian senior senator from Mississippi announced, after a period of indecision, that he would seek a seventh term. Commentators at the time anticipated that the campaign "could prove his toughest race yet."[1] The main hurdle lay not in the general election—in several recent cycles, the opposing party had not even bothered to field a candidate against him—but in the primary, where he faced a well-financed challenge from the right. Though the campaign also highlighted generational and geographic cleavages (both candidates dominated the vote in their home counties), the primary contest centered on the marked ideological differences between the candidates, who occupied opposite ends of their party's political spectrum.[2] The incumbent touted his support for federal programs that benefitted the state, while his opponent attacked him for "vot[ing] with the liberals on spending" and other issues.[3]

The intraparty battle came to a head in the first primary the following June. The vigorous contest drew strong turnout: 14% of Mississippi's voting-age population, double that in the senator's last contested primary. More than 99% of the voters were white, meaning that around a quarter of adult white Mississippians participated in the primary.[4] Though the challenger eked out a plurality, the presence of a minor third candidate

---

[1] Emily Schultheis, "Cochran to Run for Reelection," *Politico*, December 6, 2013, http://www.politico.com/story/2013/12/thad-cochran-reelection-100785.

[2] Nate Cohn, "Mississippi Primary Fight Is One of Geography as Well as Ideology," *New York Times*, June 2, 2014, https://www.nytimes.com/2014/06/03/upshot/mississippi-primary-fight-is-one-of-geography-as-well-as-ideology.html?_r=0; Jonathan Martin, "One Party, Two Factions: South's Republicans Look a Lot Like Its 1970s Democrats," *New York Times*, June 2, 2014, https://www.nytimes.com/2014/06/03/us/politics/one-party-two-factions-souths-republicans-look-a-lot-like-its-1970s-democrats.html?nrx=miss-footer; M. V. Hood III and Seth C. McKee, "Black Votes Count: The 2014 Republican Senate Nomination in Mississippi," *Social Science Quarterly* 98, no. 1 (2016): 94–95.

[3] Daniel Lippman, "The Cochran-McDaniel Ad Wars," *Politico*, June 23, 2014, http://www.politico.com/story/2014/06/thad-cochran-chris-mcdaniel-ads-federal-spending-conservative-credentials-108180.

[4] Hood and McKee, "Black Votes Count," 97.

denied him an outright majority, thus forcing a run-off. Realizing that he was likely to lose the run-off, the incumbent pursued a risky strategy of appealing, through religious leaders and other brokers, to the small number of eligible black voters, who appreciated the incumbent's support for federal spending and eschewal of overt race-baiting.[5] Ultimately, though the senator won only 49% of white ballots cast, he was able to mobilize enough support from African Americans to prevail in the run-off by 2 percentage points. His renomination secure, the incumbent glided to victory in the general election and into a seventh senatorial term.

As many readers (at least those who check footnotes) will have already surmised, the Mississippi Senate race just described did not occur in the heyday of the one-party South, or even in its twilight during and after the Second Reconstruction. Nor, for that matter, did the primary contest take place under the auspices of the Democratic Party. Rather, it occurred in the lead-up to the 2014 midterm elections and featured two Republicans: U.S. Senator Thad Cochran, a pillar of the Republican establishment, and State Senator Chris McDaniel, a Tea Party favorite.

Notwithstanding these differences from the one-party period, the fact that the Cochran–McDaniel race could be described in terms so reminiscent of that era raises intriguing and in some respects troubling questions about how much the South has really changed in the intervening years. Now that the Republicans have dismantled the last legacies of Democratic dominance, has the South entered a new period of one-party rule? Has the voting rights revolution empowered black voters, or has the South merely undergone a "shift from conservative Democrats elected by whites to conservative Republicans elected by whites," with African Americans playing at best a swing role in Republican primaries?[6] In short, is the South really any more democratic today than it used to be?

I believe the answer is clearly yes: the South *is* more democratic today, sufficiently so as to deserve classification as an unqualified democracy. As Robert Mickey chronicles, the South's democratization, accomplished through a combination of internal insurgency and external intervention, was largely complete by the early 1970s.[7] This transition to democracy

---

[5] R. L. Nave, "McDaniel Polling Ahead, Black Voters Still a Big Unknown," *Jackson (MS) Free Press*, June 23, 2014, http://www.jacksonfreepress.com/news/2014/jun/23/mcdaniel-polling-ahead-blacks-still-big-unknown/; Hood and McKee, "Black Votes Count," 94. The number of eligible black voters was limited because under Mississippi's semiclosed primary system, voters in the Democratic primary several weeks earlier were legally prohibited from participating in the Republican run-off.
[6] Quote from Black and Black, *The Rise of Southern Republicans*, 119; for speculation that blacks' participation in the Cochran–McDaniel primary may be a portent of things to come, see Hood and McKee, "Black Votes Count," 103–105.
[7] Mickey, *Paths out of Dixie*.

dismantled the legal and informal suffrage barriers that had prevented Southern blacks from voting and inhibited many whites from doing so as well. As a consequence, presidential turnout in the South increased from 24% of voting-age citizens in 1948 to 52% in 2000, as compared to a decline from 59% to 57% outside the South.[8] Moreover, Southern blacks' turnout in presidential elections had, by the early twenty-first century, matched or even surpassed that of Southern non-Hispanic whites.[9] Though blacks remain underrepresented in public office, the number of black officeholders has nevertheless increased tremendously, from below 1,000 nationwide before the Voting Rights Act to more than 10,000 today. In contemporary Alabama, for example, African Americans occupy 17% of all elected positions in the state—still well below their 26% of the state's population but a ten-fold increase over the proportion in 1970.[10]

At the same time as Southern politics has become more inclusive, the region's general elections have become more competitive. Republican inroads began at the presidential level in the 1950s and moved progressively down-ballot to include congressional, state, and local offices.[11] By 2017, Republicans controlled every state legislature in the former Confederacy and all but three of its governorships. But contemporary Republican dominance in the South is not comparable to the Democratic hegemony of yore. In the one-party South, the Democratic Party was the only game in town—the only viable arena for formal political contestation. Today's Republican Party does not have a comparable monopoly over public contestation in the South. Every state except Arkansas has least one Democratic member of Congress, and as recent elections in Louisiana and Alabama attest, even Deep South states occasionally elect Democratic governors and senators. In other words, Republicans can and do lose elections in the contemporary South. This distinguishes contemporary Southern states not only from their one-party predecessors, but also from states such as Vermont that were once dominated by Republicans but

---

[8] Calculated by summing columns 4 and 6 in tables 1 and 2 in McDonald and Popkin, "The Myth of the Vanishing Voter," 968–969.
[9] Thom File, *The Diversifying Electorate—Voting Rates by Race and Hispanic Origin in 2012 (and Other Recent Elections)*, Current Population Survey Reports, P20-569. U.S. Census Bureau, Washington, DC, 2013, 9.
[10] Khalilah Brown-Dean et al., *50 Years of the Voting Rights Act: The State of Race in Politics*, Joint Center for Political and Economic Studies, 2015, 4, 27, http://jointcenter.org/sites/default/files/VRA%20report%2C%203.5.15%20%281130%20am%29%28updated%29.pdf.
[11] Black and Black, *The Rise of Southern Republicans*.

where Democrats still polled a nontrivial percentage of the vote.[12] More-over, high-profile episodes like the Cochran–McDaniel race notwithstand-ing, Republican primaries are not the main site of ideological competition. Indeed, the exodus of conservative (white) Southerners from the Demo-cratic Party is one of the main reasons that the Southern congressional delegation is no longer centrist, but rather is divided between a majority of conservative Republicans and a minority of (mostly black and Hispanic) liberal Democrats.

It is thus fair to say that in terms of inclusiveness and contestation, the contemporary South has largely converged with the rest of the coun-try. But the region nevertheless remains distinctive in certain respects. Many Southern states, particularly in the Deep South, now exhibit an extraordinary degree of ideological and partisan polarization by race. Southern whites are now on the whole quite conservative relative to whites elsewhere, particularly on social issues, whereas Southern blacks are very liberal, particularly on economics. And in much of the South, the Democratic Party, or at least its presidential candidates, is as unpopular among whites as Republican candidates were in the one-party period.[13] The difference, of course, is that Southern electorates now include a large number of nonwhites, which makes elections much closer. But in the end, the result is still, as suggested earlier, rule by "conservative Republicans elected by whites." This is to some degree a national phenomenon: across the country, blacks are more likely than other groups to vote for losing candidates.[14] But the severity of political polarization by race in the South means that Southern blacks are particularly unlikely to be represented by a representative of their choosing. While this does not preclude black votes from exerting indirect political influence on the representation they

[12] The Republican Party controlled the legislature and every statewide office in Vermont continuously between 1856 and 1958. On the distinction between "one-party" states in the South and the non-South, see Austin Ranney and Willmoore Kendall, "The American Party Systems," *American Political Science Review* 48, no. 2 (1954): 477–485. On the importance of *potential* competition, see Sartori, *Parties and Party Systems*.

[13] This is not an exaggeration. For example, in 2012 Barack Obama probably won fewer than a fifth of white votes in the states of Louisiana, Georgia, Alabama, Mississippi, South Carolina, Tennessee, Arkansas, and Texas, which is not out of line with Republican presidential shares even in the heyday of the Solid South; Nate Cohn, "No, Obama Didn't Win One-Third of White Voters in Deep South," *New York Times*, April 24, 2014, https://www.nytimes.com/2014/04/25/upshot/rebutting-claim-that-obama-had-wider-support-among-southern-whites.html.

[14] Zoltan L. Hajnal, "Who Loses in American Democracy? A Count of Votes Demonstrates the Limited Representation of African Americans," *American Political Science Review* 103, no. 1 (2009): 37–57.

receive, it does suggest that, in a sense, a form of white rule lives on in the contemporary South.

7.1 RECONSIDERING THE ONE-PARTY SOUTH

What kind of regime, then, was the South for the first half of the twentieth century? I have argued that it is best analyzed as an exclusionary one-party enclave—a subnational one-party regime with a racially exclusive selectorate that was embedded in a far more inclusionary national two-party system. This analytic framework, however, does not specify which of the three models laid out in Chapter 2—elite dominance, ruptured linkages, or white polyarchy—best characterizes the one-party South. Unsatisfying as it may seem, there is no single answer to this question—different aspects and arenas of Southern politics conform more or less well to each model. It is certainly possible to identify local pockets of elite dominance that closely resemble the boss-controlled authoritarian enclaves in countries such as Argentina and Mexico.[15] Examples include Louisiana's Plaquemines and St. Bernard Parishes, where local magnate Leander Perez exercised strict political control, to the point of falsifying election returns at will.[16] In a less overtly corrupt but no less real way, plantation owners in the Mississippi Delta and other black-belt areas no doubt exercised great influence over local whites (not to mention blacks), many if not most of whom were directly economically dependent on the local planter elite.

Such tight top-down control, however, was more the exception than the rule.[17] As Chapter 5 argued, Southern Democratic primaries provided a forum for nonelite whites not only to participate in politics but also select among competing candidates offering distinct platforms, some of which diverged sharply from the preferences of the Southern elite. In state politics, where parties were totally absent, this vigorous competition did not

---

[15] See Gibson, *Boundary Control.*

[16] Glen Jeansonne, *Leander Perez: Boss of the Delta* (Jackson: University Press of Mississippi, 2006).

[17] Even in the Delta, "the most Southern place on Earth" in the words of James Cobb, conservative elite control was not complete. Mississippi's 3rd District, where the black proportion of the population (about 70%) was the highest in the nation, was between 1951 and 1962 represented Frank Smith, whose economic and even racial views were unusually liberal for the region, let alone the Delta. This was in part due to Smith's success in concealing his true views during his initial campaign; James C. Cobb, *The Most Southern Place on Earth: The Mississippi Delta and the Roots of Regional Identity* (New York: Oxford University Press, 1992); Dennis J. Mitchell, *Mississippi Liberal: A Biography of Frank E. Smith* (Jackson: University Press of Mississippi, 2001), chapter 6.

appear to have translated into systematic responsiveness to the white public, thus corroborating the ruptured linkages model articulated by Key and others.[18] But when we turn to Southern congressional politics, which mixed party-structured governance with partyless elections, the ruptured linkages model provides a much less compelling account than the white polyarchy model. Southern Democrats in Congress, despite facing essentially no electoral competition from Republicans, nonetheless appear to have been no less responsive to their voting-eligible constituents than members of Congress from outside the South. Thus, insofar as we consider the non-Southern United States in this period to have been polyarchal—a debatable but, I believe, reasonable claim—the best description of congressional politics in the one-party South is the one supplied by Dahl: "a more or less competitive polyarchy in which most whites were included" superimposed upon "a hegemonic system to which Negroes were subject and to which southern whites were overwhelmingly allegiant."[19]

The one-party South does *not*, I believe, deserve to be classified as a democracy. It is true that the one-party South did meet the Schumpeterian standard of selecting its leaders by competitive (intraparty) elections.[20] But as many have argued, this definition of democracy is too minimalist.[21] For while Schumpeter may have been willing to "leave it to every *populus* to define himself,"[22] most theorists regard the exclusion of large portions of the citizenry as a fundamental violation of the bedrock principle of political equality upon which democracy is premised. Juan Linz, for example, argues that so-called racial democracies, in which democratic standards are satisfied only for the dominant racial group, are in reality authoritarian regimes, as are regimes in which effective citizenship is restricted to members of a single (selective) political party.[23]

---

[18] I would emphasize, however, the tentativeness of this conclusion. For one thing, we lack good survey-based measures of Southerners' preferences with respect to *state* policymaking on economic issues. For a variety of reasons, these may have diverged substantially from the measures of New Deal liberalism I have relied on in this book.

[19] Dahl, *Polyarchy*, 93–94; for the classic debate over whether the non-South was polyarchal or elite-controlled, see C. Wright Mills, *The Power Elite* (New York: Oxford University Press, 1956); Robert Dahl, *Who Governs?* (New Haven, CT: Yale University Press, 1961); for a pessimistic assessment of contemporary American democracy, see Martin Gilens and Benjamin I. Page, "Testing Theories of American Politics: Elites, Interest Groups, and Average Citizens," *Perspectives on Politics* 12, no. 3 (2014): 564–581.

[20] Schumpeter, *Capitalism, Socialism and Democracy*, 269.

[21] But see Adam Przeworski, "Minimalist Conception of Democracy: A Defense," in *The Democracy Sourcebook*, ed. Robert Dahl, Ian Shapiro, and José Antonio Cheibub (1999; Cambridge, MA: MIT Press, 2003), 12–16.

[22] Schumpeter, *Capitalism, Socialism and Democracy*, 245.

[23] Linz, "Totalitarian and Authoritarian Regimes," 328, 183; see also Robert A. Dahl, *On Democracy* (New Haven, CT: Yale University Press, 1998), 62–82.

It is also worth bearing in mind that it was not suffrage restriction alone that rendered the one-party South undemocratic. As Robert Mickey has stressed, many of the civil liberties upon which effective democracy depends—rights such as due process, freedom of speech, free association, and even personal safety—were far from perfectly secure in the South, most obviously for African Americans but also for whites who sought to challenge Jim Crow.[24] Though lynching was less common in the period I examine than it had been previously, the regime was still ultimately backed by the threat of physical coercion and violence. For these reasons, I agree with Mickey, Linz, and others who have argued that the one-party South, like other "racial democracies," are best classified as authoritarian regimes.

Nevertheless, the binary classification of the one-party South as authoritarian should not blind us to its democratic features, which offered substantial scope for participation and contestation by, and responsiveness to, the white populace. In this regard, it is essential to recognize the qualitative distinction between the status of blacks and whites in the Jim Crow South. Put simply, Southern whites, even poor whites, were part of the political community in a way that blacks were not. This is not to say that African Americans entirely lacked political agency. Even under slavery, Southern blacks engaged in forms of collective politics and exercised forms of political power, an inheritance of contentious politics that continued through the midcentury civil rights movement and beyond.[25] But with vanishingly few exceptions, opportunities for formal participation in political decision making were closed to blacks, whereas they were open to most whites. And this mattered. Southern MCs could not ignore whites' preferences the way they did blacks', a fact with important implications for their behavior in office and, indirectly, for the course of American political development.

7.2 IMPLICATIONS

This brings us to the topic of the broader lessons of my reevaluation of the one-party South. In the text that follows, I consider the implications for three topics: American political development, the role of mass politics in authoritarian regimes, and the role of parties in democratic politics.

---

[24] Mickey, "Beginning of the End," 148–149.
[25] Steven Hahn, *A Nation under Our Feet: Black Political Struggles in the Rural South from Slavery to the Great Migration* (Cambridge, MA: Harvard University Press, 2003); Doug McAdam, *Political Process and the Development of Black Insurgency, 1930–1970* (Chicago: University of Chicago Press, 1982).

7.2.1 American Political Development

The national representatives of the one-party South played a crucial role in American political development in the middle third of the twentieth century. In the 1930s, Southern Democrats overwhelmingly supported their party's embrace of government activism in the face of a historic economic crisis. Southern MCs not only backed unprecedented state intervention to stabilize and revitalize the economy, but also helped lay the foundations for a modern welfare state and a labor market regime much more friendly to organized labor. By the 1940s, however, Southern Democrats had begun collaborating with resurgent congressional Republicans to block further reform and roll back key aspects of the New Deal order. By the end of World War II, a new political equilibrium had emerged, one in which centrist Southern Democrats collectively held the balance of power between liberal non-Southern Democrats and conservative non-Southern Republicans. With the exception of a few congresses when the non-Southern wing of one party or the other was dominant enough to control Congress, Southern Democrats retained this pivotal position through the 1970s at least.

Southern MCs' position at the fulcrum of congressional power profoundly shaped congressional politics. On one hand, it forced reform-minded liberals to design social welfare and regulatory policies to suit Southern preferences. The most salient of Southern preferences was protecting the region's system of racial hierarchy, but ensuring that New Deal programs redistributed wealth along regional lines was also a priority.[26] Southerners' pivotal position also gave them effective veto power over the scope and extent of New Deal reform, which they exercised to greatest effect by allying with Republicans to retrench the pro-union New Deal labor regime.[27] More generally, Southerners' institutional power within the congressional Democratic Party was a key to their ability to head off attacks on Jim Crow.[28] In these respects, Southern Democrats in Congress frustrated a generation of liberals. On the other hand, the fact that Southern MCs did not turn completely against the New Deal order was critical to its consolidation in the 1940s.[29] Indeed, the active

---

[26] Lieberman, *Shifting the Color Line*; Brown, *Race, Money*.

[27] Katznelson, Geiger, and Kryder, "Limiting Liberalism"; Farhang and Katznelson, "Southern Imposition."

[28] On congressional organization as an institutional solution to sectional conflict, see Richard Bensel, "Sectionalism and Congressional Development," in *The Oxford Handbook of the American Congress*, ed. Eric Schickler and Frances Lee (New York: Oxford University Press, 2011), 761–786.

[29] Plotke, *Building a Democratic Political Order*; more generally, see Orren and Skowronek, "Regimes and Regime Building."

efforts of Southern Democrats such as Arkansas's Wilbur Mills to put the New Deal state on a fiscally and politically sustainable footing were crucial to its long-term survival.[30]

Beyond the New Deal specifically, the presence of a large contingent of centrist members changed the general character of congressional politics and policymaking. Relative to most of American history, the relative lack of partisan polarization in midcentury congresses jumps out as a glaring historical anomaly.[31] And as much as liberals at the time complained of the "deadlock of democracy," it resulted in a distinctive pattern of incremental but productive policymaking.[32] As Mayhew notes, the "long 1950s," which roughly corresponds to the peak of Southern pivotality in Congress, was a distinct policy era characterized by a focus on growth, development, efficiency, and productivity and frequent cross-party or even consensual legislating.[33] The contrast with the contemporary Congress, marked as it is by polarization and in many respects dysfunction, could hardly be more stark.[34]

Southern MCs' role in shaping the New Deal order and dampening partisan polarization has been well documented by scholars. What previous accounts have largely neglected, however, are the underpinnings of these elite-level dynamics in mass politics. In some works, this is a conscious analytic decision, premised on the assumption that mass politics was essentially irrelevant to the behavior of representatives from a one-party authoritarian region. For others, it is simply a practical concession to the challenges of measuring public opinion and electoral behavior in a historical context where proxies such as partisanship and presidential vote do not have a straightforward meaning.[35] What this book has shown is that the Southern white public played a key role in these dynamics. Through their participation in Democratic primaries, nonelite Southern whites helped determine what kinds of candidates were selected into office

[30] Zelizer, *Taxing America*; Jacobs, "Policymaking as Political Constraint."
[31] Hahrie Han and David W. Brady, "A Delayed Return to Historical Norms: Congressional Party Polarization after the Second World War," *British Journal of Political Science* 37, no. 3 (2007): 505.
[32] James MacGregor Burns, *The Deadlock of Democracy: Four-Party Politics in America* (Englewood Cliffs, NJ: Prentice-Hall, 1963); Polsby, *How Congress Evolves*.
[33] David R. Mayhew, "The Long 1950s as a Policy Era," in *The Politics of Major Policy Reform*, ed. Jeffery A. Jenkins and Sidney M. Milkis (New York: Cambridge University Press, 2013), 27–47.
[34] Thomas J. Mann and Norman J. Ornstein, *It's Even Worse Than It Looks: How the American Constitutional System Collided with the New Politics of Extremism* (New York: Basic Books, 2012).
[35] Though see David R. Mayhew, *Party Loyalty among Congressmen: The Difference between Democrats and Republicans, 1947–1962* (Cambridge, MA: Harvard University Press, 1966).

and whether they remained there in subsequent elections. Thus, when the Southern public turned to the right in the late 1930s, Southern MCs followed, but without turning totally against the aspects of the New Deal that retained support in the mass public. This is not to suggest that public opinion was some sort of "unmoved mover"; the mass public reacted to and was to some extent manipulated by the actions of politicians and other elites.[36] But it does mean that scholars of American political development must take account of the ways that mass politics shaped and constrained the behavior of politicians, even in the one-party South.

7.2.2 Mass Politics in Authoritarian Regimes

The one-party South shared much in common with authoritarian regimes elsewhere in the world. The most direct comparison cases—most of which are, like the one-party South itself, no longer in existence—are regimes in which democracy is restricted to a subset of the population. These include racial or ethnic democracies such as South Africa during Apartheid, Liberia under Americo-Liberan rule, and the Baltic States after the breakdown of the Soviet Union.[37] As Samuel Huntington observes, a common response to the "bifurcation" of society into dominant and subordinate groups is the emergence of an "exclusionary one-party system." Such systems, he argues, serve a dual purpose: "mobilizing support from their constituency while at the same time suppressing or restricting political activity by the subordinate social force."[38] This description provides an apt description of Southern Democratic parties, and of the institution of the white primary in particular.

Yet the fact that the South was a subnational enclave meant that it differed from *national* exclusionary one-party systems in important respects. On one hand, Southern states faced policymaking constraints that national regimes did not.[39] In South Africa, for example, the National

---

[36] On the 1930s–40s, see Schickler and Caughey, "Public Opinion"; on MCs as participants in the public sphere, see David R. Mayhew, *America's Congress: Actions in the Public Sphere, James Madison through Newt Gingrich* (New Haven, CT: Yale University Press, 2000).

[37] On Liberia, see M. B. Akpan, "Black Imperialism: Americo-Liberian Rule over the African Peoples of Liberia, 1841–1964," *Canadian Journal of African Studies* 7, no. 2 (1973): 227–228 and *passim*; on the Baltic States, which restricted the participation of Russian ethnics, see Roeder, "Varieties of Post-Soviet Authoritarian Regimes."

[38] Huntington, "Social and Institutional Dynamics of One-Party Systems," 15. An alternative response to social bifurcation identified by Huntington is the "revolutionary one-party system," which aims to assimilate or eliminate the subordinate social force rather than merely subordinate it.

[39] Huntington notes, however, that among other conditions, "The maintenance of [a national] exclusionary one-party system depends on . . . a sympathetic or indifferent

Party—which held power continuously from 1948 to 1994—used discriminatory labor regulations and government employment in a successful bid to largely eliminate the previously widespread poverty in the Afrikaner population that was its political base (at the expense of native Africans).[40] By contrast, the democratic and egalitarian guarantees of the U.S. constitutional system, weak and incomplete as they were, nevertheless placed limits on just how overtly racist and authoritarian the South could be. In particular, the explicitly discriminatory laws that effectively guaranteed South African whites high wages and insulated them from black labor-market competition would have been declared unconstitutional if attempted in the South.[41]

On the other hand, the South's embeddedness in a larger (and richer) nation changed the potential scope of income redistribution. By wielding influence at the national level, the representatives of the one-party South could (and did) effect the implementation of policies that fostered economic development in and redistribution of wealth to their region. Though it by no means eliminated poverty among Southern whites (let alone blacks), the federal investment in the region initiated by the New Deal and continuing during and after World War II contribute heavily to the massive rise in the region's living standards over the course of the twentieth century.[42] In these respects, then, a direct comparison between exclusionary national and subnational regimes may be misleading. A broader similarity, however, remains: regimes premised on the bifurcation of society will be more likely to endure if they find ways of mobilizing and rewarding nonelite members of the dominant group.

A second natural point of comparison for the one-party South are subnational authoritarian enclaves, which exist in many countries, especially

---

international environment that does not challenge the legitimacy of the system";
Huntington, "Social and Institutional Dynamics of One-Party Systems," 18–19.
[40] Kenneth P. Vickery, "'Herrenvolk' Democracy and Egalitarianism in South Africa and the U.S. South.," *Comparative Studies in Society and History* 16, no. 3 (1974): 326–327.
[41] Even in the early twentieth century, when respect for black rights was at its postslavery nadir, the U.S. Supreme Court invalidated several Jim Crow statutes that verged to close to explicit racial discrimination; see Klarman, *From Jim Crow to Civil Rights*, chapter 2. Southern states did, of course, discriminate against blacks in innumerable ways, but the Southern labor market itself, at least for unskilled workers, appears to have been relatively free from discrimination. Where Southern states' policies exerted much of their economic influence is through unequal funding of black schools, which denied African Americans the training needed to compete for (higher-paying) skilled jobs in the first place; Wright, *Sharing the Prize*.
[42] Schulman, *Cotton Belt to Sunbelt*; Fred Bateman, Jaime Ros, and Jason E. Taylor, "Did New Deal and World War II Public Capital Investments Facilitate a 'Big Push' in the American South?," *Journal of Institutional and Theoretical Economics* 165, no. 2 (2009): 307–341; Wright, "The New Deal and the Modernization of the South."

in Latin America, that are nominally democratic at the national level.[43] The rulers of these enclaves "face two apparently contradictory tasks," Edward Gibson has noted. "They must exercise authoritarian control over the local polity while linking it institutionally to the national democratic polity."[44] Locally hegemonic parties, such as the Democratic Party in the South, often play a crucial role in managing these tasks, providing an institutional vehicle for controlling the enclave while monopolizing (in Key's words) "foreign relations" with the national polity.[45] Indeed, the "party-state" was so central to enclave governance that the South's democratization entailed (and commenced with) an attack on the party, in the form of *Smith v. Allwright*'s invalidation of the white primary.[46]

Although comparison with authoritarian enclaves elsewhere provides a revealing lens for analyzing the one-party South, it is also important to recognize the ways that the South does not fit this framework. Most saliently, Gibson's work in particular leaves little room for formal political contestation within the regime. The enclave parties he describes are far more organized and closed than the Southern Democratic parties Key described as "merely a holding-company for a congeries of transient squabbling factions."[47] Only Virginia's Byrd Organization came close to the kind of boss-directed machine rule Gibson describes in Mexico or Argentina. Notwithstanding their centrality to enclave rule, Democratic Party organizations in other Southern states were actually remarkably weak, at least at the state level, and for that reason quite permeable to opposition challenges as long as these challenges did not fundamentally threaten white hegemony.

The prevalence of electoral and other forms of popular participation is a prominent theme in the recent literature on authoritarian regimes. While in some cases elections are a mere facade, there are also many "competitive authoritarian" regimes in which incumbent officials face real electoral opposition.[48] Elections may serve a variety of functions in such regimes, including coopting potential opponents, selecting relatively popular elites,

[43] Guillermo O'Donnell, "On the State, Democratization and Some Conceptual Problems: A Latin American View with Glances at Some Postcommunist Countries," *World Development* 21, no. 8 (1993): 1355–1369.
[44] Gibson, "Boundary Control: Subnational Authoritarianism in Democratic Countries," 109.
[45] Key, *Southern Politics*; see also Gibson, *Boundary Control*, chapter 3.
[46] Mickey, "Beginning of the End"; see also Richard M. Valelly, *The Two Reconstructions: The Struggle for Black Enfranchisement* (Chicago: University of Chicago Press, 2004).
[47] Key, *Southern Politics*, 16.
[48] Steven Levitsky and Lucan A. Way, "Elections without Democracy: The Rise of Competitive Authoritarianism," *Journal of Democracy* 13, no. 2 (2002): 53–54.

and eliciting information about mass preferences.[49] There is also some evidence that authoritarian elections, like elections in democratic regimes, induce officials to respond to citizens' preferences.[50] These short-term benefits, however, may come at the long-term cost of strengthening the regime.[51] The durability of the one-party South, and particularly the loyalty of many whites to it, lends support to this hypothesis. More generally, this book underlines the value of incorporating mass opinion, electoral politics, and representation—concepts central to the study of democratic politics—into analyses of authoritarian regimes.

7.2.3 Parties and Democratic Politics

Just because the one-party South was not itself a democracy does not mean that we cannot learn something about democracy from studying it. This, indeed, is an implicit premise of scholars since Key who have sought to draw general lessons about democratic politics from the case of the South.[52] Chief among these lessons is the claim that a multiparty system—and specifically, partisan electoral competition—is a necessary condition for democracy. Notwithstanding certain theoretical[53] and empirical[54] attempts to imagine democracy without partisan competition, the general consensus among political scientists is that you cannot have the first without the second.[55] Along with nonpartisan municipal elections, the one-party South is frequently cited as Exhibit A for this claim.

My findings in this book, however, suggest that the conventional wisdom on parties and democracy requires, if not outright revision, then substantial qualification. I found no evidence that MCs from the one-party South were systematically less responsive or more conservative than non-Southern MCs with ideologically similar selectorates. This runs counter to the "ruptured linkages" view that elections without partisan competition yield poor representation. It also contrasts sharply with the results

---

[49] Jennifer Gandhi and Ellen Lust-Okar, "Elections under Authoritarianism," *Annual Review of Political Science* 12 (2009): 405.
[50] Melanie Manion, "The Electoral Connection in the Chinese Countryside," *American Political Science Review* 90, no. 4 (1996): 736–748.
[51] Gandhi and Lust-Okar, "Elections under Authoritarianism," 406.
[52] See, e.g., Aldrich and Griffin, *Why Parties Matter*.
[53] Macpherson, *The Real World of Democracy*; Ware, *Citizens, Parties, and the State*.
[54] William Tordoff, "The General Election in Tanzania," *Journal of Commonwealth Political Studies* 4, no. 1 (1966): 47–64; Schaffner, Streb, and Wright, "Teams without Uniforms."
[55] Among many others, see Schattschneider, *Party Government*; Key, *Southern Politics*; Hawley, *Nonpartisan Elections*; Aldrich, *Why Parties?*; Richard S. Katz, "Party in Democratic Theory," in *Handbook of Party Politics* (Thousand Oaks, CA: SAGE, 2006), 34–46; Wright, "Charles Adrian."

of analogous analyses of state-level representation, which conform almost perfectly to the ruptured linkages model. I have suggested that these divergent representational patterns stem from the fact that U.S. senators and representatives from the one-party South, unlike state-level officials, operated in a national political arena structured by partisan conflict. This is turn affected the informational environment of congressional politics in the South, giving voters access to ideological and other information that would normally be conveyed by party labels. In short, because congressional politics in the region lacked partisan elections but not partisan government, Southern MCs seem to have been about as responsive to their voters as non-Southerners were. The broader implication is that as long as multiple parties define political conflict in government and in the public sphere generally, parties *in elections* may not be necessary for democracy.

It is important to recognize the scope conditions for this (tentative) conclusion. Most fundamentally, it presumes that in the absence of partisan opposition, elections will continue to be held and contested. That is, once elected, officials will not use their power to eliminate the possibility of future challenges, intraparty or otherwise. The turn-of-the-century Democrats who constructed the one-party South, though they took advantage of their ascendancy by disenfranchising African Americans and eviscerating the electoral base of their partisan opponents, nonetheless failed to eliminate electoral competition entirely, and with respect to intraparty competition, actually expanded it. This was in large part because the South was not an autonomous polity, but rather was embedded in a larger (and more securely democratic) national regime. The South's subnational embeddedness was thus crucial in at least two respects: it not only allowed two-party politics to "spill over" into the one-party region, but also ensured that meaningful elections would continue to be held. Given the many examples of hegemonic-party regimes in which incumbents, once elected, never voluntarily relinquish power, I have little confidence that the lessons of the congressional politics in one-party South apply to national one-party regimes elsewhere in the world.

Where I think that the lessons do travel are to what Sartori calls "two-tier party systems," which feature a multiparty national system superimposed on one-party subnational ones.[56] Such systems are, I would guess, quite common around the world, even in fully democratic regimes, but they—along with subnational party systems more generally—have been largely neglected by party scholars.[57] To the extent that they have

---

[56] Sartori, *Parties and Party Systems*, 83–84.
[57] Edward L. Gibson and Julieta Suarez-Cao, "Federalized Party Systems and Subnational Party Competition: Theory and an Empirical Application to Argentina," *Comparative Politics* 43, no. 1 (2010): 21–39.

been studied, the focus has been on subnational units' "internal" politics (e.g., the formulation of municipal or state policies). Though some research in this vein has found results similar to mine,[58] the implications of my work are clearest for subnational units' "foreign relations" with the national polity. My findings suggest that the national representatives of one-party enclaves may be more responsive than enclave-level officials. This conclusion likely depends heavily on institutional and other factors, however, and as yet we know very little about how such institutional variation, particularly variation in the mechanisms of intraparty contestation and in the structure of the national party system, affects subnational democracy.[59] My hope is that the questions raised in this book will spur other scholars to pursue a broader research agenda on representation and democracy in one-party settings around the world. Not only are such one-party settings important in themselves, but because we cannot fully understand a phenomenon without considering its absence, they also have much to teach us about the role that partisan competition plays in multiparty democracies.

---

[58] See, e.g., the finding that municipal-level responsiveness does not seem to depend on whether elections are partisan or nonpartisan; Tausanovitch and Warshaw, "Representation in Municipal Government."

[59] Gibson and Suarez-Cao, for example, note that in Argentina's Santa Cruz province, the locally dominant Peronist Party created an electoral system that allowed party factions to compete with each other in the general election; Gibson and Suarez-Cao, "Federalized Party Systems," 32.

References

Achen, Christopher H. "Mass Political Attitudes and the Survey Response." *American Political Science Review* 69, no. 4 (1975): 1218–1231.

———. "Measuring Representation." *American Journal of Political Science* 22, no. 3 (1978): 475–510.

Akpan, M. B. "Black Imperialism: Americo-Liberian Rule over the African Peoples of Liberia, 1841–1964." *Canadian Journal of African Studies* 7, no. 2 (1973): 217–236.

Aldrich, John H. *Why Parties?* Chicago: University of Chicago Press, 1995.

———. *Why Parties? A Second Look.* Chicago: University of Chicago Press, 2011.

Aldrich, John H., and John D. Griffin. "Parties, Elections, and Democratic Politics." In *The Oxford Handbook of American Elections and Political Behavior*, edited by Jan E. Leighley, 595–610. New York: Oxford University Press, 2010.

———. *Why Parties Matter: Political Competition and Democracy in the American South.* Chicago: University of Chicago Press, 2017.

Alesina, Alberto. "Credibility and Policy Convergence in a Two-Party System with Rational Voters." *American Economic Review* 78, no. 4 (1988): 796–805.

Alsop, Joseph, and Robert Kintner. "Louisiana Switch Sank Wages Bill." *New York Times*, December 22, 1937, 20.

Alston, Lee J., and Joseph P. Ferrie. *Southern Paternalism and the American Welfare State: Economics, Politics, and Institutions in the South, 1865–1965.* New York: Cambridge University Press, 1999.

Alt, James E. "The Impact of the Voting Rights Act on Black and White Voter Registration in the South." In *Quiet Revolution in the South: The Impact of the Voting Rights Act, 1965–1990*, edited by Chandler Davidson and Bernard Grofman, 351–377. Princeton: Princeton University Press, 1994.

Amenta, Edwin, and Theda Skocpol. "Redefining the New Deal: World War II and the Development of Social Provision in the United States." In *The Politics of Social Policy in the United States*, edited by Margaret Weir, Ann Shola Orloff, and Theda Skocpol, 81–122. Princeton: Princeton University Press, 1988.

American Political Science Association. "Toward a More Responsible Two-Party System: A Report of the Committee on Political Parties." *American Political Science Review* 44, no. 3, Part 2, Supplement (1950): 1–96.

Anckar, Dag, and Carsten Anckar. "Democracies without Parties." *Comparative Political Studies* 33, no. 2 (2000): 225–247.

Ansolabehere, Stephen, John Mark Hansen, Shigeo Hirano, and James M. Snyder Jr. "More Democracy: The Direct Primary and Competition in U.S. Elections." *Studies in American Political Development* 24, no. 2 (2010): 190–205.

Ansolabehere, Stephen, John Mark Hansen, Shigeo Hirano, and James M.
Snyder Jr. "The Incumbency Advantage in U.S. Primary Elections." *Electoral
Studies* 26, no. 3 (2007): 660–668.

Ansolabehere, Stephen, and James M. Snyder Jr. *The End of Inequality: One
Person, One Vote and the Transformation of American Politics.* New York:
Norton, 2008.

Ansolabehere, Stephen, James M. Snyder Jr., and Charles Stewart III. "Candidate
Positioning in U.S. House Elections." *American Journal of Political Science* 45,
no. 1 (2001): 136–159.

AP. "Huddleston Is Defeated: Alabamian's Negative Votes on New Deal Bills
Figured in Campaign." *New York Times*, June 10, 1936, 24.

———. "New Deal Loyalty Issue in Alabama Vole Today." *New York Herald
Tribune*, June 9, 1936, 5A.

———. "Republicans to Push Poll Tax Fight to Avenge South's Vote on Income
Levy." *New York Times*, June 24, 1947, 9.

Arnold, R. Douglas. *The Logic of Congressional Action.* New Haven, CT: Yale
University Press, 1990.

Arrow, Kenneth J. *Social Choice and Individual Values*, 2nd ed. 1951. New
Haven, CT: Yale University Press, 1963.

Ashworth, Scott. "Electoral Accountability: Recent Theoretical and Empirical
Work." *Annual Review of Political Science* 15, no. 1 (2012): 183–201.

Ashworth, Scott, and Ethan Bueno de Mesquita. "Informative Party Labels with
Institutional and Electoral Variation." *Journal of Theoretical Politics* 20, no. 3
(2008): 251–273.

Badger, Anthony J. "*Brown* and Backlash." In *Massive Resistance*, edited by
Clive Webb, 39–55. Oxford: Oxford University Press, 2005.

———. "How Did the New Deal Change the South?" In *New Deal/New South*,
31–44. Fayetteville: University of Arkansas Press, 2007.

———. "Huey Long and the New Deal." In *New Deal/New South*, 1–30.
Fayetteville: University of Arkansas Press, 2007.

———. *The New Deal: The Depression Years, 1933–1940.* Chicago: Ivan R.
Dee, 2002.

———. "The Rise and Fall of Biracial Politics in the South." In *The Southern
State of Mind*, edited by Jan Nordby Gretlund, 23–35. Columbia: University
of South Carolina Press, 1999.

———. "Southerners Who Refused to Sign the Southern Manifesto." *The
Historical Journal* 42, no. 2 (1999): 533–534.

———. "Whatever Happened to Roosevelt's New Generation of Southerners?"
In *New Deal/New South*, 58–71. Fayetteville: University of Arkansas Press,
2007.

Bafumi, Joseph, and Michael C. Herron. "Leapfrog Representation and
Extremism: A Study of American Voters and Their Members in Congress."
American Political Science Review 104, no. 3 (2010): 519–542.

Bailey, Robert J. "Theodore G. Bilbo and the Senatorial Election of 1934."
Southern Quarterly 10 (October 1971): 91–105.

Bailey, Stephen Kemp. *Congress Makes a Law: The Story behind the
Employment Act of 1946.* New York: Columbia University Press, 1950.

Barnard, William D. *Dixiecrats and Democrats: Alabama Politics, 1942–1950.* Tuscaloosa: University of Alabama Press, 1974.

Bartels, Larry M. "Democracy with Attitudes." In *Electoral Democracy*, edited by Michael B. MacKuen and George Rabinowitz, 48–82. Ann Arbor: University of Michigan Press, 2003.

Bateman, Fred, Jaime Ros, and Jason E. Taylor. "Did New Deal and World War II Public Capital Investments Facilitate a 'Big Push' in the American South?" *Journal of Institutional and Theoretical Economics* 165, no. 2 (2009): 307–341.

Battistin, Erich, Richard Blundell, and Arthur Lewbel. "Why Is Consumption More Log Normal than Income? Gibrat's Law Revisited." *Journal of Political Economy* 117, no. 6 (2009): 1140–1154.

Baum, Matthew A., and Samuel Kernell. "Economic Class and Popular Support for Franklin Roosevelt in War and Peace." *Public Opinion Quarterly* 65, no. 2 (2001): 198–229.

Bawn, Kathleen, Martin Cohen, David Karol, Seth Masket, Hans Noel, and John Zaller. "A Theory of Political Parties: Groups, Policy Demands and Nominations in American Politics." *Perspectives on Politics* 10, no. 3 (2012): 571–597.

Bell, Jonathan W. "Conceptualising Southern Liberalism: Ideology and the Pepper–Smathers 1950 Primary in Florida." *Journal of American Studies* 37, no. 1 (2003): 17–45.

Bensel, Richard. *Sectionalism and American Political Development: 1880–1980.* Madison: University of Wisconsin Press, 1984.

———. "Sectionalism and Congressional Development." In *The Oxford Handbook of the American Congress*, edited by Eric Schickler and Frances Lee, 761–786. New York: Oxford University Press, 2011.

Berinsky, Adam J. "American Public Opinion in the 1930s and 1940s: The Analysis of Quota-Controlled Sample Survey Data." *Public Opinion Quarterly* 70, no. 4 (2006): 499–529.

Bernhardt, Dan, Larissa Campuzano, Francesco Squintani, and Odilon Câmara. "On the Benefits of Party Competition." *Games and Economic Behavior* 66, no. 2 (2009): 685–707.

Besley, Timothy, and Stephen Coate. "An Economic Model of Representative Democracy." *Quarterly Journal of Economics* 112, no. 1 (1997): 85–114.

Besley, Timothy, Torsten Persson, and Daniel M. Sturm. "Political Competition, Policy and Growth: Theory and Evidence from the US." *Review of Economic Studies* 77, no. 4 (2010): 1329–1352.

Biles, Roger. *The South and the New Deal.* Lexington: University Press of Kentucky, 1994.

Black, Earl, and Merle Black. *Politics and Society in the South.* Cambridge, MA: Harvard University Press, 1987.

———. *The Rise of Southern Republicans.* Cambridge, MA: Belknap, 2002.

Blackwell, Matthew, James Honaker, and Gary King. "A Unified Approach to Measurement Error and Missing Data: Overview and Applications." *Sociological Methods & Research* 46, no. 3 (2017): 303–341.

Bloch Rubin, Ruth. *Building the Bloc: Intraparty Organization in the U.S. Congress*. New York: Cambridge University Press, 2017.

Blondel, Jean. *An Introduction to Comparative Government*. New York: Praeger, 1969.

Boix, Carles. *Democracy and Redistribution*. New York: Cambridge University Press, 2003.

Boynton, George Robert. "Southern Conservatism: Constituency Opinion and Congressional Voting." *Public Opinion Quarterly* 29, no. 2 (1965): 259.

Brady, David W., and Charles S. Bullock III. "Is There a Conservative Coalition in the House?" *Journal of Politics* 42, no. 2 (1980): 549–559.

Brattain, Michelle. "Making Friends and Enemies: Textile Workers and Political Action in Post-World War II Georgia." *Journal of Southern History* 63, no. 1 (1997): 91–138.

Breaux, David A., and Stephen D. Shaffer. "Southern Political Attitudes." In *The Oxford Handbook of Southern Politics*, edited by Charles S. Bullock III and Mark J. Rozell, 235–254. New York: Oxford University Press, 2012.

Brinkley, Alan. *The End of Reform: New Deal Liberalism in Recession and War*. New York: Vintage Books, 1995.

Brooks, Jennifer E. "Winning the Peace: Georgia Veterans and the Struggle to Define the Political Legacy of World War II." *Journal of Southern History* 66, no. 3 (2000): 563–604.

Brown, Michael K. *Race, Money, and the American Welfare State*. Ithaca, NY: Cornell University Press, 1999.

Brown-Dean, Khalilah, Zoltan Hajnal, Christina Rivers, and Ismail White. *50 Years of the Voting Rights Act: The State of Race in Politics*. Joint Center for Political and Economic Studies, 2015. http://jointcenter.org/sites/default/files/VRA%20report%2C%203.5.15%20%281130%20am%29%28updated%29.pdf.

Brownlee, W. Elliot. *Federal Taxation in America: A Short History*, 2nd ed. Washington, DC and New York: Woodrow Wilson Center Press/Cambridge University Press, 2004.

———. "Tax Regimes, National Crises, and State-Building in America." In *Funding the Modern American State, 1941–1995*, edited by W. Elliot Brownlee, 37–104. New York: Cambridge University Press, 1996.

Bryan, Frank M. *Yankee Politics in Rural Vermont*. Hanover, NH: University Press of New England, 1974.

"Bryson Says Nobody Questioning Him on How He Stands on Political Bolt." *Florence Morning News* (Florence, SC), October 17, 1948, 12–A.

Bueno de Mesquita, Bruce, Alastair Smith, Randolph M. Siverson, and James D. Morrow. *The Logic of Political Survival*. Cambridge, MA: MIT Press, 2003.

Burns, James MacGregor. *The Deadlock of Democracy: Four-Party Politics in America*. Englewood Cliffs, NJ: Prentice-Hall, 1963.

Caldeira, Gregory A. "Public Opinion and the U.S. Supreme Court: FDR's Court-Packing Plan." *American Political Science Review* 81, no. 4 (1987): 1139–1153.

Calvert, Randall L. "Robustness of the Multidimensional Voting Model: Candidate Motivations, Uncertainty, and Convergence." *American Journal of Political Science* 29, no. 1 (1985): 69–95.

Canes-Wrone, Brandice. "From Mass Preferences to Policy." *Annual Review of Political Science* 18, no. 1 (2015): 147–165.

Canes-Wrone, Brandice, David W. Brady, and John F. Cogan. "Out of Step, Out of Office: Electoral Accountability and House Members' Voting." *American Political Science Review* 96, no. 1 (2002): 127–140.

Canes-Wrone, Brandice, and Kenneth W. Shotts. "When Do Elections Encourage Ideological Rigidity?" *American Political Science Review* 101, no. 2 (2007): 273–288.

Cantril, Hadley, ed. *Public Opinion, 1935–1946*. Prepared by Mildred Strunk. Princeton: Princeton University Press, 1951.

Carleton, William G. "The Southern Politician—1900 and 1950." *Journal of Politics* 13, no. 2 (1951): 215–231.

Caro, Robert A. *Master of the Senate*. New York: Vintage Books, 2002.
———. *Means of Ascent*. New York: Vintage Books, 1990.
———. *The Path to Power*. New York: Vintage Books, 1981.

Carroll, Royce, and Jason Eichorst. "The Role of Party: The Legislative Consequences of Partisan Electoral Competition." *Legislative Studies Quarterly* 38, no. 1 (2013): 83–109.

Cascio, Elizabeth U., and Ebonya Washington. "Valuing the Vote: The Redistribution of Voting Rights and State Funds Following the Voting Rights Act of 1965." *Quarterly Journal of Economics* 129, no. 1 (2014): 379–433.

Castro, J. Justin. "Mexican Braceros and Arkansas Cotton: Agricultural Labor and Civil Rights in the Post-World War II South." *Arkansas Historical Quarterly* 75, no. 1 (2016): 27–46.

Caughey, Devin. "Congress, Public Opinion, and Representation in the One-Party South, 1930s–1960s." PhD dissertation, University of California, Berkeley, 2012.

Caughey, Devin, and Sara Chatfield. "Creating a Constituency for New Deal Liberalism: The Policy Feedback Effects of the Tennessee Valley Authority." Paper presented at the APSA Annual Meeting, Philadelphia, September 1, 2016.

Caughey, Devin, and Eric Schickler. "Substance and Change in Congressional Ideology: NOMINATE and Its Alternatives." *Studies in American Political Development* 30, no. 2 (2016): 128–146.

Caughey, Devin, and Christopher Warshaw. "Dynamic Estimation of Latent Opinion Using a Hierarchical Group-Level IRT Model." *Political Analysis* 23, no. 2 (2015): 197–211.
———. "The Dynamics of State Policy Liberalism, 1936–2014." *American Journal of Political Science* 60, no. 4 (2016): 899–913.
———. "Policy Preferences and Policy Change: Dynamic Responsiveness in the American States, 1936–2014." *American Political Science Review*, 2017. doi:10.1017/S0003055417000533.

Christian, Ralph J. "The Folger-Chatham Congressional Primary of 1946." *North Carolina Historical Review* 53, no. 1 (1976): 25–54.

Clapp, Charles L. *The Congressman: His Work As He Sees It*. Garden City, NY: Anchor Books, 1963.

Clausen, Aage R. *How Congressmen Decide: A Policy Focus*. New York: St. Martin's, 1973.

Clinton, Joshua D. "Representation in Congress: Constituents and Roll Calls in the 106th House." *Journal of Politics* 68, no. 2 (2006): 397–409.

Clinton, Joshua, Simon Jackman, and Douglas Rivers. "The Statistical Analysis of Roll Call Data." *American Political Science Review* 98, no. 2 (May 2004): 355–370.

Cobb, James C. *The Most Southern Place on Earth: The Mississippi Delta and the Roots of Regional Identity*. New York: Oxford University Press, 1992.

———. *The South and America since World War II*. New York: Oxford University Press, 2010.

Cohn, Nate. "Mississippi Primary Fight Is One of Geography as Well as Ideology." *New York Times*, June 2, 2014. https://www.nytimes.com/2014/06/03/upshot/mississippi-primary-fight-is-one-of-geography-as-well-as-ideology.html?_r=0.

———. "No, Obama Didn't Win One-Third of White Voters in Deep South." *New York Times*, April 24, 2014. https://www.nytimes.com/2014/04/25/upshot/rebutting-claim-that-obama-had-wider-support-among-southern-whites.html.

Collier, David, and Steven Levitsky. "Democracy with Adjectives: Conceptual Innovation in Comparative Research." *World Politics* 49, no. 3 (1997): 430–451.

Committee on Political Education Research Department Collection, George Meany Memorial AFL-CIO Archives, University of Maryland, College Park, MD.

"Congressional Quarterly Polls." In *CQ Almanac 1949*, 5th ed., 06-462–06-463. Washington, DC: Congressional Quarterly, 1950. http://library.cqpress.com/cqalmanac/cqal49-1400486.

Converse, Jean M. *Survey Research in the United States: Roots and Emergence*. Berkeley: University of California Press, 1987.

Coode, Thomas H. "Bryant Thomas Castellow of Georgia." *Georgia Advocate* 8, no. Fall (1971): 16–20.

Cox, Gary W. *Making Votes Count: Strategic Coordination in the World's Electoral Systems*. New York: Cambridge University Press, 1997.

Cox, Gary W., and Mathew D. McCubbins. *Legislative Leviathan*. Berkeley: University of California Press, 1993.

Cutler, Fred. "The Simplest Shortcut of All: Sociodemographic Characteristics and Electoral Choice." *Journal of Politics* 64, no. 2 (2002): 466–490.

Dahl, Robert. *Who Governs?* New Haven, CT: Yale University Press, 1961.

Dahl, Robert A. *Democracy and Its Critics*. New Haven, CT: Yale University Press, 1989.

———. *On Democracy*. New Haven, CT: Yale University Press, 1998.

———. *Polyarchy: Participation and Opposition*. New Haven, CT: Yale University Press, 1971.

Dallek, Robert. *Lone Star Rising: Lyndon Johnson and His Times, 1908–1960.* Vol. 1. New York: Oxford University Press, 1991.

Dangerfield, Royden J., and Richard H. Flynn. "Voter Motivation in the 1936 Oklahoma Democratic Primary." *Southwestern Social Science Quarterly* 17, no. 2 (1936): 97–105.

Davies, Gareth, and Martha Derthick. "Race and Social Welfare Policy: The Social Security Act of 1935." *Political Science Quarterly* 112, no. 2 (1997): 217–235.

DeWitt, Larry. "The Decision to Exclude Agricultural and Domestic Workers from the 1935 Social Security Act." *Social Security Bulletin* 70, no. 4 (2010): 49–68.

Diamond, Larry, and Richard Gunther. "Types and Functions of Parties." In *Political Parties and Democracy*, edited by Larry Diamond and Richard Gunther, 3–39. Baltimore: Johns Hopkins University Press.

DiSalvo, Daniel. "Party Factions in Congress." *Congress & the Presidency* 36, no. July (2010): 27–57.

Doherty, Herbert J., Jr. "Liberal and Conservative Voting Patterns in Florida." *Journal of Politics* 14, no. 3 (1952): 403–417.

Domhoff, G. William, and Michael J. Webber. *Class and Power in the New Deal: Corporate Moderates, Southern Democrats, and the Liberal-Labor Coalition.* Stanford, CA: Stanford University Press, 2011.

Douglas, Paul H., and Joseph Hackman. "The Fair Labor Standards Act of 1938 I." *Political Science Quarterly* 53, no. 4 (1938): 491–515.

Downs, Anthony. *An Economic Theory of Democracy.* New York: Harper, 1957.

Dubofsky, Melvyn. *The State and Labor in Modern America.* Chapel Hill: University of North Carolina Press, 1994.

Duggan, John. "Repeated Elections with Asymmetric Information." *Economics & Politics* 12, no. 2 (2000): 109–135.

Dunham, James, Devin Caughey, and Christopher Warshaw. dgo: *DynamicEstimation of Group-Level Opinion. R package version 0.2.3.,* 2016. https://jamesdunham.github.io/dgo/.

Dunn, Susan. *Roosevelt's Purge: How FDR Fought to Change the Democratic Party.* New York: Cambridge University Press, 2010.

Eckstein, Harry. "Case Studies and Theory in Political Science." In *Handbook of Political Science*, edited by Fred I. Greenstein and Nelson W. Polsby, 7:94–137. Reading, MA: Addison-Wesley, 1975.

Eguia, Jon X. "Endogenous Parties in an Assembly." *American Journal of Political Science* 55, no. 1 (2010): 16–26.

Ellis, Christopher, and James A. Stimson. "Symbolic Ideology in the American Electorate." *Electoral Studies* 28, no. 3 (2009): 388–402.

Epstein, Leon D. *Political Parties in the American Mold.* Madison: University of Wisconsin Press, 1986.

Erikson, Robert S., Michael B. MacKuen, and James A. Stimson. *The Macro Polity.* New York: Cambridge University Press, 2002.

Erskine, Hazel Gaudet. "The Polls: Some Gauges of Conservatism." *Public Opinion Quarterly* 28, no. 1 (1964): 154–168.

Ewing, Cortez A. M. *Primary Elections in the South: A Study in Uniparty Politics*. Norman: University of Oklahoma Press, 1953.

Farhang, Sean. "The Political Development of Job Discrimination Litigation, 1963–1976." *Studies in American Political Development* 23, no. 1 (2009): 23.

Farhang, Sean, and Ira Katznelson. "The Southern Imposition: Congress and Labor in the New Deal and Fair Deal." *Studies in American Political Development* 19, no. 1 (2005): 1–30.

Fearon, James D. "Electoral Accountability and the Control of Politicians: Selecting Good Types versus Sanctioning Poor Performance." In *Democracy, Accountability, and Representation*, edited by Adam Przeworski, Susan Carol Stokes, and Bernard Manin, 55–97. New York: Cambridge University Press, 1999.

Fenno, Richard F., Jr. *Congress at the Grassroots: Representational Change in the South, 1970–1998*. Chapel Hill: University of North Carolina Press, 2000.

———. *Congressmen in Committees*. Boston: Little, Brown, 1973.

———. "U.S. House Members in Their Constituencies: An Exploration." *American Political Science Review* 71, no. 3 (1977): 883–917.

File, Thom. *The Diversifying Electorate—Voting Rates by Race and Hispanic Origin in 2012 (and Other Recent Elections)*. Current Population Survey Reports, P20-569. U.S. Census Bureau, Washington, DC, 2013.

Finley, Keith M. *Delaying the Dream: Southern Senators and the Fight against Civil Rights, 1938–1965*. Baton Rouge: Louisiana State University Press, 2008.

———. *Southern Opposition to Civil Rights in the United States Senate: A Tactical and Ideological Analysis, 1938–1965*. PhD dissertation, Louisiana State University, Baton Rouge, 2003.

Fiorina, Morris P. "The Decline of Collective Responsibility in American Politics." *Daedalus* 109, no. 3 (1980): 25–45.

Fishback, Price V., Michael R. Haines, and Shawn Kantor. "The Impact of the New Deal on Black and White Infant Mortality in the South." *Explorations in Economic History* 38, no. 1 (2001): 93–122.

Fleck, Robert K. "Democratic Opposition to the Fair Labor Standards Act of 1938." *Journal of Economic History* 62, no. 1 (2002): 25–54.

Fontenay, Charles L. *Estes Kefauver: A Biography*. Knoxville: University of Tennessee Press, 1980.

Fowler, Anthony. "Electoral and Policy Consequences of Voter Turnout: Evidence from Compulsory Voting in Australia." *Quarterly Journal of Political Science* 8, no. 2 (2013): 159–182.

Frantz, Joe B. "Opening a Curtain: The Metamorphosis of Lyndon B. Johnson." *Journal of Southern History* 45, no. 1 (1979): 3–26.

Frederickson, Kari. *The Dixiecrat Revolt and the End of the Solid South*. London: University of North Carolina Press, 2001.

Friedman, Gerald. "The Political Economy of Early Southern Unionism: Race, Politics, and Labor in the South, 1880–1953." *Journal of Economic History* 60, no. 2 (2000): 384–413.

Gailmard, Sean, and Jeffery A. Jenkins. "Agency Problems, the 17th Amendment, and Representation in the Senate." *American Journal of Political Science* 53, no. 2 (2009): 324–342.

Gall, Gilbert J. *The Politics of Right to Work: The Labor Federations as Special Interests, 1943–1979*. New York: Greenwood Press, 1988.

———. "Southern Industrial Workers and Anti-Union Sentiment: Arkansas and Florida in 1944." In *Organized Labor in the Twentieth-Century South*, edited by Robert H. Zieger, 223–249. Knoxville: University of Tennessee Press, 1991.

Gandhi, Jennifer, and Ellen Lust-Okar. "Elections under Authoritarianism." *Annual Review of Political Science* 12 (2009): 403–422.

Gans, Curtis, ed. *Voter Turnout in the United States 1788–2009*. CQ Press, 2011. http://dx.doi.org/10.4135/9781608712700.

Garson, Robert A. *The Democratic Party and the Politics of Sectionalism, 1941–1948*. Baton Rouge: Louisiana State University Press, 1974.

Geer, John G. *From Tea Leaves to Opinion Polls*. New York: Columbia University Press, 1996.

Gibson, Edward L. "Boundary Control: Subnational Authoritarianism in Democratic Countries." *World Politics* 58, no. 1 (2005): 101–132.

———. *Boundary Control: Subnational Authoritarianism in Federal Democracies*. New York: Cambridge University Press, 2012.

Gibson, Edward L., and Julieta Suarez-Cao. "Federalized Party Systems and Subnational Party Competition: Theory and an Empirical Application to Argentina." *Comparative Politics* 43, no. 1 (2010): 21–39.

Gilens, Martin, and Benjamin I. Page. "Testing Theories of American Politics: Elites, Interest Groups, and Average Citizens." *Perspectives on Politics* 12, no. 3 (2014): 564–581.

Gilliam, Thomas Jasper, Sr. "The Second Folsom Administration: The Destruction of Alabama Liberalism, 1954–1958." PhD dissertation, Auburn University, 1975.

Gonzales, William E. "The South Is Still Solid: South Carolina." *Review of Reviews* 93 (January 1936): 38–39.

Grantham, Dewey W. *The Life and Death of the Solid South: A Political History*. Lexington: University Press of Kentucky, 1988.

Graves, John Temple. "This Afternoon." *Birmingham Post*, August 9, 1946.

Grofman, Bernard. "Downs and Two-Party Convergence." *Annual Review of Political Science* 7 (2004): 25–46.

Gross, Donald, and David Breaux. "Historical Trends in U.S. Senate Elections, 1912–1988." *American Politics Quarterly* 19, no. 3 (1991): 284–309.

Grynaviski, Jeffrey D. "The Impact of Electoral Rules on Factional Competition in the Democratic South, 1919–48." *Party Politics* 10, no. 5 (2004): 499–519.

Hagen, Michael G., Edward L. Lascher Jr., and John F. Camobreco. "Response to Matsusaka: Estimating the Effect of Ballot Initiatives on Policy Responsiveness." *Journal of Politics* 63, no. 4 (2001): 1257–1263.

Hahn, Steven. *A Nation under Our Feet: Black Political Struggles in the Rural South from Slavery to the Great Migration*. Cambridge, MA: Harvard University Press, 2003.

Hajnal, Zoltan L. "Who Loses in American Democracy? A Count of Votes Demonstrates the Limited Representation of African Americans." *American Political Science Review* 103, no. 1 (2009): 37–57.

Hall, Wade. *The Rest of the Dream: The Black Odyssey of Lyman Johnson*. Lexington: University Press of Kentucky, 1988.

Hamby, Alonzo L. *Beyond the New Deal: Harry S. Truman and American Liberalism*. New York: Columbia University Press, 1973.

Hamilton, Virginia Van der Veer. *Lister Hill: Statesman from the South*. Chapel Hill: University of North Carolina Press, 1987.

Han, Hahrie, and David W. Brady. "A Delayed Return to Historical Norms: Congressional Party Polarization after the Second World War." *British Journal of Political Science* 37, no. 3 (2007): 505.

Hansen, John Mark, Shigeo Hirano, and James M. Snyder Jr. "Parties within Parties: Parties, Factions, and Coordinated Politics, 1900–1980." In *Governing in a Polarized Age: Elections, Parties, and Political Representation in America*, edited by Alan S. Gerber and Eric Schickler, 143–190. New York: Cambridge University Press, 2017.

Hardeman, D. B., and Donald C. Bacon. *Rayburn: A Biography*. Austin: Texas Monthly Press, 1987.

Hawley, Willis D. *Nonpartisan Elections and the Case for Party Politics*. New York: Wiley, 1973.

Henderson, John Arthur. "Downs' Revenge: Elections, Responsibility and the Rise of Congressional Polarization." PhD dissertation, University of California–Berkeley, Department of Political Science, 2013.

Hero, Alfred O. *The Southerner and World Affairs*. Baton Rouge: Louisiana State University Press, 1965.

Hofstadter, Richard. *The Idea of a Party System: The Rise of Legitimate Opposition in the United States, 1780–1840*. Berkeley: University of California Press, 1969.

Holmans, A. E. *United States Fiscal Policy, 1945–1959: Its Contribution to Economic Stability*. London: Oxford University Press, 1961.

Honaker, James, Gary King, and Matthew Blackwell. "Amelia II: A Program for Missing Data." *Journal of Statistical Software* 45, no. 7 (2011): 1–47. http://www.jstatsoft.org/v45/i07/.

Hood, M. V., III, and Seth C. McKee. "Black Votes Count: The 2014 Republican Senate Nomination in Mississippi." *Social Science Quarterly* 98, no. 1 (2016): 89–106.

Hughes, L. Patrick. "West Texas Swing: Roosevelt Purge in the Land of the Lone Star?" In *The West Texas Historical Association Year Book*, 75:41–53. Abilene, TX: West Texas Historical Association, 1999.

Huntington, Samuel P. "Social and Institutional Dynamics of One-Party Systems." In *Authoritarian Politics in Modern Society: The Dynamics of Established One-Party Systems*, edited by Samuel P. Huntington and Clement H. Moore, 3–47. New York: Basic Books, 1970.

Husted, Thomas A., and Lawrence W. Kenny. "The Effect of the Expansion of the Voting Franchise on the Size of Government." *Journal of Political Economy* 105, no. 1 (1997): 54–82.

Jackman, Simon. *Bayesian Analysis for the Social Sciences*. Hoboken, NJ: Wiley, 2009.

Jackson, John E. *Constituencies and Leaders in Congress: Their Effects on Senate Voting Behavior*. Cambridge, MA: Harvard University Press, 1974.

Jacobs, Alan. "Policymaking as Political Constraint: Institutional Development in the U.S. Social Security Program." In *Explaining Institutional Change: Ambiguity, Agency, and Power*, edited by James Mahoney and Kathleen Thelen, 94–131. New York: Cambridge University Press, 2010.

Jeansonne, Glen. *Leander Perez: Boss of the Delta*. Jackson: University Press of Mississippi, 2006.

Jenkins, Jeffery A. "Examining the Bonding Effects of Party: A Comparative Analysis of Roll-Call Voting in the U.S. and Confederate Houses." *American Journal of Political Science* 43, no. 4 (1999): 1144–1165.

Jessee, Stephen A. "(How) Can We Estimate the Ideology of Citizens and Political Elites on the Same Scale?" *American Journal of Political Science* 60, no. 4 (2016): 1108–1124.

Johnson, Kimberly. *Reforming Jim Crow: Southern Politics and State in the Age before Brown*. New York: Oxford University Press, 2010.

Johnston, Marguerite. "Alabama's Congr. John Sparkman Is One of Three Top Men in House." *Birmingham News Age-Herald*, March 10, 1946.

Karol, David. "Has Polling Enhanced Representation? Unearthing Evidence from the Literary Digest Issue Polls." *Studies in American Political Development* 21 (Spring 2007): 16–29.

Katz, Richard S. "Party in Democratic Theory." In *Handbook of Party Politics*, 34–46. Thousand Oaks, CA: SAGE, 2006.

———. *A Theory of Parties and Electoral Systems*. Baltimore: Johns Hopkins University Press, 1980.

Katznelson, Ira. *Fear Itself: The New Deal and the Origins of Our Time*. New York: Liveright, 2013.

———. "Was the Great Society a Lost Opportunity?" In *The Rise and Fall of the New Deal Order, 1930–1980*, edited by Steve Fraser and Gary Gerstle, 185–211. Princeton: Princeton University Press, 1989.

———. *When Affirmative Action Was White: An Untold History of Racial Inequality in Twentieth-Century America*. New York: Norton, 2005.

Katznelson, Ira, Kim Geiger, and Daniel Kryder. "Limiting Liberalism: The Southern Veto in Congress, 1933–1950." *Political Science Quarterly* 108, no. 2 (1993): 283–306.

Katznelson, Ira, and Quinn Mulroy. "Was the South Pivotal? Situated Partisanship and Policy Coalitions during the New Deal and Fair Deal." *Journal of Politics* 74, no. 2 (2012): 604–620.

Kennedy, David M. *Freedom from Fear: The American People in Depression and War, 1929–1945*. New York: Oxford University Press, 1999.

Key, V. O. *The Responsible Electorate: Rationality in Presidential Voting 1936–1960*. Cambridge, MA: Harvard University Press, 1966.

Key, V. O., Jr. *Politics, Parties & Pressure Groups*. 434–454. New York: Crowell, 1964.

———. *Public Opinion and American Democracy*. New York: Knopf, 1961.

Key, V. O., Jr. *Southern Politics in State and Nation*. New York: Knopf, 1949.

Keyssar, Alexander. *The Right to Vote: The Contested History of Democracy in the United States*. New York: Basic Books, 2000.

Klarman, Michael J. *From Jim Crow to Civil Rights: The Supreme Court and the Struggle for Racial Equality*. New York: Oxford University Press, 2004.

Koeniger, A. Cash. "The New Deal and the States: Roosevelt versus the Byrd Organization in Virginia." *Journal of American History* 68, no. 4 (1982): 876–896.

Korstad, Robert, and Nelson Lichtenstein. "Opportunities Found and Lost: Labor, Radicals, and the Early Civil Rights Movement." *Journal of American History* 75, no. 3 (1988): 786–811.

Kousser, J. Morgan. "Origins of the Run-Off Primary." *The Black Scholar* 15, no. 5 (1984): 23–26.

———. "Progressivism—For Middle-Class Whites Only: North Carolina Education, 1880–1910." *Journal of Southern History* 46, no. 2 (1980): 169–194.

———. *The Shaping of Southern Politics: Suffrage Restriction and the Establishment of the One-Party South*. New Haven, CT: Yale University Press, 1974.

Krehbiel, Keith. "Party Discipline and Measures of Partisanship." *American Journal of Political Science* 44, no. 2 (2000): 212–227.

———. *Pivotal Politics: A Theory of U.S. Lawmaking*. Chicago: University of Chicago Press, 1998.

Ladd, Everett Carll, and Charles D. Hadley. *Transformations of the American Party System: Political Coalitions from the New Deal to the 1970s*. New York: Norton, 1975.

Lee, Brian E. "A Matter of National Concern: The Kennedy Administration and Prince Edward County, Virginia." Master's thesis, Virginia Commonwealth University, Department of History, 2009.

Lee, David S., Enrico Moretti, and Matthew J. Butler. "Do Voters Affect or Elect Policies? Evidence from the U.S. House." *Quarterly Journal of Economics* 119, no. 3 (2004): 807–859.

Leemhuis, Roger P. "Olin Johnston Runs for the Senate." *Proceedings of the South Carolina Historical Association*, 1986, 57–69.

Leip, David. "Dave Leip's Atlas of U.S. Presidential Elections." 2013. http://www.uselectionatlas.org.

Lenz, Gabriel. *Follow the Leader? How Voters Respond to Politicians' Performance and Policies*. Chicago: University of Chicago Press, 2012.

Leuchtenburg, William E. "Franklin D. Roosevelt's Supreme Court 'Packing' Plan." In *Essays on the New Deal*, edited by Harold M. Hillingsworth and William F. Holmes, 69–115. The Walter Prescott Webb Memorial Lectures. Austin: University of Texas Press, 1969.

Leuchtenburg, William Edward. *The White House Looks South: Franklin D. Roosevelt, Harry S. Truman, Lyndon B. Johnson*. Baton Rouge: Louisiana State University Press, 2005.

Levitsky, Steven, and Lucan A. Way. *Competitive Authoritarianism: Hybrid Regimes after the Cold War*. New York: Cambridge University Press, 2010.

———. "Elections without Democracy: The Rise of Competitive Authoritarianism." *Journal of Democracy* 13, no. 2 (2002): 51–65.

Lewis, Jeffrey B., and Chris Tausanovitch. "When Does Joint Scaling Allow for Direct Comparisons of Preferences?" Paper presented at the Conference on Ideal Point Models, Massachusetts Institute of Technology, Cambridge, MA, May 1, 2015. http://idealpoint.tahk.us/papers/lewisTausanovitch.pdf.

Lichtenstein, Nelson. "From Corporatism to Collective Bargaining: Organized Labor and the Eclipse of Social Democracy in the Postwar Era." In *The Rise and Fall of the New Deal Order, 1930–1980*, edited by Steve Fraser and Gary Gerstle, 122–152. Princeton: Princeton University Press, 1989.

Lieberman, Robert C. *Shifting the Color Line: Race and the American Welfare State*. Cambridge, MA: Harvard University Press, 1998.

Linden, Frank van den. "'Baby' Of Next Congress, Ex-Paratrooper, Plans to Be Real Working Representative." *Olean Times Herald* (Olean, NY), October 14, 1948, 19.

Lindert, Peter H. *Growing Public: Social Spending and Economic Growth since the Eighteenth Century*. New York: Cambridge University Press, 2004.

Link, Henry C. "A New Method for Testing Advertising and a Psychological Sales Barometer." *Journal of Applied Psychology* 18, no. 1 (1934): 1–26.

Linz, Juan J. "Totalitarian and Authoritarian Regimes." In *Handbook of Political Science*, edited by Fred I. Greenstein and Nelson W. Polsby, Vol. 3: Macropolitical Theory, 175–411. Reading, MA: Addison-Wesley, 1975.

Lippman, Daniel. "The Cochran-McDaniel Ad Wars." *Politico*, June 23, 2014. http://www.politico.com/story/2014/06/thad-cochran-chris-mcdaniel-ads-federal-spending-conservative-credentials-108180.

Logan, Rayford W., ed. *The Attitude of the Southern White Press toward Negro Suffrage 1932–1940*. Washington, DC: Foundation Publishers, 1940.

Londregan, John. "Political Income Distribution." In *The Oxford Handbook of Political Economy*, edited by Barry R. Weingast and Donald A. Wittman, 84–101. New York: Oxford University Press, 2006.

Lupia, Arthur, and Mathew D. McCubbins. "The Institutional Foundations of Political Competence: How Citizens Learn What They Need to Know." In *Elements of Reason*, edited by Arthur Lupia, Mathew D. McCubbins, and Samuel L. Popkin, 47–66. New York: Cambridge University Press, 2000.

Lupu, Noam, and Jonas Pontusson. "The Structure of Inequality and the Politics of Redistribution." *American Political Science Review* 105, no. 2 (2011): 316–336.

Macpherson, C. B. *The Real World of Democracy*. Oxford: Clarendon, 1966.

Maney, Patrick J. "Hale Boggs, Organized Labor, and the Politics of Race in South Louisiana." In *Southern Labor in Transition, 1940–1995*, 230–250. Knoxville: University of Tennessee Press, 1997.

Manion, Melanie. "The Electoral Connection in the Chinese Countryside." *American Political Science Review* 90, no. 4 (1996): 736–748.

———. "'Good Types' in Authoritarian Elections: The Selectoral Connection in Chinese Local Congresses." *Comparative Political Studies* 47 (2014): 1–33.

Mann, Thomas J., and Norman J. Ornstein. *It's Even Worse Than It Looks: How the American Constitutional System Collided with the New Politics of Extremism*. New York: Basic Books, 2012.

Manza, Jeff. "Political Sociological Models of the U.S. New Deal." *Annual Review of Sociology* 26 (2000): 297–322.

Marcello, Ronald E. "The Politics of Relief: The North Carolina WPA and the Tar Heel Elections of 1936." *North Carolina Historical Review* 68, no. 1 (1991): 17–37.

Margo, Robert A. *Race and Schooling in the South, 1880–1950: An Economic History.* Chicago: University of Chicago Press, 1990.

Markley, Gregory Michael. "Senators Hill and Sparkman and Nine Alabama Congressmen Debate National Health Insurance, 1935–1965." Master's thesis, Auburn University, Department of History, 2008.

Martin, Andrew D., and Kevin M. Quinn. "Dynamic Ideal Point Estimation via Markov Chain Monte Carlo for the U.S. Supreme Court, 1953–1999." *Political Analysis* 10, no. 2 (2002): 134–153.

Martin, Andrew D., Kevin M. Quinn, and Jong Hee Park. "MCMCpack: Markov Chain Monte Carlo in R." *Journal of Statistical Software* 42, no. 9 (2011): 1–21.

Martin, Jonathan. "One Party, Two Factions: South's Republicans Look a Lot Like Its 1970s Democrats." *New York Times*, June 2, 2014. https://www.nytimes.com/2014/06/03/us/politics/one-party-two-factions-souths-republicans-look-a-lot-like-its-1970s-democrats.html?nrx=miss-footer.

Martin, Julien D. "Topics of the Week: Sims to Have Mobile Office." *Aiken Standard and Review* (Aiken, SC), February 16, 1949, 4.

Martis, Kenneth C., Clifford Lee Lord, Ruth Anderson Rowles, and Historical Records Survey (New York, N.Y.) *The Historical Atlas of United States Congressional Districts, 1789–1983.* New York: Free Press, 1982.

Marx, Karl to Dr. Ludwig Kugelmann, "Confidential Communication on Bakunin," March 28, 1870. https://www.marxists.org/archive/marx/works/1870/03/28.htm.

Mason, Robert. *The Republican Party and American Politics from Hoover to Reagan.* New York: Cambridge University Press, 2012.

Mayhew, David R. *America's Congress: Actions in the Public Sphere, James Madison through Newt Gingrich.* New Haven, CT: Yale University Press, 2000.

———. *Congress: The Electoral Connection.* New Haven, CT: Yale University Press, 1974.

———. "Congressional Elections: The Case of the Vanishing Marginals." *Polity* 6, no. 3 (1974): 295–317.

———. *Party Loyalty among Congressmen: The Difference between Democrats and Republicans, 1947–1962.* Cambridge, MA: Harvard University Press, 1966.

———. "Supermajority Rule in the U.S. Senate." *PS: Political Science & Politics* 36, no. 1 (2003): 31–36.

———. "The Long 1950s as a Policy Era." In *The Politics of Major Policy Reform*, edited by Jeffery A. Jenkins and Sidney M. Milkis, 27–47. New York: Cambridge University Press, 2013.

———. "Wars and American Politics." *Perspectives on Politics* 3, no. 3 (September 2005): 473–493.

———. "Why Did V. O. Key Draw Back from His 'Have-Nots' Claim?" In *Parties and Policies: How the American Government Works*, 73–93. New Haven, CT: Yale University Press, 2008.

McAdam, Doug. *Political Process and the Development of Black Insurgency, 1930–1970*. Chicago: University of Chicago Press, 1982.

McDonald, Michael P., and Samuel L. Popkin. "The Myth of the Vanishing Voter." *American Political Science Review* 95, no. 4 (2001): 963–974.

McMillan, George. "Three Southern Portraits: Liberal Congressman." *The Reporter*, March 28, 1950, 13–15.

Mead, Howard N. "Russell vs. Talmadge: Southern Politics and the New Deal." *Georgia Historical Quarterly* 65, no. 1 (1981): 28–45.

Meltzer, Allan H., and Scott F. Richard. "A Rational Theory of the Size of Government." *Journal of Political Economy* 89, no. 5 (1981): 914–927.

Mickey, Robert W. *Paths out of Dixie: The Democratization of Authoritarian Enclaves in America's Deep South*. Princeton: Princeton University Press, 2015.

———. "The Beginning of the End for Authoritarian Rule in America: *Smith v. Allwright* and the Abolition of the White Primary in the Deep South, 1944–1948." *Studies in American Political Development* 22, no. 2 (2008): 143–182.

Mill, John Stuart. *Considerations on Representative Government*. People's edition, London: Longmans, Green, 1867.

Miller, Warren E., and Donald E. Stokes. "Constituency Influence in Congress." *American Political Science Review* 57, no. 1 (1963): 45–56.

Millis, Harry A., and Harold A. Katz. "A Decade of State Labor Legislation 1937–1947." *University of Chicago Law Review* 15, no. 2 (1948): 282–310.

Mills, C. Wright. *The Power Elite*. New York: Oxford University Press, 1956.

Mitchell, Dennis J. *Mississippi Liberal: A Biography of Frank E. Smith*. Jackson: University Press of Mississippi, 2001.

Morgan, Chester M. *Redneck Liberal: Theodore G. Bilbo and the New Deal*. London: Louisiana State University Press, 1985.

Morgan, Edmund S. "Slavery and Freedom: The American Paradox." *Journal of American History* 59, no. 1 (1972): 5–29.

Morgan, Sammy L. "Elite Dominance in the Arkansas Delta, from the New Deal to the New Millennium." PhD dissertation, University of Mississippi, Department of History, 2005.

National Industrial Conference Board. *A Statistical Survey of Public Opinion: Regarding Current Economic and Social Problems as Reported by Newspaper Editors in August and September, 1934*. Study no. 205. New York: National Industrial Conference Board, 1934.

———. *A Statistical Survey of Public Opinion: Regarding Current Economic and Social Problems as Reported by Newspaper Editors in the First Quarter of 1936*. Study no. 222. New York: National Industrial Conference Board, 1936.

National Labor Relations Board. *Legislative History of the Labor Management Relations Act, 1947*. Reprint of the 1959 edition, Vol. I. Washington, DC: U.S. Government Printing Office, 1985.

National Labor Relations Board. *Legislative History of the National Labor Relations Act, 1935*. reprint of the 1959 edition, Vol. II. Washington, DC: U.S. Government Printing Office, 1985.

Nave, R. L. "McDaniel Polling Ahead, Black Voters Still a Big Unknown." *Jackson (MS) Free Press*, June 23, 2014. http://www.jacksonfreepress.com/news/2014/jun/23/mcdaniel-polling-ahead-blacks-still-big-unknown/.

Neustadt, Richard E. "The Fair Deal: A Legislative Balance Sheet." *Public Policy: A Yearbook of the Graduate School of Public Administration, Harvard University* 5 (1954): 349–381.

Nixon, H. C. "Politics of the Hills." *Journal of Politics* 8, no. 2 (1946): 123–133.

Nolen, Roy. "Confidential Memoranda for Senator Lister Hill," January 15, 1938, Box 267, Folder 1, Lister Hill Senatorial Collection, W. S. Hoole Library, University of Alabama,

Norrell, Robert J. "Labor at the Ballot Box: Alabama Politics from the New Deal to the Dixiecrat Movement." *Journal of Southern History* 57, no. 2 (1991): 201–234.

O'Donnell, Guillermo. "On the State, Democratization and Some Conceptual Problems: A Latin American View with Glances at Some Postcommunist Countries." *World Development* 21, no. 8 (1993): 1355–1369.

Oestreicher, Richard. "The Rules of the Game: Class Politics in Twentieth-Century America." In *Organized Labor and American Politics, 1894–1994: The Labor-Liberal Alliance*, edited by Kevin Boyle, 19–50. Albany: SUNY Press, 1998.

Orren, Karen, and Stephen Skowronek. "Regimes and Regime Building in American Government: A Review of Literature on the 1940s." *Political Science Quarterly* 113, no. 4 (December 1998): 689–702.

Packer, George. *Blood of the Liberals*. New York: Farrar, Straus and Giroux, 2000.

Patterson, James T. "A Conservative Coalition Forms in Congress, 1933–1939." *Journal of American History* 52, no. 4 (1966): 757–772.

———. *Congressional Conservatism and the New Deal: The Growth of the Conservative Coalition in Congress, 1933–1939*. Lexington: University of Kentucky Press, 1967.

———. *Mr. Republican: A Biography of Robert A. Taft*. Boston: Houghton Mifflin, 1972.

Pearson, Drew. "The Daily Washington Merry-Go-Round." *Southeast Missourian* (Cape Girardeau, MO), September 25, 1948, 4.

Pearson, Kathryn, and Eric Schickler. "Discharge Petitions, Agenda Control, and the Congressional Committee System, 1929–76." *Journal of Politics* 71, no. 4 (2009): 1238–1256.

Perman, Michael. *Pursuit of Unity: A Political History of the American South*. Chapel Hill: University of North Carolina Press, 2009.

Pitkin, Hanna Fenichel. *The Concept of Representation*. Berkeley: University of California Press, 1967.

Plotke, David. *Building a Democratic Political Order: Reshaping American Liberalism in the 1930s and 1940s*. Cambridge: Cambridge University Press, 1996.

Polsby, Nelson W. *How Congress Evolves: Social Bases of Institutional Change.* New York: Oxford University Press, 2004.

Pomper, Gerald. "Labor and Congress: The Repeal of Taft–Hartley." *Labor History* 2, no. 3 (1961): 323–343.

Poole, Keith T., and Howard Rosenthal. *HCODES.TXT.* Text file downloaded from http://voteview.com/page2c.htm. 1998.

———. *Houses 1–106 Outcome Coordinates and Issue Codes.* ftp://voteview .com/h01106xx.dat. Last updated July 3, 2001.

———. *Ideology & Congress.* New Brunswick, NJ: Transaction Publishers, 2007.

———. "The Polarization of American Politics." *Journal of Politics* 46, no. 4 (1984): 1061–1079.

Powell, Daniel A. "PAC to COPE: Thirty-Two Years of Southern Labor in Politics." In *Essays in Southern Labor History: Selected Papers, Southern Labor History Conference, 1976,* edited by Gary M. Fink and Merle E. Reed, 244–257. Westport, CT: Greenwood Press.

Przeworski, Adam. "Minimalist Conception of Democracy: A Defense." In *The Democracy Sourcebook,* edited by Robert Dahl, Ian Shapiro, and José Antonio Cheibub, 12–16. 1999. Cambridge, MA: MIT Press, 2003.

Przeworski, Adam, Susan Carol Stokes, and Bernard Manin. "Introduction." In *Democracy, Accountability, and Representation,* edited by Adam Przeworski, Susan Carol Stokes, and Bernard Manin, 1–26. New York: Cambridge University Press, 1999.

Quadagno, Jill. *The Color of Welfare.* New York: Columbia University Press, 1994.

———. "From Old-Age Assistance to Supplemental Security Income: The Political Economy of Relief in the South, 1935–1972." In *The Politics of Social Policy in the United States,* edited by Margaret Weir, Ann Shola Orloff, and Theda Skocpol, 235–263. Princeton: Princeton University Press, 1988.

Quadagno, Jill S. "Welfare Capitalism and the Social Security Act of 1935." *American Sociological Review* 49, no. 5 (1984): 632–647.

Ranney, Austin, and Willmoore Kendall. "The American Party Systems." *American Political Science Review* 48, no. 2 (1954): 477–485.

Reiter, Howard L. "The Building of a Bifactional Structure: The Democrats in the 1940s." *Political Science Quarterly* 116, no. 1 (2001): 107–129.

"Revenue Act of 1950." In *CQ Almanac 1950,* 6th ed., 573–595. Washington, DC: Congressional Quarterly, 1951. http://library.cqpress.com/cqalmanac/ cqal50-1375509.

Riker, William H. *Liberalism against Populism.* San Francisco: W. H. Freeman, 1982.

Robertson, David. *Sly and Able: A Political Biography of James F. Byrnes.* New York: Norton, 1994.

Roeder, Philip G. "Varieties of Post-Soviet Authoritarian Regimes." *Post-Soviet Affairs* 10, no. 1 (1994): 61–101.

Rogers, William Warren, Robert David Ward, Leah Rawls Atkins, and Wayne Flynt. *Alabama: The History of a Deep South State.* Tuscaloosa: University of Alabama Press, 1994.

Roosevelt, Franklin D. "Fireside Chat (June 24, 1938)." *The American Presidency Project*, ed. Gerhard Peters and John T. Woolley. http://www.presidency.ucsb.edu/ws/?pid=15662.

Rosenfarb, Joseph. "Labor's Role in the Election." *Public Opinion Quarterly* 8, no. 3 (1944): 376.

Rowe, James H., Jr. "Interview by Joe B. Frantz." Interview I, transcript, Lyndon Johnson Oral History Collection, Lyndon Johnson Presidential Library, Washington, DC, September 9, 1969. http://millercenter.org/scripps/archive/oralhistories/detail/2952.

Saloutos, Theodore. "The American Farm Bureau Federation and Farm Policy: 1933–1945." *Southwestern Social Science Quarterly* 28, no. 4 (1947/1948): 313–333.

Sams, Ferrol, Jr. "God as Elector: Religion and the Vote." In *The Prevailing South: Life and Politics in a Changing Culture*, edited by Dudley Clendinen, 48–59. Atlanta: Longstreet, 1988.

Sanders, Elizabeth. *Roots of Reform: Farmers, Workers, and the American State, 1877–1917*. Chicago: University of Chicago Press, 1999.

Sartori, Giovanni. *Parties and Party Systems: A Framework for Analysis*. New York: Cambridge University Press, 1976.

Schaffner, Brian F., and Matthew J. Streb. "The Partisan Heuristic in Low-Information Elections." *Public Opinion Quarterly* 66, no. 4 (2002): 559–581.

Schaffner, Brian F., Matthew Streb, and Gerald Wright. "Teams without Uniforms: The Nonpartisan Ballot in State and Local Elections." *Political Research Quarterly* 54, no. 1 (2001): 7–30.

Schattschneider, E. E. *Party Government*. Westport, CT: Greenwood, 1942.

———. *The Semi-Sovereign People*. New York: Hold, Rinehart, Winston, 1960.

Schickler, Eric. *Racial Realignment: The Transformation of American Liberalism, 1932–1965*. Princeton: Princeton University Press, 2016.

Schickler, Eric, and Devin Caughey. "Public Opinion, Organized Labor, and the Limits of New Deal Liberalism, 1936–1945." *Studies in American Political Development* 25, no. 2 (2011): 1–28.

Schickler, Eric, and Kathryn Pearson. "Agenda Control, Majority Party Power, and the House Committee on Rules, 1937–52." *Legislative Studies Quarterly* 34, no. 4 (2009): 455–491.

Schulman, Bruce J. *From Cotton Belt to Sunbelt: Federal Policy, Economic Development, and the Transformation of the South, 1938–1980*. Durham, NC: Duke University Press, 1994.

Schultheis, Emily. "Cochran to Run for Reelection." *Politico*, December 6, 2013. http://www.politico.com/story/2013/12/thad-cochran-reelection-100785.

Schumpeter, Joseph A. *Capitalism, Socialism and Democracy*. 1942. Reprint, New York: Routledge, 2003.

Schwartz, Jordan A. *The New Dealers: Power Politics in the Age of Roosevelt*. New York: Vintage Books, 1993.

"Second Income Tax Reduction Bill." In *CQ Almanac 1947*, 3rd ed., 09-507–09-509. Washington, DC: Congressional Quarterly, 1948. http://library.cqpress.com/cqalmanac/cqal47-1398910.

Seltzer, Andrew J. "Democratic Opposition to the Fair Labor Standards Act: A Comment on Fleck." *Journal of Economic History* 64, no. 1 (2004): 226–230.

Shafer, Byron E., and Richard Johnston. *The End of Southern Exceptionalism: Class, Race, and Partisan Change in the Postwar South*. Cambridge, MA: Harvard University Press, 2006.

Shapley, L. S., and Martin Shubik. "A Method for Evaluating the Distribution of Power in a Committee System." *American Political Science Review* 48, no. 3 (1954): 787–792.

Shepsle, Kenneth A. "Congress Is a 'They,' Not an 'It': Legislative Intent as Oxymoron." *International Review of Law and Economics* 12, no. 2 (1992): 239–256.

Shott, John G. *How 'Right-to-Work' Laws Are Passed: Florida Sets the Pattern*. Washington, DC: Public Affairs Institute, 1956.

Simpson, Kirke L. "Capital Watching Primary in Florida as Political Straw." *Atlanta Constitution*, May 1, 1938.

Sinclair, Barbara. *Congressional Realignment: 1925–1978*. Austin: University of Texas Press, 1982.

Sitkoff, Harvard. "Harry Truman and the Election of 1948: The Coming of Age of Civil Rights in American Politics." *Journal of Southern History* 37, no. 4 (1971): 597–616.

Skocpol, Theda, and Edwin Amenta. "Did Capitalists Shape Social Security?" *American Sociological Review* 50, no. 4 (1985): 572–575.

Smith, Jason Scott. *Building New Deal Liberalism: The Political Economy of Public Works, 1933–1956*. New York: Cambridge University Press, 2006.

Snyder, James M., Jr., and Michael M. Ting. "Electoral Selection with Parties and Primaries." *American Journal of Political Science* 55, no. 4 (2011): 782–796.

———. "An Informational Rationale for Political Parties." *American Journal of Political Science* 46, no. 1 (2002): 90–110.

———. "Roll Calls, Party Labels, and Elections." *Political Analysis* 11, no. 4 (2003): 419–444.

Southwick, Leslie H. "John Sparkman." In *Presidential Also Rans and Running Mates, 1788–1980*, 582–589. Jefferson, NC: McFarland, 1984.

Sparkman, John. "Interview by Paige E. Mulhollan." Transcript, Lyndon Johnson Oral History Collection, Lyndon Johnson Presidential Library, Washington, DC, October 5, 1968. http://web1.millercenter.org/poh/transcripts/sparkman_john_1968_1005.pdf.

Stanley, Harold W. "Reflections on Reading V. O. Key Jr.'s *Southern Politics*." In *Unlocking V. O. Key, Jr.: Southern Politics for the Twenty-First Century*, 105–125. Fayetteville: University of Arkansas Press, 2011.

———. *Voter Mobilization and the Politics of Race: The South and Universal Suffrage, 1952–1984*. New York: Praeger, 1987.

Stanley, Harold W., and Richard G. Niemi. "House and Senate Incumbents Retired, Defeated, or Reelected, 1946–2010." In *Vital Statistics on American Politics 2011–2012*, edited by Harold W. Stanley and Richard G. Niemi. Washington, DC: CQ Press, 2011. http://library.cqpress.com/elections/vsap11%5C_tab1-18.

Stanley, Harold W., and Richard G. Niemi. "Table 1-4 Party Competition, by Region, 1860–2008 (percent)." In *Vital Statistics on American Politics 2009–2010*, edited by Harold W. Stanley and Richard G. Niemi. Washington, DC: CQ Press, 2009. http://library.cqpress.com/vsap/vsap09%5C_tab1-4.

"Stewart E. McClure: Chief Clerk, Senate Committee on Labor, Education, and Public Welfare (1949–1973)." Oral History Interviews, Senate Historical Office, Washington, 1982–1983.

Stimson, James A., Michael B. MacKuen, and Robert S. Erikson. "Dynamic Representation." *American Political Science Review* 89, no. 3 (1995): 543–565.

Stokes, Donald E. "Spatial Models of Party Competition." *American Political Science Review* 57, no. 2 (1963): 368–377.

Stokes, S. C. "Political Parties and Democracy." *Annual Review of Political Science* 2 (1999): 243–267.

Stokes, Thomas. "Government and Politics." *Reno Evening Gazette*, March 19, 1949, 4.

Sulkin, Tracy. *Issue Politics in Congress*. New York: Cambridge University Press, 2005.

Sullens, Frederick. "The South Is Still Solid: Mississippi." *Review of Reviews* 93 (January 1936): 39.

Sullivan, Patricia. *Days of Hope: Race and Democracy in the New Deal Era.* Chapel Hill: University of North Carolina Press, 1996.

Sundquist, James L. *Politics and Policy: The Eisenhower, Kennedy, and Johnson Years*. Washington, DC: The Brookings Institution, 1968.

Swain, Martha H. "Hubert D. Stephens: Mississippi's 'Quiet Man' in the Senate, 1923–1935." *Journal of Mississippi History* 63, no. 4 (2001).

Sweeney, James R. "'Sheep without a Shepherd': The New Deal Faction in the Virginia Democratic Party." *Presidential Studies Quarterly* 29, no. 2 (1999): 438–458.

Syvertsen, Thomas Hamilton. "Earle Chester Clements and the Democratic Party, 1920–1950." PhD thesis, Department of History, University of Kentucky, 1982.

"Taft–Hartley Repeal Attempts." In *CQ Almanac 1949*, 5th ed., 06-444–06-455. Washington, DC: Congressional Quarterly, 1950. http://library.cqpress.com/cqalmanac/cqal49-1400386.

Tausanovitch, Chris, and Christopher Warshaw. "Representation in Municipal Government." *American Political Science Review* 108, no. 3 (2014): 605–641.

"Tax Reduction." In *CQ Almanac 1947*, 3rd ed., 09-101–09-104. Washington, DC: Congressional Quarterly, 1948. http://library.cqpress.com/cqalmanac/cqal47-1397733.

"Tax Reduction." In *CQ Almanac 1948*, 4th ed., 344–350. Washington, DC: Congressional Quarterly, 1949. http://library.cqpress.com/cqalmanac/cqal48-1407007.

Thompson, Dennis F. *The Democratic Citizen*. Cambridge: Cambridge University Press, 1970.

Thornton, J. Mills, III. "Alabama Politics, J. Thomas Heflin, and the Expulsion Movement of 1929." *Alabama Review* 21 (1968): 83–112.

———. *Dividing Lines: Municipal Politics and the Struggle for Civil Rights in Montgomery, Birmingham, and Selma.* Tuscaloosa: University of Alabama Press, 2002.

Time. "At Home on Wheels." November 14, 1949, no. 20, 27.

Tindall, George Brown. *The Emergence of the New South, 1913–1945.* Baton Rouge: Louisiana State University Press, 1967.

Tordoff, William. "The General Election in Tanzania." *Journal of Commonwealth Political Studies* 4, no. 1 (1966): 47–64.

Treaster, Joseph B. "James E. Folsom, Colorful Politician and Twice Governor of Alabama, Is Dead at 79." *New York Times*, November 22, 1987. http://www.nytimes.com/1987/11/22/obituaries/james-e-folsom-colorful-politician-and-twice-governor-of-alabama-is-dead-at-79.html.

Unger, Irwin, and Debi Unger. *LBJ: A Life.* New York: Wiley, 1999.

United Press. "Multi-Billion Job Measure Ready Today." *Washington Post*, January 10, 1949, 1.

Valelly, Richard M. *The Two Reconstructions: The Struggle for Black Enfranchisement.* Chicago: University of Chicago Press, 2004.

Van den Berghe, Pierre L. *Race and Racism.* New York: Wiley, 1967.

Vickery, Kenneth P. "'Herrenvolk' Democracy and Egalitarianism in South Africa and the U.S. South." *Comparative Studies in Society and History* 16, no. 3 (1974): 309–328.

Wald, Kenneth D. "The Visible Empire: The Ku Klux Klan as an Electoral Movement." *Journal of Interdisciplinary History* 11, no. 2 (1980): 217–234.

Walker, Henry James. "Beyond the Call of Duty: Representative John Sparkman of Alabama and World War II, 1939–1945." *Southern Historian* 11 (1990): 24–42.

Ware, Alan. *Citizens, Parties, and the State: A Reappraisal.* Cambridge: Polity, 1987.

Warner, Albert L. "Court Bill Battle Opens with Robinson Defying Opposition to Filibuster." *New York Herald Tribune*, July 7, 1937, 1.

Wawro, Gregory J., and Eric Schickler. *Filibuster: Obstruction and Lawmaking in the U.S. Senate.* Princeton: Princeton University Press, 2006.

Weaver, John C. "Lawyers, Lodges, and Kinfolk: The Workings of a South Carolina Political Organization, 1920–1936." *The South Carolina Historical Magazine* 78, no. 4 (1977): 272–285.

Webb, Samuel L. "Hugo Black, Bibb Graves, and the Ku Klux Klan." *Alabama Review*, October 2004, 243–283.

———. "Southern Politics in the Age of Populism and Progressivism: A Historiographical Essay." In *A Companion to the American South*, edited by John B. Boles, 317–335. Malden, MA: Blackwell, 2007. http://dx.doi.org/10.1002/9780470996300.ch19.

Weir, Margaret. "The Federal Government and Unemployment: The Frustration of Policy Innovation from the New Deal to the Great Society." In *The Politics of Social Policy in the United States*, edited by Margaret Weir, Ann Shola Orloff, and Theda Skocpol, 149–190. Princeton: Princeton University Press, 1988.

Weiss, Stuart L. "Maury Maverick and the Liberal Bloc." *Journal of American History* 57, no. 4 (1971): 880–895.

Weissberg, Robert. "Collective vs. Dyadic Representation in Congress." *American Political Science Review* 72, no. 2 (1978): 535–547.

Werner, Timothy. "Congressmen of the Silent South: The Persistence of Southern Racial Liberals, 1949–1964." *Journal of Politics* 71, no. 1 (2009): 70–81.

White, Bill. *America's Fiscal Constitution: Its Triumph and Collapse*. New York: PublicAffairs, 2014.

Wilkerson, John D., and Barry Pump. "The Ties That Bind: Coalitions in Congress." In *The Oxford Handbook of the American Congress*, edited by Eric Schickler and Frances Lee, 618–640. New York: Oxford University Press, 2011.

Williams, T. Harry. *Huey Long*. New York: Vintage, 1969.

Wolfinger, James. "War Labor Disputes Act (Smith-Connally Act)." In *Historical Encyclopedia of American Labor*, 2:537–538. Westport, CT: Greenwood, 2004.

Wolfinger, Raymond E., and Steven J. Rosenstone. *Who Votes?* New Haven, CT: Yale University Press, 1980.

Woodward, C. Vann. *Origins of the New South, 1877–1913*. Baton Rouge: Louisiana State University Press, 1951.

Wright, Gavin. *Old South, New South: Revolutions in the Southern Economy since the Civil War*. New York: Basic Books, 1986.

———. "The New Deal and the Modernization of the South." *Federal History* 2010, no. 2 (2010): 58–73.

———. *Sharing the Prize: The Economics of the Civil Rights Revolution in the American South*. Cambridge, MA: Harvard University Press, 2013.

Wright, Gerald C. "Charles Adrian and the Study of Nonpartisan Elections." *Political Research Quarterly* 61, no. 1 (2008): 13–16.

Wright, Gerald C., and Brian F. Schaffner. "The Influence of Party: Evidence from the State Legislatures." *American Political Science Review* 96, no. 2 (2002): 367–379.

Wrighton, J. Mark, and Peverill Squire. "Uncontested Seats and Electoral Competition for the U.S. House of Representatives over Time." *Journal of Politics* 59, no. 2 (1997): 452–468.

Young, Julia Marks. "A Republican Challenge to Democratic Progressivism in the Deep South: Alabama's 1962 United States Senatorial Contest." Master's thesis, Auburn University, 1978.

Young, Nancy Beck. "Change and Continuity in the Politics of Running for Congress: Wright Patman and the Campaigns of 1928, 1938, 1962, and 1972." *East Texas Historical Journal* 34, no. 2 (1996): 52–64.

Zaller, John R. *The Nature and Origins of Mass Opinion*. New York: Cambridge University Press, 1992.

Zelizer, Julian E. "Review of *Race, Money, and the American Welfare State*, by Michael K. Brown." *Journal of American History* 87, no. 2 (2000): 722.

————. "The Forgotten Legacy of the New Deal: Fiscal Conservatism and the Roosevelt Administration, 1933–1938." *Presidential Studies Quarterly* 30, no. 2 (2000): 331–358.

————. *Taxing America: Wilbur D. Mills, Congress, and the State, 1945–1975.* New York: Cambridge University Press, 1998.

Index

212 ◆— Index

PRINCETON STUDIES IN AMERICAN POLITICS
HISTORICAL, INTERNATIONAL, AND COMPARATIVE PERSPECTIVES

SERIES EDITORS
Ira Katznelson, Eric Schickler, Martin Sheffer, and Theda Skocpol

*Looking for Rights in All the Wrong Places: Why State Constitutions
Contain America's Positive Rights*
by Emily Zackin

*Paths out of Dixie: The Democratization of Authoritarian
Enclaves in America's Deep South, 1944–1972*
by Robert Mickey

*Fighting for the Speakership: The House and the
Rise of Party Government*
by Jeffery A. Jenkins and Charles Stewart III

*Three Worlds of Relief: Race, Immigration, and the American
Welfare State from the Progressive Era to the New Deal*
by Cybelle Fox

*Building the Judiciary: Law, Courts, and the Politics
of Institutional Development*
by Justin Crowe

Still a House Divided: Race and Politics in Obama's America
by Desmond S. King and Rogers M. Smith

*The Litigation State: Public Regulations and Private
Lawsuits in the United States*
by Sean Farhang

*Reputation and Power: Organizational Image
and Pharmaceutical Regulation at the FDA*
by Daniel Carpenter

*Presidential Party Building: Dwight D. Eisenhower to
George W. Bush*
by Daniel J. Galvin

*Fighting for Democracy: Black Veterans and the Struggle
against White Supremacy in the Postwar South*
by Christopher S. Parker

*The Fifth Freedom: Jobs, Politics, and Civil Rights
in the United States, 1941–1972*
by Anthony Chen

*Reforms at Risk: What Happens after
Major Policy Changes Are Enacted*
by Eric Patashnik

The Hidden Welfare State: Tax Expenditures and
Social Policy in the United States
by Christopher Howard

Morning Glories: Municipal Reform in the Southwest
by Amy Bridges

Imperiled Innocents: Anthony Comstock and Family
Reproduction in Victorian America
by Nicola Beisel

The Road to Nowhere: The Genesis of President Clinton's
Plan for Health Security
by Jacob Hacker

The Origins of the Urban Crisis: Race and
Inequality in Postwar Detroit
by Thomas J. Sugrue

Party Decline in America: Policy, Politics, and the Fiscal State
by John J. Coleman

The Power of Separation: American Constitutionalism
and the Myth of the Legislative Veto
by Jessica Korn

Why Movements Succeed or Fail: Opportunity, Culture,
and the Struggle for Woman Suffrage
by Lee Ann Banaszak

Kindred Strangers: The Uneasy Relationship between
Politics and Business in America
by David Vogel

From the Outside In: World War II and the American State
by Bartholomew H. Sparrow

Classifying by Race
edited by Paul E. Peterson

Facing Up to the American Dream: Race, Class,
and the Soul of the Nation
by Jennifer L. Hochschild

Political Organizations
by James Q. Wilson

Social Policy in the United States: Future
Possibilities in Historical Perspective
by Theda Skocpol

*Experts and Politicians: Reform Challenges to Machine
Politics in New York, Cleveland, and Chicago*
by Kenneth Finegold

*Bound by Our Constitution: Women, Workers,
and the Minimum Wage*
by Vivien Hart

*Prisoners of Myth: The Leadership of the Tennessee
Valley Authority, 1933–1990*
by Erwin C. Hargrove

Political Parties and the State: The American Historical Experience
by Martin Shefter

*Politics and Industrialization: Early Railroads in the
United States and Prussia*
by Colleen A. Dunlavy

The Lincoln Persuasion: Remaking American Liberalism
by J. David Greenstone

*Labor Visions and State Power: The Origins of
Business Unionism in the United States*
by Victoria C. Hattam